Cross~Cultural Perspectives

UNIVERSITY CORE READINGS

Fifth Edition

Edited by
Indira Govindan and James Kuehl

FAIRLEIGH
DICKINSON
UNIVERSITY
THE LEADER IN GLOBAL EDUCATION

Copley Custom Textbooks

An imprint of XanEdu Custom Publishing

ISBN 13: 978-1-58152-533-5
ISBN 10: 1-58152-533-8

Acknowledgments:
p. 3–20: From *My Freshman Year: What a Professor Learned by Becoming a Student* by
Rebekah Nathan. Copyright © 2005 by Rebekah Nathan. Used by permission of the
publisher, Cornell University Press.
pp. 24–76: From *Reading National Geographic* by Catherine A. Lutz and Jane L.
Collins. Copyright © 1993 by Chicago University Press. Reprinted by permission.
pp. 77–92: From *Dress and Popular Culture* edited by Patricia A Cunningham.
Copyright © 1991 by The University of Wisconsin Press. Reprinted by permission
of the publisher.
pp. 93–96: As appeared in *Economic and Political Weekly*, December 9, 2006. Copyright © 2006 by Imtiaz Ahmad. Reprinted by permission of the author.
pp. 102–107: From *The King in Every Man: Evolutionary Trends in Ibo Society and
Culture.* Copyright © 1972 by Yale University Press. Reprinted by permission of the
publisher.
pp. 108–131: From *Buddhist Missionaries in the Era of Globalization* by Cristina Rocha.
Copyright © 2005 by University of Hawaii Press. Reprinted by permission.
pp. 132–144: From *Darsan: Seeing the Divine Image in India* by Diana Eck. Copyright
© 1998 by Columbia University Press. Reprinted by permission of the publisher via
the Copyright Clearance Center.
pp. 145–162: From *Sources of Chinese Tradition* edited by Wm. Theodore De Bary.
Copyright 1987, 1960 by Columbia University Press. Reprinted by permission of the
publisher via the Copyright Clearance Center.
pp. 181–262: From *Mao's Children in the New China: Voices from the Red Guard
Generation* edited by Yarong Jiang and David Ashley. Copyright © 2000 by Taylor
& Francis Group. Reprinted by permission of the publisher.

Copley Custom Textbooks
An imprint of XanEdu Custom Publishing
138 Great Road
Acton, MA 01720
800-562-2147

CROSS-CULTURAL PERSPECTIVES FACULTY

The readings in this book were selected by a committee of the faculty
teaching Cross-Cultural Perspectives and approved by a majority
of members voting.

Gbolohan Akinsanya, *History*

Patricia Bazan-Figueras, *Languages*

Sylvia Belen-Ramos, *Languages*

Madera Edwards-Adams, *History*

Indira Govindan, *History*

Judith Granger, *English*

Susan Hastings, *English*

Krista Hughes, *Theology*

Francis Ingledew, *English*

Judith Kaufman, *Psychology*

Delicia Koeneke, *Languages*

Dorothy Mabey, *Mathematics*

Rendell Mabey, *Philosophy*

Judith Manton, *English*

Ronald Miller, *Theology*

Mutiara Mohamad, *Education*

Austin Ogunsuyi, *Political Science*

Azly Rahman, *Education*

Neil Salzman, *History*

Sheila Schoenbrun, *Fine Arts*

CONTENTS

INTRODUCTION

Ever since Edward B. Tylor (1832–1917) defined culture as "that complex whole which includes knowledge, belief, art, morals, laws, custom, and any other capabilities and habits acquired by man as a member of society," anthropologists and others who study cultures have progressively moved towards a more complex definition and understanding of culture. This reformulation has been stimulated and accelerated by the political, social and economic changes in the second half of the 20th century marked by the dissolution of European empires, the emergence of newly independent former colonies and the struggles of disenfranchised and marginal groups for social justice, human dignity and equality. Students of culture became increasingly aware that culture could not be understood as a fixed set of acquired capabilities and habits. In an increasingly interdependent world, marked by considerable "inter-cultural borrowing and lending," culture study must now include attention to complex political and historical processes. Any analysis of these processes must also take into account differences of gender, age, ethnicity, race and class. The more recent understandings of culture which stress its dynamic and changing character offer the promise of better ways to communicate across cultural differences and perhaps learn to tolerate ambiguity at the limit of those new understandings.

This text follows the pattern of other courses in the University Core program. Like the other texts it offers a range of topics that explore the subject of the course, in this case culture, in a variety of contexts. The readings and course are designed to help students recognize that:

. . . they are part of a global series of cultures and subcultures and this fact of their situation poses opportunities and problems of communication and understanding within and across diverse groups of many kinds.

. . . that cultures and subcultures to some extent make or shape people, and do so according to principles that include the way that power works (who has it and who does not) and the available technologies.

. . . that culture by nature changes, and that people are among the agents of change, so that awareness of the ways that cultural systems work, and of how to negotiate sameness and difference, is indispensable to cultural coexistence.

Indira Govindan and James Kuehl

UNIT ONE
CULTURE AND YOU

CULTURE AND YOU

Professor Rebekkah Nathan, an anthropologist, enrolled as a freshman at an American university to study the culture of present-day students. The reading that follows is from her book *My Freshman Year*. Finding it somewhat difficult to make friends with American students she was able to relate personally to international students at the university. In the fourth chapter of her book *As Others See Us* she describes the results of her interviews with students from twelve countries. The international students express remarkably similar impressions of the nature of American friendship, American college courses, and professors. Their assessment of American students is focused and balanced. Some of the observations the international students make are disturbing, but at the same time they provoke an awareness of American culture which is often, in Nathan's words, "invisible to its natives."

You will understand the students' observations on friendship if you can answer the following question: "Why are American students good at group work in courses whereas the international students are not?"

AS OTHERS SEE US

Rebekah Nathan

As a partial outsider in college owing to my age, I found myself drawn to other partial outsiders, and vice versa. Those of us who in some way deviated from the norm perceived something in common and ended up, I noted, seeking one another out. Thus, the transfer student on my hall became a friend; I was close, too, to the more withdrawn and rural students at Previews, the lone African American student in my freshman seminar, and the international students in my dorms and classes.

My conversations with students from other countries were often illuminating. As anthropologists have come to know, culture can be invisible to its natives—so taken for granted that it seems unworthy of comment. Although I could view student life with an outsider-professor's eye, there was much about the U.S. college scene that, in its familiarity, was invisible to me as well. The more I spoke with international students, the more I noticed familiar refrains that both educated me and reminded me about my own U.S. and academic culture. After having many such informal conversations with both international students and teachers, I decided to add formal interviews of international students to my investigation of U.S. college life. In all, I conducted thirteen formal interviews, as well as several informal conversations, which included perspectives from Somalia, England, Japan, Germany, China, Mexico, Spain, the United Arab Emirates, India, Malaysia, France, and Korea. In this chapter I share the comments made and stories told by international students as they grappled to understand and to fit in at AnyU.[1] Their struggles, surprises, and dilemmas pointed to both mundane and profound revelations about U.S. students, professors, and the college education system.

Getting to Know "American" Students

One of my earliest international contacts was with a young Japanese woman, Toshi, who lived on my floor. During Welcome Week, after we played volleyball together, I introduced myself and began a casual conversation. When I saw her again at a workshop, we eyed each other like long-lost friends, and

3

she introduced me to two Japanese friends accompanying her who lived in other dorms. The four of us talked enjoyably for a while, and it was clear that the three exchange students were pleased to be engaged by an American student in this first week of activities.[2] I told them that I'd like to make dinner for them, and departed intending to stop by Toshi's room and ask her to invite her two friends to a Friday night dinner at our dorm. As I left, though, one of the women (whom I'll call Chiho) asked me a brave question in slightly halting English: "Excuse me but I don't understand. How can we have dinner together if you don't have my phone number and I don't have yours?"

I saw her confusion. After exchanging telephone numbers with all three women for assurance, I asked Chiho whether people had invited her before without following up. "I think so," she responded "but I'm not sure. I have been here for two months and I am still very confused by the customs. American students are so friendly and so nice. They are so open about wanting to get together, but they never take my phone number and they never contact me again. When I see a woman I met two days ago, she does not seem to know me or remember my name."

I winced at the truth of the friendly American veneer. "Nice to meet you," "Drop by," "See you soon," all sounded like authentic invitations for further contact. And yet the words were without social substance. It was not just Japanese, or even non-Western, students for whom deciphering friendliness was a problem. One German student commented: "There are some surface things about American friendliness. Like 'How are you?' A girl asked me that one day when I was feeling sick, and I answered that I wasn't too good but she just went on like I had never said that. Maybe it's a sign of caring to say that. But in Germany, 'How are you?' is the actual start of a conversation rather than just a hi/good-bye."

Meeting and befriending Americans in more than a superficial way presented challenges to many international students. Even in class, students found it difficult. One Asian student told me how, in her linguistics class, the teacher had told the class that the native speakers should try to include international students in their groups for the study project. "But when we formed the groups," she recounted, "nobody even responded or asked us to be in their groups, so the international students had to make their own group."

In some ways, their dilemma was like my own. Where is community in the American university, and how does one become a part of it? International students learned quickly that being a student, being a dorm mate, being a classmate—none of it automatically qualifies you as a "member of the community," that is, someone whom others will seek out for activities.

"In Korea," one woman told me, "if we all take class together and our class ends at lunchtime, we would go out together as a group." No such group outing was available as a way for new students to meet others in their classes. Because in Japan, creating a network of friends and contacts is a major purpose of going to college, Midori found it surprising that U.S. students "leave the classroom right after class is over. They come to class to get a grade, not to meet people or talk to people. They leave right away and don't talk to other people. I don't get why students run out of class, packing up and running out immediately."

Many students expressed surprise at the dull reception they received and the lack of interest they perceived from American students about their experiences and backgrounds. "Students don't ask me anything about my life," a Somali student lamented. "Even my friends . . . they don't ask me questions about how I got here, or my life in other places." A student from the United Arab Emirates observed: "Here everyone minds their own business. They're not that hospitable. Like if someone from the U.S. came to the UAE, people would take them out to eat and ask questions. It would be a long time before they paid for their own meal." A Mexican student concurred: "I'm lonely here. I don't think an American coming to Mexico would have the same experience as I've had here. We're more social, more curious. We'd be talking to him and asking questions."

"When I talk to them," one Japanese woman noted with dismay about her American classmates, "they don't try to understand what I say or keep up the conversation. They don't keep talking, and I realize that they don't want to take the trouble to talk with me." She thought that maybe the problem had to do with her thick accent. When I asked another Japanese student what questions students had asked him about his country, he answered: "Well, mostly nobody asks me anything about Japan. Some Americans don't care about other worlds. They don't ask questions, but those that do sometimes know more about Japan than I do."

Almost all international students discovered some individuals who were interested in their lives, but it was much more the exception than the rule, and these tended to be U.S. students who were well traveled or who had been exchange students themselves. "What I miss most," admitted one student, "is to have someone to talk to, to feel that someone else is interested in you." A

Mexican student agreed: "I've met people who are interested in me, but for a lot of other people it's . . . 'whatever'! My [car] mechanic is more interested in my life and my background than other students."

It was difficult, even for someone born in the United States, to see that the outward openness of both college and American life was often coupled with a closed attachment to a small set of relationships, many of them (as we saw in chapter 2) developed early in college and focused on people of very similar background. International students were often forced into the same structure, finding that despite their interest in forming friendships with Americans, they seemed to end up in relationships with other "foreigners." In many ways the active international programs, which ran socials and trips for its students, reinforced a pattern in which international students came in contact mostly with other non-U.S.-born students.

It was interesting to me that, echoing the camaraderie I felt with "others," a number of international students indicated that they found it easier to get to know U.S. minority students than white students. One student told me, "They [minorities] seem to be less gregarious than other Americans, in the sense that they seem not to have as many friends and they are looking [shyly] for people themselves." In practice, despite the fact that many students had come to the United States expressly for the "international experience," the majority fraternized with other foreign students.

"I think I know how to meet Americans," Beniko, a Japanese student, told me, "because my boyfriend meets people and has some American friends. It's his interests." Beniko explained to me that Americans find relationships when they identify hobbies or elective interests in common. She went on: "My boyfriend likes playing the drums, and he plays them in the dorms and people come into his room. They're like a friend magnet. It's the same with martial arts. He likes that, and other boys do too, and they watch videos together, like Jackie Chan. If you don't have a hobby in this country, it's harder to meet people. I need to develop a hobby."

Relationships and Friendships

Both Midori and Reiko had been excited, if a little nervous, to be assigned an American roommate. It was surprising to Reiko that there was no formal introduction; roommates met, instead, when they both happened to be in the room at the same time. Midori had heard that many Americans were messy and loud, but she knew that wasn't true across the board and hoped her roommate would not fit the stereotype.

As it turned out, Midori's roommate—neat and fairly quiet—*was* different from her expectations, but she presented challenges on another level. She spent most days and nights at her boyfriend's apartment, returning only one or two days a week to their room. And when she did, as Midori explained, her personal and spatial boundaries were sharp:

> It bothers her if I change anything in the room, even though she only came to the room one or two times a week. She would say, "This is my window—don't open it"—even if she is not there and I am very hot! "Don't change the heater setting." I ask her, "Can I turn on the light now?" "Can I put some food in your refrigerator?" It had almost nothing in it. After a while, she just comes back to the room and ignores me. She let me know that I am her roommate and nothing more.

The separateness and individualism of the roommate relationship was something that Reiko encountered as well, albeit without the hostility. Her roommate had also communicated that they would be "roommates and nothing more," but Reiko came to appreciate the advantages of this arrangement:

> I like the American system. My roommate is just my roommate. In [my country] I would be worrying and thinking all the time about my roommate. If I want to go to dinner, I feel I have to ask my roommate, "Have you eaten yet? Would you like to go to dinner?" I must ask her about her classes and help her if she has a problem. Here I have a roommate and I work separately. I don't have to care about her. It's easier.

International students saw "individualism" and "independence" as characteristic not only of roommate interactions but of relations with family and friends as well. When Arturo was asked about how AnyU students differed from those in his own country, he responded: "There's much more independence here. At home, students live with their parents. Here families aren't that tied together. My roommates call their dads and moms maybe once a week, and that's it. It would be different if they were Mexican." Alicia, another Mexican student, thought similarly that "Americans have a lot of independence. At eighteen in Mexico, I can't think of living by myself. Maybe it's the money, but we think united is better, for both family ties and for expenses."

For Peter from Germany, Nadif from Somalia, and Nigel from England, the disconnection from family had repercussions for social life with friends. Americans, they felt, sharply distinguished their family from their friends and schoolmates; more than one international student remarked about the dearth of family photos on student doors, as if family didn't exist at school. International students generally saw family as more naturally integrated into their social lives. "When you're not near your family," Peter told me, "it's hard to know where do I invite people. No one here says, 'Come on and meet my family.' Here I have to invite people to come to a home with two other people I don't know. It's strange."

Nadif continued in a similar vein:

> I have American friends, but I haven't been to their houses. I don't know their parents or their brothers and sisters or families. Back home, if I have a friend, everyone in their family knows me and I know them. If I go over to visit [friends] and they're not there, I still stay and talk with their family. Here friendship doesn't involve families. I don't know where my friends live and who their families are.

Nigel found the American system peculiar, much less similar to his own culture than he had expected. "My friends come to my house, and they just walk in. It's like they're friends not just with me but with my family. You know, a lot of my friends' parents buy me Christmas presents." He went on:

> If I have a party—like at Christmas I had a big party—my mum and dad, they'd just join in and drink with everyone else and have a good time. My American friends would think that's daft. I have friends [at AnyU] who have all grown up in the same city near one another. They wouldn't know how to have a conversation with anyone else's parents. They get their friends to come over when their parents are out, like, "Hey, my parents are away, come on over." At home, it doesn't make a difference whether your parents are there or not.

For Alicia from Mexico, this was all evidence of American "independence." But "independence," she argued, was one side of the coin. The other side "is that I'm not sure that they have real friendships."

The issue of real friendship was often more problematic in interviews than I had anticipated. I typically asked what I considered to be a straightforward question: "Do you have friends who are American?"

"I'm not sure," answered one Japanese girl. "My American roommate might be a friend."

"What makes you unsure?" I queried further.

"Well, I like my roommate," she explained, "and sometimes even I cook and we eat together at home, but since August [six months earlier] we have

gone out together three times. That's really not much, not what friends would do in my country, so I don't know."

Another student responded to my question about friends with one of his own. "What do you mean by 'friend,'" he asked, "*my* version or the American version?" A French student responded quickly to my query about friends: "Sure I have friends. It's so easy to meet people here, to make friends." Then she added: "Well, not really friends. That's the thing. Friendship is very surface-defined here. It is easy to get to know people, but the friendship is superficial. We wouldn't even call it a friendship. In France, when you're someone's friend, you're their friend for life." Their trouble answering my question taught me something: There were recurring questions about what constitutes friendship for Americans.

A prime difficulty in sorting out the concept centered on judgments surrounding what one did for a friend. When Maria made her first American "friends," she expected that they would be more active in helping her settle in her new home.

> I was living in a new country and I needed help. Like with setting up a bank account and doing the lease. It was new for me. And looking for a mechanic to fix my car. Or going shopping—I didn't know what to buy [for my room]. And when I tell my friends that I had a hard day trying to figure out all the things they say, "Oh, I'm so sorry for you."

Maria found it unfathomable. "In Mexico, when someone is a friend, then regardless of the situation, even if I would get in trouble, I would help them. American people are always busy. 'Oh, I like you so much,' they say. But then if I'm in trouble, it's, 'Oh, I'm so sorry for you.' 'So sorry for you' doesn't help!"

Geeta's roommates seemed just the opposite. When she told them that she was planning on buying a used car, they told her, "Oh, you don't need a car. We have two cars and one of us will take you where you want to go." But then after a while, she explained,

> I see how life is here. It's like I'm a little eight-year-old girl, and I have to say. "Could someone please take me here?" "Could someone take me there?" So I don't ask much. One day I said that I need a ride to school, and my roommate says, "Fine, but you have to leave right now," and now isn't when I want to go. After a while, I saw that I needed my own car.

Nigel told me: "I don't understand the superficiality in friendships here. Americans are much friendlier than the English, but then it doesn't really go anywhere. As far as deep friendships are concerned—I know there are people who have deep friendships, but it's a lot harder to figure out who those people will be." I asked him, "What's so different about friendship at home?"

> I think friends at home are closer. We're in touch every day, for one thing. For another, when one person is doing something, the others are supporting them. Here one of my American friends graduated, and I went to the graduation to support him. A lot of our other friends were here for graduation, but they didn't even go to watch him graduate, and they weren't even doing anything. That upset me. There's a lot of incidents like that. It's confusing.

"Confusing," "funny," "peculiar" were all words used to describe American social behavior. "Why do so many students eat alone in their rooms rather than go out or cook together?" "Why don't any of the guys on my hall know how to cook anything?" "Why does everyone here use computers [Instant Messaging] to communicate with people who are down the hall or in the same dorm?" "Why do young Americans talk so much about *relationships*?"

The *way* that Americans socialized was also a prime subject of comment. Two points stood out. First, Americans don't socialize as much, tending to spend more time alone, as this British student explained:

> People back home of my age socialize a lot more. On a free night, you'd go out and meet friends and be doing something together. You'd probably go out as a big group. In a week of seven days, I'd probably go out two or three nights. It's all student-based and promoted. Here, in the evenings, you walk down the hall and people are sitting in their rooms playing video games and watching television.

The second thing consistently noticed by international students is how Americans seem to separate socializing and partying from the rest of their lives. "Social life in Japan," explained one student, "is different. It's not like, 'This is party time.' It's more integrated with the rest of your day and your life." A French student noted this same pattern, but with regard to clothing. "We'll be hanging out; and then we decide to go out. The American girl in the group says, 'I need to go home and change.' I think, why? It's the same people. We're just going to a different place now. We're not going to anyplace fancy. What is so different now that you have to go change your clothes?"

For one British student as well, the American "party time" mentality was perplexing:

I don't understand this party thing in the U.S. When you go out here, it's get drunk or nothing. If people go out with people and drink, they have to get drunk. If they don't get falling-down drunk, they think, "What's the point of doing it?" I find it difficult to understand. It's really a European thing. You socialize, have a few drinks together, and go home.

For many international students, then, there was more flow between family and friends, school and home, and between academics and social life.

Classroom Life

In the classroom, most foreign students notice what U.S. adults, if they have been away long from academia, would probably notice too: there is an informality to the U.S. college classroom that some, including professors, would interpret as bordering on disrespect. A Japanese student giggled as she told me: "It makes me laugh when I see how students come to class: shorts, flip-flops . . . torn T-shirts. Some students come to class in pajamas!" A Middle Eastern student exclaimed: "You have so much freedom here. You can step out of class in the middle of the class! We could never do that." For one Asian student, one of the surprises was how often students interrupt the professor in the middle of a lecture to ask their own questions. This would not be tolerated in his country. An African student shared his thoughts: "There are certain things that surprise me about American students. I look at how they drink and eat during class. They put their feet up on the chairs. They pack up their books at the end of class before the teacher has finished talking." One European student noted, "We used to eat and drink in class sometimes, but at least we hid it!"

Indeed, as any American college student knows, stepping out of class or interrupting a lecture with questions is now quite acceptable. Eating and drinking during class, sleeping openly, packing up books before the teacher has finished talking have come to be standard behavior that most professors will ignore.

For the most part, international students liked the American classroom and American professors. U.S. professors were described by different international students as "laid-back," "helpful," "open," "tolerant" (of scant clothing and sleeping in class), "casual," and "friendly." Some, like the UAE and Somali students, appreciated that "teachers are not as involved in your lives— they don't see where you live or try to force you to study." For others, including the Japanese and Korean students, it was the interest in listening to students' problems and opinions and in helping students that was refreshing:

Teachers think helping students is their job. In Japan they don't think that way. I e-mailed my prof in Japan because I am doing an independent study and I asked her to send me an article. She got mad at me and thought this was very rude for me to ask her to do this.

American professors are more open; they give you their phone numbers and some let you call them at home. You can really talk to them outside of class and they are willing to give you extra help.

Although American professors and the American classroom received high marks for openness and helpfulness, they received mixed reviews on course content, including its rigor, organization, and modes of evaluation. Although one Indian student appreciated that "profs tell me which points to concentrate on when I read; they sometimes give chapter summaries so I know what to focus my attention on," more than one other mentioned the controlled way in which the American college classroom is run. The student is given a small chunk of reading and lecture to absorb, and then there is a test, usually short-answer format. Then there is another chunk of reading and a test. It is a system that one student described as "forced study," but one in which it's generally fairly easy to master the material and do well.

Engagement Most international students were used to a less pre-digested academic diet. Their course content was delivered by lecture, and it was students' responsibility to fully understand the content without the benefit of outlines, projected overhead notes, and other aids, as in the American classroom. Their grades for the semester would be based only on two long comprehensive essay exams and sometimes a lengthy theme paper. The American approach—frequent small short-answer tests sometimes coupled with study guides and lecture outlines—was criticized by different international students:

> [It works but] in some ways . . . it's like elementary school or grade school. The teacher tells you exactly which chapters to study, and then you review just those chapters. The advisers tell you the courses to take and approve your schedule. Sometimes it's annoying.

> Students here have lots of exams, really small quizzes. The quizzes make you study. You learn a little bit for the quiz, then you learn a little bit different for the next quiz. But people forget from week to week. Once the quiz is over, they forget. . . . Really, I wonder at the end of the semester what people remember when they leave.

> I find it difficult to take the exams here seriously. You can go into a multiple-choice exam without studying really and still come out all right from things you remember from class, and a process of elimination. You could never go into an exam back home knowing nothing. They're essay, and you start from a blank page; you wouldn't know

what to write. Knowing almost nothing there, you'd get a 20 percent. Here you could pass the test!

Still some students appreciated the American grading system, with smaller, non-comprehensive exams and a syllabus, serving almost as a contract that laid out exactly how tests, papers, and presentations would bear on the final grade. As one Asian student explained:

> We don't know what we're getting for a grade in [my country]. We don't have small quizzes, just one final exam or sometimes two, and there's no class participation. I had a class that I thought I was doing well in but I got a C. Expectations are much clearer in the U.S. They are much clearer about grading. It's easier to see results of a test or paper and how it related to a grade in a course.

"Teaching in America is like a one-man show," argued Élène, a French student, in the middle of our interview. "Teachers tell jokes; they do PowerPoint. There is audience participation."

"I thought you just said that in France it was a one-man show," I followed up, "because the teacher basically just stood up with a microphone and lectured."

"Yeah, that's true" Élène went on, "but it's not entertainment. It's a lecture. They're not trying to interest and entertain the students, and where I went to school we never rated the professors, like entertainers, with evaluations at the end of every course."

Opinions of the U.S. system varied somewhat with a student's country of origin. While Mexican students found U.S. professors and advisers a little formal, most international students noted their easy informality. A Chinese student was alone in mentioning that "the profs don't seem to prepare as much. There is little in the way of class notes or handouts for the students." And while the UAE and Somali students believed that "U.S. students are more serious about school because it makes more of a difference to your future," for most international students, either the lack of rigor of American classes or the work attitudes of American students presented a different sort of surprise.

"When I was in Japan, I heard how hard it was to go to university in the U.S.," said one student, "but now I'm here and I see that many students don't do the work."

"How do you know that?" I asked.

She responded, "When I talk about an assignment, they say they didn't do it!" It's confusing, though, she admitted: "Students in my class complain a lot about the time commitment while, at the same time, they talk about the parties they go to and the drinking. Some students make the effort, but I see that many others don't do the work."

Most European students agreed that U.S. classes were less demanding. "My first two years of classes in this country," said Élène, "were at the high school level. What a joke! Only at the 300 and 400 level am I seeing much better and harder material." A British student commented: "My involvement within my actual classes is a lot higher here, but as far as the content of work, it's actually a lot easier. I didn't work nearly as hard as I could, and I got Bs and better in all of my classes." According to Li, Chinese students work harder and do more homework: "I don't think the American students work that hard. I did a group project with an American student and I see he follows. I organize. I suggest the books we should read because I want a good grade. He just comes to meetings but doesn't really prepare. At the end, he thanks me for carrying the project."

"Group work" was one of three points that were often repeated when I asked what if anything is different about the "academic approach" in the American classroom. I had never really thought about it until I saw how many international students noted the frequency of group projects and presentations in their classes. One European recounted: "Here they keep telling you to get into groups; do a presentation. I've done so many presentations while I've been here I can't believe it. . . . Many of them aren't even marked— we just do them as an exercise. I think it's a good thing, because people here get a lot more confident about talking in front of others."

"It's funny," I mused with Beniko, a Japanese student, "that in such an individual culture students do so much work in groups."

"I think I understand why you can," she answered. "It is because of your individualism. In Japan, we don't and couldn't do much group work because we would consider each other TOO MUCH, and the project would get very complicated because of that." Only American students, she suggested, would have the necessary boundaries and sense of their own preferences to be able to negotiate the demands of a group project.

Individualism and individual choice also figured into both of the other mentioned themes. For Asian students in particular, one formidable challenge of the American classroom was in the number of times people were asked to "say what they think." "Professors are always asking what you think of this and think of that," maintained one Japanese student. "It's great, but it's scary when you're not used to this. I don't always know what I think."

One Korean woman remarked to me:

Everything here is: "What do you want?" "What do you think?" "What do you like?" Even little children have preferences and interests in this country. I hear parents in restaurants. They ask a three-year-old child, "Do you want French fries or potato chips?" Every little kid in this country can tell you, "I like green beans but not spinach, I like vanilla but not chocolate, and my favorite color is blue." They're used to thinking that way.

"Choice" abounds in the U.S. educational system in ways that most American-born students are unaware of. "You can take [courses] that interest you here," affirmed one student. "If I like archaeology—good, I take it. But then I also like astronomy, so I take that." A Japanese student explained that at home she "can't take a ceramics course just because I like it." The courses she takes are determined by her major and not subject to choice. In Europe, another student told me, "when we get electives, we are able to choose from a very short list which course from the list you will take. You get very few 'open credits'—what *you* call electives—where you can actually pick the course, and it is usual for someone to take a course that is related to their major so it helps them with other courses."

In their home countries, most international students could not change their major, nor could they liberally choose classes outside their major, nor could they double-major or double-minor. Most could not drop courses after they were enrolled. For some international students, even being able to pick one's major was a luxury. In countries that rely heavily on test scores for entry into specific fields, one's major often depends on rankings on exams. A Japanese student reported: "Many people in Japan pick majors they don't want. My friend is studying to be an English teacher, but she wants to be a dog groomer. She picked her major based on her test results and what she did well in."

"There's a lot of choice in your curriculum," one Spanish student maintained, "and even in the time you take classes. In Spain, certain courses MUST be taken, and a class is given at one time and that's it."

The same choice inherent in the curriculum was seen in the extra-curriculum. "There are so many clubs to choose from here—you can pick any interest and there will be a club for it!" remarked an African student. "If you want to join a sport in my country," said another, "we have one or two sports you can join (soccer and cricket), but here you can choose from so many different ones like climbing, snowboarding, basketball, soccer, football—and so many more."

There were few detractors from the benefits of choice in the American system, but a couple of students pointed out the downside of having so *much* choice. One suggested: "Your system is much more complicated, and it's much less specialized. Because you take so many different kinds of courses, you are spread thinner and have less focused knowledge in particular areas." Another looked at the implications of students' freedom to drop a course at will: "People here can drop a class whenever they want. If I don't like it, I drop it. If I don't like the teacher, I drop it. If I'm not doing well, I drop it. In Spain, once you sign, you pay, and you can't drop. I think it affects attitude."

Indeed, as one foreign-born teacher confided, "I take time to talk to my students who didn't do well on an exam or who are having trouble. I suggest that they set up an appointment with me, and I tell them what skills they need to work on extra. The minute I do that, it has the opposite effect in your system. Instead of coming to my office, they drop the class. It's really quite surprising!"

Worldliness and Worldview

The single biggest complaint international students lodged about U.S. students was, to put it bluntly, our ignorance. As informants described it, by "ignorance" they meant the misinformation and lack of information that Americans have both about other countries and about themselves. Although most international students noted how little other students asked them about their countries, almost all students had received questions that they found startling: "Is Japan in China?" "Do you have a hole for a bathroom?" "Is it North Korea or South Korea that has a dictator?" "Where exactly is India?" "Do you still ride elephants?" "Do they dub American TV programs into British?"

These are just a few of the questions American students actually asked of international students. While they no doubt came from the less sophisticated among their classmates, it was clear that international students across the board felt that most Americans—even their own friends—are woefully ignorant of the world scene. It is instructive to hear how students from diverse countries discuss their perceptions of American students' views of themselves and the world.

JAPAN: Really, they don't know very much about other countries, but maybe it's just because a country like Japan is so far away. Japanese probably don't know about the Middle East. Sometimes, students keep asking about ninjas.

UAE: American students are nice, but they need to stop being so ignorant about other countries and other cultures. Americans need to look at the world around them, and even the cultures around them in their own country.

MEXICO: The U.S. is not the center of the world. [Americans] don't know anything about other countries. Many of them don't have an interest in learning about other cultures. The only things students ever ask me about in my culture is food.

CHINA: Americans know very little about China or its culture. Most people think China is still very poor and very communist-controlled, with no freedom. There is a very anticommunist feeling, and people know little about today's China, which is quite changing and different. New Zealanders know much more about China—perhaps it's their proximity. I think that older people here have more of a sense of history, and that history, about the wars, about the cold war, makes them understand more about the world. Younger people seem to have no sense of history.

ENGLAND: People here know surprisingly little about England, and they assume a lot of things, some true, some not. People's impressions of me when I say I'm from England is that I might drink tea off a silver tray, and maybe live in a castle, and use a red telephone box. That's the honest truth. The questions that I've been asked are unbelievable.

MALAYSIA: I tell people that I am Muslim, and they take for granted that I'm an Arab. How can they not realize that not all Muslims are Arabs when they have many Muslims here who are American?

GERMANY: American students are much more ignorant of other countries and cultures. I suppose it's because it's so big, and knowing about California for you is like us knowing about France. It's a neighbor. The U.S. is less dependent on other cultures, and maybe that's why they need to know less. Still, Americans come across as not interested in other cultures, like they don't really care about other countries. So they think things like Swedish people are only blonds.

INDIA: Somebody asked me if we still ride on elephants. That really bothered me. If I say I'm Indian, they ask which reservation? I say I'm from Bombay. "Where is Bombay?" Some people don't even know where India is. A friend of mine and I tried to make these Americans see what it was like and we asked them where they're from. They said California. And we said, Where was that?

FRANCE: People here don't know where anything is. For World War II, the teacher had to bring in a map to show where Germany and England are—it was incredible! I read somewhere a little research that said only 15 to 20 percent of Americans between the ages eighteen to twenty-five could point out Iraq on a map. The country will go to war, but it doesn't know where the country is!

Despite the critical consensus in these comments, it would be unfair of me to represent international student perspectives as roundly negative. In general, students from outside the United States warmly appreciated the American educational system as well as the spirit of the American college student. The criticisms that they did have, though, were pointed and focused. Taken together, they amounted to nothing less than a theory of the relationship among ignorance, intolerance, and ethnocentrism in this country, one that international eyes saw bordering on profound self-delusion. When I asked the linked questions, "What would you want American students to see about themselves?" and "What advice would you give them?" one German student stated succinctly what many students communicated to me at greater length: "Americans seem to think they have the perfect place to live, the best country, the best city. I hear that all the time. I used to think you just got that from politicians, but now I see it's from regular people too. The patriotism thing here really bothers me."

It is sobering to hear these words from a German student, whose country's historical experience in the 1930s and 1940s taught him the dangers of hypernationalism. To his fellow U.S. students he offered this recommendation: "I'd give them advice to live elsewhere. They should recognize that the way of living in the U.S. is fine, but it isn't necessarily the best way for everyone. I don't like to evaluate, and I'd like that applied to me. Be more informed. Information leads to tolerance."

It bothered a Chinese student who read in an article that American students don't want to study a foreign language because they believe that the world language will be English. "I think they need to learn about the world, to learn a foreign language," he urged. It bothered a British student, who lamented how much of world music American students seem to miss. "Everything here [on his corridor] is either black gangster rap or punk rock, and that's basically it. They don't want to hear other music—contemporary music from around the world."

The connection between lack of information and intolerance translated occasionally into personal stories of frustration, hitting home in the lives of some students. "I wish they [his hall mates] were accepting of more different music," said an Indian student. "I play my own music. I play it loud just like they do—Arabic and Punjabi and other stuff—and they complain to the RAs. But it's my right to play that too. Why don't they understand that?"

"They don't accept other cultures," speculated one Japanese student.

> Once I was eating the food I had made—Japanese noodles—and we Japanese eat noodles with a noise. Somebody else in the kitchen area looked at me funny. She asked, "Why are you making so much noise?" I told her that's the way Japanese eat their noodles, and I can see by her face that she is disapproving. It hurt me to see that. Some Americans don't care about other worlds.

One key toward creating a more positive cycle of information, self-awareness, and tolerance was for many the university and university education itself. Learn a foreign language and study overseas, many recommended for individual students. Use your education to expand your purview beyond your own country. For the university, other students recommended a greater emphasis on self-awareness, including a more critical eye directed to our own institutions and history.

For one Chinese student, the need to be more reflective about the media representation of news and issues was critical: "Media coverage has a very great influence here. In China, it has less influence because everyone knows it's propaganda. Here it is not seen that way because there is a free press. But it's curious." In American newspaper articles and TV news, "the individual facts are true often, but the whole is not sometimes. I can see how Americans need to question the way stories are being represented to them."

A French student beseeched us to examine our own educational system:

> Americans teach like the only important thing is America. There is no required history course in college. The history course I took on Western civ. at AnyU was middle-school level, and it was very biased. I mean they taught how, in World War II, America saved France and saved the world, how they were so great. The courses don't consider what

Americans have done wrong. All the current events here is news about America and what America is doing. If it's about another country, it's about what America is doing there. There's nothing about other countries and their histories and problems. [In France] we had lots of history and geography courses, starting very young. I learned about France, but then we had to take a course in U.S. industrialization, in China, Russia, Japan, too. We got the history and geography of the world, so we could see how France now fits into the bigger picture.

Thesis= For the international students I interviewed, American college culture is a world of engagement, choice, individualism, and independence, but it is also one of cross-cultural ignorance and self-delusion that cries out for remediation. It was a Somali student who summed up all of their hopes for "America": "You have so much here, and so many opportunities. I wish America would ask more what this country can do to make the world a better place."

Notes

[1]   Some comments in this chapter appear in edited form. I took notes during international student interviews, and tried to get comments down verbatim, but did not tape the interviews. As a result, I often imposed my own native English on them, so, for instance, a Japanese woman saying, "Excuse but not understand," would be written as "Excuse me but I don't understand." I did not record in my notes "uhs," "you knows," and other interjections and hesitations that would have been preserved in a taped record. This chapter contains many snippets of conversations. For a fuller feeling for the thinking of international students, and more complete narrative from individuals, see Garrod and Davis 1999.

[2]   I employ the vernacular use of "American" to mean U.S., but, as international students are well aware, there are many countries in the Americas, and making "American" equivalent with only the United States is one aspect of the egocentricity international students identify with the U.S. system. Nevertheless, this term accurately represents how students themselves talk about the United States.

UNIT TWO
CULTURE AND THE THINGS WE MAKE

CULTURE AND THE THINGS WE MAKE

This set of readings is about photographs, blue jeans and the practice of many Muslim women of wearing a veil. It is also about how photographs reflect the attitudes of their creators and how they affect the mindsets of their viewers and how clothes become personal and historical symbols. In the first reading Lutz and Collins describe their study of photographs that appeared in *The National Geographic* from 1950 to 1986. The authors looked for patterns in the ways in which non-Western people were presented in this popular magazine. Each of 594 photographs was coded for twenty characteristics. One of the codings was for skin color of non-Westerners depicted in the photographs. Subjects in the photographs were classified as dark-skinned, white, or bronze. In every case anyone who was neither very dark-skinned nor obviously white was classified as bronze. The coding in this case shows a remarkable regularity. For twenty-five years 28 percent of non-Western subjects pictured were dark-skinned, 60 percent bronze, and 12 percent white. Could this simply be coincidental or does this reflect an editorial policy? Lutz and Collins claim that the marketing department of the magazine during the twenty-five years had surveyed readers about which articles they liked and disliked. Articles about Africa were the least popular according to findings of the marketing department.

The authors supplement their quantitative study with descriptions that are qualitative and evaluative. They also connect their generalizations about the photographs to historical events and trends of those decades.

While one may disagree about aspects of the method and scope of the generalizations made by Lutz and Collins, it is important to emphasize the categories which the authors generate. Consider the way in which background is treated in a photograph. For example, zooming in on subjects thereby leaving very little background sets the subject outside of a social and historical context. It gives the impression of an idealized subject, outside history and social change, a timeless, natural person. The reader is provoked to think about the way in which photographs induce the perceiver to make certain conscious and subconscious interpretations of the people pictured. A goal of the course is to stimulate critical self-awareness of the bases on which we make our interpretations of the Other. Pursuing context, asking for more detail, suspending immediate impressions are marks of the serious student of other cultures and of the global citizen.

The dynamic quality of the things we make is illustrated by the American blue jean. Beverly Gordon offers a lively biography of the denim pants from their creation by Levi Strauss in the 1850s to their "worn to death" look in the 1980s. From its childhood as an attire only for work to its adolescence as anti-fashion and counter culture statement, to its adulthood: "abused," "distressed" "sabotaged," "blasted," "washed out," "polar washed,"—but a designer fashion, the blue jean has carried meanings tied to American history. Contrast the portrait which freezes the subject with the dynamic cultural object which can embody so much historical human meaning. As others have observed, there is an internal contradiction in putting cultural artifacts in a museum where they become lifeless portraits. Gordon invites us to link the blue jean to our personal histories and our country's as well.

Clothing is sometimes an expression of deeply held rules for living as in the case of the veil. Imtiaz Ahmad argues that the requirement of women to wear the veil is not in original Islam but came to be mandated only in those societies which required that women be secluded before Islam became the religion of those societies. According to the author what was merely a "form of dress" in Muslim countries became a symbol of resistance to the Western charge, often made in the nineteenth century, that this form of dress was backward and that Islam itself was backward. Gordon and Ahmad invite us to study the ways in which events in history charge and change practical arrangements and clothes into powerful symbols.

from READING NATIONAL GEOGRAPHIC

Catherine A. Lutz and Jane L. Collins

A WORLD BRIGHTLY DIFFERENT:
PHOTOGRAPHIC CONVENTIONS
1950—1986

To make an exact image is to insure against disappearance, to cannibalize life until it is safely and permanently a specular image, a ghost.

(Haraway 1984/85:42)

The result of the production practices and institutional history just described is a rich and voluminous corpus of magazine issues and photographs. Even decades-old issues of the magazine have a significant continuing life. Millions of copies are archived in public libraries, and millions more inhabit the bookshelves and attics of private homes. Current copies are scattered liberally across America's coffee tables and doctors' waiting rooms. This corpus has, then, both historical significance and contemporary impact. To understand it, we begin with an analysis of the surface content of the photos. We ask how people in other lands have been depicted, what they have been photographed doing, and how the photo has been composed. The goals of this exploration are to describe the genre, to glean some clues as to the models of difference held by the producers of the magazine, and to relate both of these aspects to historical sociocultural processes and changes of the postwar period.

. . . We look at photographs as they relate to each other (that is, the set of *National Geographic* magazines of the period) and to their historical and social context (the United States since 1950). We develop our own critical sense of the photograph as an artifact that can be analyzed with some reference to—but not reducible to—its makers' institutional context, constraints, intentions, and unconscious motives on the one hand, or, on the other, its readers' construction of meaning. In reading the photographs in this way, we have drawn on the insights of the social historians and theoreticians of images, including especially Benjamin (1985), Gaines (1988), Geary (1988), Graham-Brown (1988),

Modleski (1988), Sekula (1981), Shapiro (1988), Sontag (1977), Tagg (1988), Traube (1989), and Williamson (1978).[1] These scholars have drawn our attention to the many ways in which photographs signify—through formal elements such as color, composition, and vantage point; through narrative structure, including what is internal to the shot and what results from setting photographs in a sequence; through specific items in photo and caption that relate directly to cultural ideas and phenomena outside the picture; through their position in a cultural hierarchy that includes art, television, and consumer goods; and through their ability to assume or ignore, to evoke or discount, their readers' social experience and values.

In addition to this kind of analysis of individual *Geographic* photographs, we took a large set from the period 1950 through 1986 and systematically asked a series of questions about each. We chose this period because we wanted to trace effects of the decolonization process and the Vietnam War. Another consideration was that only after World War II did a large number of people contribute to each issue. Photographs before the war reflect individual as much as truly institutional behavior.

Our method consisted of randomly sampling one photograph from each of the 594 articles featuring non-Western people published in that period.[2] Each photo was coded independently by two people for twenty-two characteristics.[3] . . . Although at first blush it might appear counterproductive to reduce the rich material in any photograph to a small number of codes, quantification does not preclude or substitute for qualitative analysis of the pictures. It does allow, however, discovery of patterns that are too subtle to be visible on casual inspection and protection against an unconscious search through the magazine for only those which confirm one's initial sense of what the photos say or do.

An important set of themes runs through all *National Geographic* renderings of the non-Euramerican world. The people of the third and fourth worlds are portrayed as *exotic*; they are *idealized*; they are *naturalized* and taken out of all but a single historical narrative; and they are *sexualized*. Several of these themes wax and wane in importance through the postwar period, but none is ever absent. While each region, country, or ethnic group has received some distinctive treatment, the magazine's global orientation means that readers may be likely to see all regions, even those occasionally not so depicted, as exotic, ideal, and so on. Together these themes establish *National Geographic*'s style of coverage, and they have, over the course of a century, helped to set an important cornerstone of its readers' definitions of the world. By looking more closely at some of these features of the photos, we can begin to see how the process of world definition is achieved.

An Exotic World

The eye of *National Geographic*, like the eye of anthropology, looks for cultural difference. It is continually drawn to people in brightly colored, "different" dress, engaged in initially strange-seeming rituals or inexplicable behavior. This exoticism involves the creation of an other who is strange but—at least as important—beautiful. At other times and in other media outlets, the exoticism of other people has been framed visually and verbally as less beautiful and more absurdly or derisively different. Movies, television news, and other post-war cultural artifacts have frequently trafficked in revolting ethnic difference. Take, for example, the evil penumbra painted around the eventually self-immolating Arabs in "Raiders of the Lost Ark" or the pathos and ugliness communicated by news images of Latin American poverty or Ethiopia's starvation (see also Postone and Traube 1986). These kinds of ugliness are relatively rare in the *National Geographic*.

The exotic other is by definition attractive, albeit in a special, threefold sense. When the camera looks for the unusual, it ensures a reader whose attention is riveted by the intriguing scene. It draws attention, at least implicitly, to things that define "us" in our unmarked and usual state of humanness, that is, as people who dress and act in "standard" ways. It also creates a distance that the magazine may or may not have attempted to bridge in other ways. The distance is a product of making the pictured person a kind of spectacle, the latter defined as something that both demands attention and "offers an imagistic surface of the world as a strategy of containment against any depth of involvement with that world" (Polan 1986b:63). One of the effects of the emphasis on spectacle is to discredit the significance of the foreign, even to create a sense of its fictitiousness.

A World of Ritual. No single feature renders the third world exotic more forcefully than the magazine's focus on ritual. Nearly one-fifth of all photographs with non-Westerners in them feature people engaged in or preparing for a ritual—ritual being defined in the narrow sense of sacred and formally organized group behavior. These pictures are among the most dramatic in the magazine, often chosen by the editors to spread across two pages in brilliant polychrome. A director in the photography department explained that all photographers naturally gravitate to ritual events because color and action make for intrinsically more interesting material. The interest also derives from cultural themes and helps reproduce them. The non-Westerner comes to be portrayed as a ritual performer, embedded (perhaps some would read encrusted) in tradition and living in a sacred (some would say superstitious) world. This is an emphasis that *National Geographic* has shared with earlier photography of the non-Western world, whose focus on ritual "reflected the assumption of Boas's generation that ritual contained distilled history and cultural wisdom, that it was the most conservative and thus the most mean- ingful remnant of culture" (Banta and Hinsley 1986:106). In other instances, this focus on non-Western ritual can be consistent with a view of the other as superstitious or irrational and might be responsible for contempt for the native mind (Drinnon 1980:442). *National Geographic* appears not to have taken this perspective, at least in the postwar period and in relation to the world's "great religions."

Much of the text accompanying pictures of ritual in the *National Geographic* makes explicit reference to an area's rituals and religion(s) as part of a long, ancient tradition. So the caption to a 1962 photograph of a New Guinea marriage feast notes that "tribal life still lies locked in millenniums- old patterns." Context for a Tibetan shaman at prayer in a 1977 photo is pro- vided by a caption which asserts that "the ancient Tibetan way of life . . . combines animism with the teachings of Buddha." The magazine tends to downplay a ritual's contemporary actuality and the historical changes that preceded its current form, although religious syncretism is often highlighted as a special kind of contrast narrative. Fascination with ritual stems from the sense that it is a key to the past and a sign of the trip through time taken by the photographer and writer. Anthropology has made parallel connections between past time and other people (Fabian 1983; Price 1989). Two primary features of exoticism—living close to the sacred or supernatural and living with the past—are actually combined in many of these pictures. By present- ing the ritual as a feature of custom or tradition, these pictures can also have, for many readers, the unintended effect of flattening the emotional life of the people depicted. This is because the ritual procession can be seen as a routine that people follow rather than as an expression of individual and group faith. The funeral becomes a moment of cultural display (of special paraphernalia or dress, as well as custom more generally) rather than a moment of grief (Rosaldo 1989).

Indexical Dress. In more than half of the photographs in the sample set, the non-Westerner is shown in indigenous dress, tribal fashion, and/or ritual costume. The *National Geographic* searches out native clothing in its most elaborate form. The Indian woman is often dressed not simply in an everyday sari, but in a gold-embroidered one, and she is festooned with jewelry. A Tibetan couple in the July 1955 issue stand, arms down, in a full-front portrait with little in the background or their gestures to distract from their bright silk and brocade outfits. A photograph such as that of a Masai woman (1954) is cropped so as to narrate a story about native styles of dress.

Exotic dress alone often stands for an entire alien life-style, locale, or mind-set. This is true not only of the *National Geographic* but of other Western photographic work on the third world as well. Local costume suggests something about the social stability and timelessness of the people depicted (Graham-Brown 1988), and in a story drawing attention to the social transformation of a people, changes from native to western-style dress are often highlighted by photographs that set locals in the two styles of dress in explicit contrast. A photo from the January 1983 *Geographic* shows young South American Indians dancing, some in native skirts and loincloths, some in jeans and T-shirts. A central story of the picture, told by way of dress, is of an encounter or passage between an exotic cultural pattern and a familiar one. The Western observer is likely to see Western dress as saying something about the mind-set of the person wearing those clothes. The man in Western dress can be understood as desiring social change, material progress, and Westernization in other spheres. Exotic dress can stand for a premodern attitude, Western dress for a forward-looking Western orientation.

The highlighting of native dress contributes not only to a view of others as different, but also to their framing as picturesque and erotic, beautiful and sexually alluring (Graham-Brown 1988:118). The orange silks and fur-trimmed shirts of the local elite wrap whole peoples in an imagined sensuality and luxurious beauty. Because differences in dress can easily be interpreted as questions of style and because they draw attention away from such matters as conflict of interest, they make the entire notion of difference among people easily digestible (Bolton 1990:269). Difference becomes assimilable to the idea of taste, and, like that concept, allows the renaming of poverty as "bad taste" and unlike values as matters of consumer choice.

The focus on native dress in *National Geographic* shows some fluctuations during the postwar period, dropping slowly over two decades to 44 percent of the total in 1970. A sudden reversal of this trend put the figure at 63 percent in the early seventies, but that increase was again steadily eroded through the next fifteen years. It is not until the mid-eighties that the proportion of native dress found in photographs reached the lower levels of the late sixties. The editors of the magazine now face a substantial challenge in how they will deal with the theme of exoticism as differences in dress play less and less into defining cultural difference and as more and more tourists have already seen the dress and the festivals that have done the work of painting an exotic other.

The Role of Color Photography. Contemporary *National Geographic* photographs display vibrant, striking colors. Advanced printing techniques now allow ink to be laid down in such a way that color virtually hovers above the glossy page. Giving the magazine its allure and self-definition, color has distinctive qualities both for those who take the pictures and those who read them. Polan (1986a) contrasts the glamorous and wish-fulfilling qualities of color with the mundane factuality suggested by black and white. Advertising photos have, since the 1950s, almost always been made in color, while news photography has until recently almost always been reproduced in black and white. Through these practices, color has become the language of consumption and plenty, black and white the conduit of facts, often spare or oppressive. Color is the vehicle of spectacle, black and white of the depth of facts behind the screen. Accordingly, for journalists and some artists, color photography came to be seen as "frivolous and shallow," black and white, with its focus on light and shape, as "more artistic and creative" (Bryan 1987:295).

On the whole, however, color photography has been perfectly suited to the *National Geographic* project of presenting an exotically peopled world. While photographs of animals, geological formations, and American and European subjects are also, of course, presented in color, color in relation to people in exotic places can and does lend different potential meaning to a photograph. The color of an orange shirt on an American man can be absorbed as a visual pleasure in itself, while orange-colored robes on a Buddhist monk might become "saffron" in caption or in the reader's imagination, thereby underlining cultural difference.

Some photos continued to appear in black and white into the period we are examining, particularly through 1960,[4] and it is instructive to note what subjects the editors have tended to portray in black and white when its use was declining. A significant number of these pictures show the Western narrator of the article, often explorer or anthropologist. It is almost as though the black-and-white photo says, "This is a person of a distinct type, standing to his 'colored' brethren as the factual black and white does to the fantasy, multicolor shot." Here, more clearly than elsewhere, the Western observer or explorer is portrayed as scientist, whose presence needs to be reported but whose appearance need not be examined in detail. Rarely treated in black and white are the ritual, the spectacle par excellence; and the portrait, a study of personality, the "colorful" individual.[5] Declining use can also mean that a black-and-white photo is likely to be interpreted as an old photo by contemporary readers.

Idealizations: From Noble Savage to a Middle-class World

The American Museum of Natural History bears striking similarities to the *National Geographic* magazine (on the former, see Haraway 1984/85). Both began as scientific institutions in the last third of the nineteenth century, with the aim of collecting natural artifacts from around the world and making them available to a public much wider than an educated or scientific elite. Both made extensive use of photographs, and both were concerned to present nature as highly ordered rather than random, creating, in effect, a world without blemish or handicap. Just as the Museum's dioramas never included old or feeble exemplars of elephants or zebras, so too has *National Geographic* presented, until the late 1970s, photographs that virtually eliminate the ill, the pockmarked, the deformed, or the hungry.

The idealization of the non-Westerner, like the idealization of nature, has its roots in the magazine's explicit editorial policy. More broadly, we can see this beautification of the world's people as linked to a number of themes in American cultural history. The first is the notion that nature represented a spiritual domain in which the ills of civilization could be cured (Nash 1982). Since at least some non-Western people were subsumed under the category natural rather than cultural, their perfection and beauty would be represented. There are in the magazine traces of the nineteenth-century religious scientism in which nature was considered divine. These pieties, once centered in the wilderness concept and now in some kinds of environmentalism, echo Schiller's statement, "Everything that nature achieves is divine" (cited in Monti 1987:80). The ambivalence toward modernity that arose with the new middle class at the turn of the century (Lears 1981) could also be played out in these views of beauty and nature in a simpler, more natural overseas world.

Another factor in idealizing is an anxiety about threats of chaos or decay. An ideal world, free of suffering, does not require work to bring about change. Connectedness and responsibility are downplayed, as the world's peoples become aesthetic objects to appreciate. The act of appreciating them lets the viewer see himself or herself as both humane (because the photographed are still recognized as people) and as cultured (because the photograph is like a museum piece, a work of art). The beauty of these pictures can also be seen, as Haraway (1984/85) points out for nature photography and taxidermy and as Stewart (1984) points out for the souvenir, as the attempt to simultaneously arrest time and decay and to allay elite and middleclass fears that the wealth of the American twentieth century might be lost.

Finally, in looking for and finding perfection, the *National Geographic* camera may prevent the reader from finding the exotic other *too* different. Motivated by its classic humanism, the *Geographic* has cleaned up the culturally different person in the same way that other photographers have created images of gays and lesbians in America, presenting "clean-cut, shiny-haired, Land's End *citizens with a difference*" (Grover 1990:168). The move to create a beautiful image can stir up new problems, however, for the search for beauty can produce an intensification of the "fracture, partial identification, pleasure and distrust" (Rose 1986:227) that might accompany much visual experience.

We can now consider some of the techniques by which the magazine achieves its idealization of others.

The Smile. Though *National Geographic* editors see themselves as documenting naturally occurring behavior, the non-Westerners they photograph often acknowledge and turn to the camera. Twenty percent of all pictures have at least one foreground figure looking at the camera, and almost one-third of all photos show one or more people smiling. The smile, like the portrait, follows cultural conventions in defining and depicting the person. The smiling, happy person evokes the goal of the pursuit of happiness, written into the Declaration of Independence. These conventions stand in marked contrast to other ethnopsychologies (Lutz 1988) and other, more serious modes of composing the self for the photograph (King 1985). The smile is a key way of achieving idealization of the other, permitting the projection of the ideal of the happy life.

Portraiture. The portrait often aims to capture the subject at that person's best; because it is posed, it allows for maximum control by both photographer and subject. Moreover, the goal of humanizing the other—giving the reader a sense that these are real people—is furthered when people are photographed as individuals and encountered as readable faces. *National Geographic* staff, recognizing the value of the portrait, makes it a staple of virtually all articles. Nine percent of the photos we examined show a person close up and often outside of a recognizable context, and this percentage has remained relatively constant.[6] Many of the photographs that National Geographic staff have selected as classic examples of photographs of the non-West are portraits. Portraits frequently adorn the walls of editorial offices; they are heavily reproduced in the book *Images of the World* (1981), which was published to define and celebrate *National Geographic* photographers; and they dominate in a centennial article on the magazine's photography (Livingston 1988). Of the twenty photographs in the article, which describes an exhibit in 1988 of *National Geographic* photos at the Corcoran Gallery in Washington, D.C., thirteen were of people, and nine of those were portraits.

The portrait allows for scrutiny of the person, the search for and depiction of character. It gives the ideology of individualism full play, inviting the belief that the individual is first and foremost a personality whose characteristics can be read from facial expression and gesture. In a related, although seemingly incongruous way, the portrait may also communicate a message of universal brotherhood. Many at the *Geographic* might agree with Cartier–Bresson's assessment of portraits: "They enable us to trace the sameness of man" (Galassi 1987). They do this by stripping away culture and leaving the universal, individual person.

Benjamin (1985:682) notes that portraits were very popular when the camera was first invented as part of a "cult of remembrance," a kind of ancestor worship. The *National Geographic* portrait may likewise be related to what Rosaldo (1989) calls imperialist nostalgia, that is, mourning the passing of what we ourselves have destroyed. But the *National Geographic* portrait, like all close-ups of only a part of the body, leaves us with a fragment of a person. According to Mulvey, the close-up "gives flatness [and] the quality of a cut-out or icon" (1985:809) to the depicted. This can sometimes be amplified by the namelessness and exoticism of the photographed non-Westerners in past *National Geographics*.

The portrait, then, has potentially paradoxical or different effects on viewers, highlighting the other as a personality, that central feature of the Western self, which yet remains unnamed, unapproachable, and fragmented. The portrait humanizes and yet constantly threatens to be absorbed into a taxonomic outcome—the mode of much previous photographic work on non-Westerners, which has "presented[ed] them as ethnic types rather than individuals" (Geary 1988:50).

Group Size. When going beyond the portrait, the *National Geographic* still prefers to photograph non-Westerners in small groups. Almost sixty percent of the sample photos show people in intimate groups of one to three persons, twenty-five percent in medium-size groups of four to twelve, and less than seventeen percent in large groups. Although *National Geographic's* photographic subjects were rarely named until the 1980s (the exceptions were famous figures such as Imelda Marcos or King Hussein), individuals and small groups are nonetheless often depicted in what might be read as rugged individualist stances. An African man is shown working alone plowing a field; a Japanese couple in their fishing boat reel in a heavy net. By contrast, print and television photojournalism often shows large groups engaged in mass protests and the like, limiting small group photos to celebrities or the elite. Individuals or small groups appearing in other photojournalism often come in "human interest" stories, where they may include families undergoing a calamity such as a fire or earthquake.

Gentle Natives and Wars Without Brutalized Bodies. In keeping with the stated policy of showing people at their best, very few *National Geographic* photographs show their subjects engaged in, being victimized by, or in the obvious aftermath of violent encounters. Only four photographs from the entire sample show local people fighting or threatening to fight or giving evidence of previous violence. This does not necessarily indicate that the American audience for these images sees violence or militarism as negative; it may, though, when the violence is perpetrated or threatened by foreigners. Thus, to show *these* people at their best requires a nonaggressive subject. Western photographers in other periods and genres have also hesitated to record militant non-Westerners, as when German photographers hesitated to depict King Njoya of central Africa in uniform during a period of anticolonial tension after 1909 (Geary 1988:53–59). In fully twelve percent of our sample photographs, however, there is some military presence, particularly men in uniform. In these photos, the military is presented as a regular, not unpleasant part of everyday life in the third world, but is rarely seen in internal or cross-national conflict. The military as an institutional force has been normalized, anger or aggression erased.

The *National Geographic* represses what some other representations of non-Westerners prominently feature—the violent potential of the savage other. Aggressivity could be and has been seen as a sign of regression, a primitive loss of control (Gilman 1985:99). Violent resistance to empire building, American or European, has usually been treated as a personality trait of natives rather than a situational response to the theft of land or other mode of attack (Drinnon 1980). This view of aggression as lack of control has led to non-Westerners being culturally constructed, like women and mental degenerates, as both physically strong and characterologically weak (cf. Taussig 1987). While other cultural venues have portrayed the "violent nature" of the Latin American, Middle Easterner, or Asian through the twentieth century, this is not the *National Geographic* beat.

Its avoidance of depicting violence between persons has not deterred the *National Geographic* from giving extensive coverage to wars, especially those in Korea and Vietnam, and the Cambodian genocide.[7] Korean coverage focuses on American soldiers, with the country treated as an interesting backdrop and Koreans as a group receiving needed American help. As Sontag (1977:18) points out, the audience for Korean war images had not been prepared by other media to see Asians as victims. A significant number of these and other photos in the *Geographic* show GIs feeding, entertaining, or enjoying local children.[8] One photograph in a 1956 article on the U.S. defense of Formosa is cheerfully titled "U.S. Navy gives an ice cream party."

National Geographic's Vietnam war photography has been called innocent by one of its official chroniclers, in contrast to the grimmer standards of *Life* and other publications (Bryan 1987). In fact, the difference is stark. The *Geographic*'s wars are shown through the anxious faces of civilians rather than the corpses of soldiers as published in other media outlets (Moeller 1989). An early article in October 1961 shows little evidence of the war itself. Only two of its forty-two pictures show soldiers, one of training exercises, the other of a patrol headed through and dwarfed by a magnificently ornate city gate in Hue. Three pictures, on the other hand, focus on beautiful young women, with captions describing one with a "face as radiant as the moon" or generalizing to "the grace and charm of Vietnamese women."

No Vietnam War photograph was ever innocent or apolitical, however, for all images of that country at war, whether graphic or not, emerged out of and circulated in the highly politicized atmosphere of the late 1960s and early 1970s. The claim of innocence itself involves a politics. As in much other American media coverage, the editorial intent was to support the government's version of the goals and values of the war effort and, in line with the "kindly light" policy, to make the war appear less unpleasant than it was.[9]

All war photography can potentially suggest parallels between gun and camera. It can also make visible atrocities that would otherwise be hidden. The former effect may be seen in a *Life* magazine photo published in 1969 (reprinted in Drinnon 1980:453) showing the anguished faces of a small group of people from My Lai village just before they were murdered. It is captioned in the photographer's words, "Guys were about to shoot these people. I yelled, 'Hold it,' and shot my picture. As I walked away, I heard M-16s open up. From the corner of my eye I saw bodies falling, but I didn't turn to look."

Such pictures—with their vivid depiction of suffering and their exposure of the passive, even accepting gaze of the photographer—are absent from the *Geographic*'s Vietnam articles. *National Geographic* photographs rarely show wounded civilians or soldiers. A 1966 photograph of a war victim's funeral has a festive air, owing to the bright colors of the clothing and the absence of obvious grief in the crowd. The armed soldiers who defend the casket, a potentially ominous element, stand small, squeezed to the side of the frame (February 1966).

This soft coverage may or may not contradict Wilbur Garrett's claim that his photographs have been "stripping away romantic notions and exposing war as a horrible, futile depravity" and that they aim to temper, "at least for one generation of readers, the fascination, the excitement, and the glory too often associated with war" (National Geographic Society 1981:317). This rendition ignores, however, the ambiguity of photos (even those of horrifying subjects); given some readers' politics and some historical contexts, most war photos can validate more hatred of and effort against the "enemy." Garrett's comment also ignores the heavily prowar text and captions wrapped around virtually all pictures of American wars in the magazine. In the 1961 "Red Tide" article, for example, captions suggest a subhuman nature in the North Vietnamese through metaphors of "prowling Communists" and "enemy-infested jungle[s]." And there is no more celebratory set of pictures than those in the September 1968 article showing the resolute, compassionate, and handsome young American men of the Air Rescue unit.

To see the *Geographic* editorial hand at work, one has only to contrast James Nachtwey's images of war published in the magazine (June 1988) with those of his published elsewhere (Nachtwey 1989). Captions also soften the potential impact of his pictures: a line of war captives in Guatemala, whose faces could be read as fearful of state torture, is captioned "Trying on a new life through a government amnesty program, former guerrillas and supporters receive donated clothing at Coban army base, where they will begin indoctrination toward resettlement in government-established villages."

Images of brutalized bodies, a stock-in-trade of much war photography, are missing from *National Geographic*. In Vietnam and Korea, the magazine dealt only through denial with the fact that warfare "is waged on tangible human flesh and inscribed in pain" and agreed with readers on "the living wounded body as the final *untellable* legend" of war (Trachtenberg 1989:118; emphasis added). While wounded bodies proliferate elsewhere in American popular culture, nonfiction family magazines are the last place they will be found. For such pictures to appear in the media, what seems to be required is either the frame of fantasy or adult status in viewers, as well as a certain politics.

When in November 1986 *National Geographic* hesitantly returned to cover the area of the Vietnam War after a hiatus of a decade, it inquired into the MIA question in Laos. Showing the discovery of the wreck of a U.S. jet in the jungle, the local Laotians appear not as enemies, survivors or victims but as helpmates to the U. S. team searching for military remains. One photograph has a U.S. soldier holding up a rusted American handgun, suggesting both the archaeological status of the war rather than its recency and continuing reverberations in, for example, dioxin effects of Agent Orange, and the harmlessness of the American, now standing in civilian clothes amid sun-dappled greenery.

A Middle-Class World. The *National Geographic* has presented a world that is predominantly middle class, in which there is neither much poverty nor great wealth (see Figure 4.1). It is a world comfortable to contemplate. Like the absence of violence or illness, these pictures reflect back to Americans their own self-image as a relatively classless society, one in which most citizens define themselves as either working class or middle class (Davis and Smith 1986:218).[10] At another level, of course, readers know that there are radical gaps between rich and poor in the United States and abroad, and there may be ways that this implicit awareness is addressed by the magazine as well.

There seems to have been a ban on picturing hungry or blemished individuals until the recent past. Exceptions began to appear in the mid-seventies. A 1978 article on smallpox shows its "last victim," a man from Somalia. The

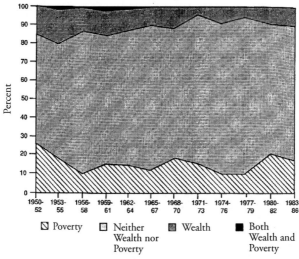

Figure 4.1 Indicators of wealth in photographs, 1950–86

picture, small by magazine standards, might show a hint of a smile on the man's lips. Since 1950 a number of articles have focused on famine, including several in 1953, five between 1972 and 1975, and three in the 1980s, but not until a July 1975 article do the first visibly malnourished children show up in our sample of six hundred photos. By the mid-eighties, several articles had focused on hunger or featured some photographic evidence of systemic, non-episodic, hunger. In general, a much sharper turn to coverage of human misery has occurred in the 1980s. . . . Many of the strong images of poverty are found in articles by James Blair on Haiti and South Africa, Steve Raymer on Bangladesh, and Steve McCurry on several countries. The distress of viewers that is associated with hunger continues to weigh heavily in editorial decision making, as in the downsizing of a photo of Guatemalans eating in a garbage dump.

The *Geographic*'s shunning of the poor, the ill, and the hungry throughout much of the fifties, sixties, and seventies stands in marked contrast to images in other media portraits of the third world, both contemporary and historical. Take, for example, *Life* magazine's published review of photography in the 1980s. Looking at all sources, the editors selected 118 of the "best photographs" of the decade. Of those, one-third were taken in non-Western settings. More than half of these depict death, disease, poverty, and war, often in a graphic and wrenching way, as in the picture of the frozen body of a small girl killed in the Iran-Iraq war, overlaid by the dead body of what must be her mother, or that of a dying Colombian girl chest-deep in landslide mud. The decade's best photos taken in Western settings are much less likely to show dead, diseased, or physically grotesque bodies.

Gilman (1985) presents evidence that all forms of physiognomic difference between themselves and non-Europeans were objects of intense interest to Europeans in the nineteenth and twentieth centuries. Both drawings and photos accentuated the differences, from Chinese men's queues to the skin color of Africans, often portraying them as pathologies. For many contemporary Americans, the most familiar image of the non-European commoner is a starving African child. *National Geographic* images have stood in pointed contrast to such pictures, the ideal set against the degenerate other found elsewhere. As in the case of violence, the media present a common cultural pattern of vacillation from angelic to demonic representation of others (Bhabha 1983; Taussig 1987)—from *National Geographic's* unblemished and sunny middle-class smiles to the television program *Nightline's* more than four hundred hours of angry, moblike Iranians (often transmitted in black and white or washed-out color) presented through the 1980s.

This duality can be seen in the context of JanMohamed's (1985) useful argument (contra Bhabha [1983]) that the ambivalence of colonial representations does not represent genuine confusion within the colonial mind over the value of the other. Rather, he maintains, "the imperialist is not fixated on specific images or stereotypes of the Other but rather on the affective benefits proffered by the manichean allegory," which include the ability to create an Other whose goodness and badness seem absolute and not merely social, or so extreme as to be neither human nor historical. Accordingly, "those who have fashioned the colonial world are themselves reduced to the role of passive spectators in a mystery not of their making" (1985:68).

A World of Work. In a less obvious way, the magazine's photographs also idealize through focusing on people's industriousness. While other historical and contemporary forms of Western representation of the non-Western world frequently show people at rest or engaged in newsworthy behavior, often violent or episodic, the *National Geographic* favors the view of a world at work (see Table 4.1). Of the pictures which clearly suggest that people are either at work or play (that is, excluding portraits, shots of ritual, or ambiguous pictures), two-thirds focus on people working at productive tasks. Correspondingly, 63 percent of all pictures were coded as showing people in an active mode, whether walking, engaged in vigorous recreation, or working.

Table 4.1 Activity type of main foreground figure in *National Geographic* photos (non-Westerners only)

	%	N
At work or in work context (includes ritual preparation)	37	204
At rest or leisure activity (includes eating)	19	101
Ritual Activity	16	88
Portrait	9	48
Neither clearly work nor play or both work and play	18	99
Not ascertainable	1	5
Total	100	545

The passive or lazy native favored in much colonialist discourse (Gilman 1985) is seldom in evidence. The pragmatic reasons for this emphasis were pinpointed by an editor who noted that photos of people at work provide information on the economy of a country; they allow for more candid shots, as people are absorbed in their tasks; and the fact that they are in action provides more intrinsically interesting photographic material. Such pragmatic incentives, however, do not cancel out the role of the photographs in broader cultural discourses about the industriousness of the native.

The Ideal of Virility. Through *National Geographic*'s eyes, as through the filter of much mass media, the world is mostly male. Nearly two-thirds of all photographs focus chiefly on men, while about one quarter show all or mostly women.[11] While in some cultures there are constraints on the entrance of male photographers into groups of women, it is no doubt also the case that the world of men is seen as of greater interest to readers. The *National Geographic* here follows the androcentric pattern identified in a host of cultural productions, from television serials and school textbooks to movie characters and news accounts. The focus on men, at least in part, emerges from the Western model in which things cultural are masculine and things natural are feminine (Ortner 1974). To search for exotic cultural practices, then, is to search for males. The representation of the tribal person as somewhere between nature and culture makes the issue more complex.

Almost 80 percent of all photographs show all or mostly adults, although pictures of smiling children are a staple of the magazine, with 14 percent of photos focused mainly or exclusively on children. Most commonly, infants are shown in their mother's arms and older children doing chores. Relatively scarce in the *National Geographic* are the elderly, with only 10 percent of the photos including at least one older person and a small fraction of that number foregrounding them.

In many ways, the age structure of the non-Westerners photographed reflects Western cultural attitudes. The invisibility of the elderly in American society, that is, their relative absence from larger households and from media images, accompanies a cultural emphasis on youthful beauty and on productivity defined as the ability to earn wages. The Geographic's treatment of children likewise reflects a cultural set. Its focus on the child alone or in groups of other children is consonant with the sociological reality in which children are not integrated into the adult world of work or leisure and with the cultural belief that the child is a special kind of person rather than a miniature or even protoadult. The romanticizing of childhood is also reflected in their often lyrical photographic treatment, as in the December 1984 shot of two Indonesian girls in the rain, brimming to the edges of both the pages it occupies, with a soft haze of blurred greenery behind them. The girls are huddled warmly against each other and against the rain, their eyes huge as they look out from under a flat basket held gracefully by one of them.

Natural Humans without History

National Geographic has typically focused on those whom Eric Wolf (1982) has called the people without history. Wolf's thesis is that Western culture often presents non-Europeans as having timeless societies and personalities. Only now are they seen as responding to the "onslaught" of civilization or modernization; hitherto all dynamism, change, and agency have been ideologically apportioned to the West. This view of the non-Westerner as unchanging and as more primitive than civilized lends itself to the portrayal of the people without history as also the people of nature. Those without history, seated in the natural rather than the cultural realm, have a morphology rather than a trajectory.

Rosaldo (1989) draws a related but more complex picture when he notes that a kind of tripartite scheme has been in use in which the evolutionary ladder has bottom rungs that are precultural (for example, the Tasaday or Papuans); more thoroughly cultural middle rungs, because some historical dynamism is attributed to their societies (India and Japan); and a top occupied by the Western observer, who is presented as postcultural. This latter perspective on American identity is evident in the melting-pot norm that sees immigrants as gradually shedding, perhaps over generations, their cultural veneers on the way to becoming simply modern people. We might say that

Americans see themselves as no longer in possession of a culture but as holding on to history through their scientific advancements and their power to influence the evolutionary advance of other peoples to democracy and market economies. The National Geographic Society headquarters in Washington clearly organizes the visitor's experience around these notions in its opening exhibit—portraits of the Tasaday on the left, a floating American astronaut on the right (time, like English text, reads left to right). The magazine's soft evolutionism contrasts, however, with harder types still in use elsewhere, as in a cartoon in the *New York Times* in 1991 showing the devolutionary process as a descent from Clark Gable to ape to Saddam Hussein as snake.

We can now look in more detail at how naturalization and this evolutionary scenario have been achieved through the images.

The Halo of Green. One of the most distinctive features of *National Geographic's* coverage of the world is its sharp focus on the people of the fourth world as peoples of nature. This was often explicitly the case in the colonial period, as when an April 1953 article on New Guinea interspersed photos of Papuans in elaborate, sometimes feathered dress, with photos of local birds. In more recent years, local people are sometimes portrayed as conservators, holding a special relationship with nature, rather than directly in and of it. In either mode, the magazine's attempt to cover the earth comprehensively may have lent itself to shoring up some preexisting cultural notions about the naturalness of the non-Westerner, many readers already having an answer to the question of what the following articles in a typical issue have in common: "The Planets," "Koko [the gorilla]'s Kitten," "Yosemite—Forever?" and articles on Jamaica and Baghdad (January 1985). Aside from the effect of juxtaposition, the magazine's self-presentation as a scientific journal has drawn on the equation of science with the study of nature rather than of society, which might suggest why people construed as natural so frequently occupy its pages.

In nearly a third of all photos, the non-Westerner is presented against a background that gives no evidence of social context. This includes pictures in which there is no recognizable background at all, only an aestheticized blur of color produced by a narrow depth of field. It also includes photographs of people against purely natural backgrounds. Such pictures can pass as depictions of the "natural man" of earlier centuries' imaginings about the people beyond Europe and can evoke in readers the nostalgia for an imagined condition of humanity before the industrial revolution and environmental degradation broke the link between humans and nature (MacFarlane 1987).

These pictures of naturalized societies stand in marked contrast to the reverse strategy of anthropomorphism employed in *National Geographic* nature photography. In one series of such pictures, a lioness is described as running a cub "day care center," and a group of chimps is captioned as a "family portrait." Standing more directly at the crossroads of what Haraway (1989) terms the "traffic" between nature and culture is the picture that follows, in which a pair of tawny stallions rear wildly. The caption tells us that the photographer intentionally used the image "to capture the proud spirit of the Spanish men" in his magazine piece on that country (National Geographic Society 1981:334).

National Geographic has focused heavily on people in rural settings (68 percent of the total of sample pictures whose location could be determined). The rural backdrop can serve to tell different kinds of stories, from the jungle fecundity of a sexualized other, to his or her innocence, to the similarity to a Western farmer or frontiersman. Rural photos are more common in certain regions than others, in particular Africa and the Pacific. Regardless of the actual urbanization rate in any world area, these regional differences in pictorial representation are susceptible to characterological interpretations and, even more, to estimates about the degree of civilization of a region.

For the magazine to avert its gaze from the massive urbanization of the planet during the postwar period was standard practice until recently. After 1977, a year marked by the beginnings of change in editorial policy, there is a sudden drop in the number of rural photos presented to just over half of what had been the norm (see Figure 4.2). The rural focus had been crucial to erasing a view of class relations within the third world. Increased urban coverage has gone hand in hand with the partial erosion of the picture of a middle-class world painted by the *Geographic*.

There Are Only Two Worlds. Although the magazine focuses on exotic differences, at many points there appear to be only two worlds—the traditional and the modern; the world before "the West" and its technological and social progress came to "the rest" and the world after. The narrative structure of many images is one of progress or modernization, as demonstrated in the titles of two articles: "Yemen opens the door to progress: American scientists visit this Arabian land at the invitation of its king to improve the health of his people" (1952) and "Progress and Pageantry in Changing Nigeria:

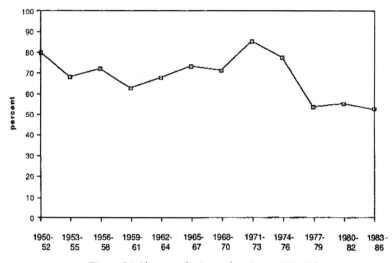

Figure 4.2 Photographs in rural settings, 1950–86

Bulldozers and penicillin, science and democracy come to grips with color-ful age-old customs in Britain's largest colony" (1956). These celebrations of progress exist side by side with articles suggesting the more nearly equal value of both traditional and modern and holding out a kind of promise of stasis. The caption for a 1965 photo of an Indian woman in nose ring and sari describes her as "Wife of two worlds: Though married in the old tradition, the new Maharani of Rajpipla is a matron of progress. She holds a master's degree in philosophy from Rajasthan University." This framework of balance becomes increasingly common, as when the Apache are said to live, perhaps permanently, in "two worlds" (February 1980).

Why has the *Geographic* focused so relentlessly on photographs and text that set up and explore a contrast between the traditional and the modern, particularly in the post-World War II period? While we will return to this question in more depth later, we can begin here to consider how these pic-tures play a role in dealing with the changing national identity of the American state in the same period. Increasingly it is correlated with capital-ism and contrasted to other economic systems. When *Geographic* photogra-phers and writers talk about their travels as trips through time, the main sign-post is often the commodity. When Thomas Abercrombie describes his decades of work in the Middle East, he writes that

> what makes the Middle East a joy is the time warp. . . . Often I found [people] living out
> what seemed chapters in the history of mankind. Over dusty tracks or down four-lane

expressways, a Land-Rover became my time machine. I drove across the centuries, from Stone Age Bedouin in the sand mountains of Saudi Arabia's Empty Quarter to the old walled cities of Oman; then back to the computerized refineries of Algeria's Sahara, the Rolls Royce traffic of Bahrain's financial district, or the boutiques of war-torn Beirut. (National Geographic Society 1981:143)

The center and the commodity stand for the future, the simple periphery for the past, and the contrast builds an American identification of both itself and its market system with the world's future.

Wolf suggests how contrast pictures might have functioned in the context of cold war conflict between the superpowers. He notes that the distinctions between a traditional, developing, and modern world "became intellectual instruments in the prosecution of the Cold War . . . [with] communism a 'disease of modernization' (Rostow 1960)" (E. Wolf 1982:7). The therapeutic goal could then be to push the third world toward the Western model of modernity, even to the point of saturation bombing of the countryside in Vietnam to advance, according to one political scientist, "urbanization and modernization which rapidly brings the country in question out of the phase in which a rural revolutionary movement can hope to generate sufficient strength to come to power" (Huntington 1968 in Drinnon 1980:373). The contrast between traditional and modern also allows readers to model the melting-pot imperative for immigrants to the United States. The traditional immigrant, these contrast pictures say, is not a threat but simply a stage on the way to full Americanization.

Decolonization brought interesting changes in the structure of contrast pictures, something Pratt drew our attention to with her brilliant analysis of landscape descriptions in Western travel literature (1982). Pratt finds that in both colonial and contemporary postcolonial travel accounts the narrator is often looking down on an exotic scene from mountaintop or hotel balcony. This stance and its related stylistics she calls the-monarch-of-all-I-survey scene, giving its narrator the opportunity to examine and evaluate the whole and to thereby assert dominance over it. Pratt discerns a dramatic change, however, between the colonial and postcolonial travel literature; while both view the landscape from above, the colonial observer glorifies it, seeing a country which is beautiful, rich in resources, and therefore "worth taking." Sir Richard Burton describes his first view of Lake Tanganyika from a hilltop in 1860:

> Nothing, in sooth, could be more picturesque than this first view of the Tanganyika Lake, as it lay in the lap of the mountains, basking in the gorgeous tropical sunshine. Below and

beyond a short foreground of rugged and precipitous hillfold, down which the foot-path zigzags painfully, a narrow strip of emerald green, never sere and marvelously fertile, shelves towards a ribbon of glistening yellow sand. (Cited in Pratt 1982:145)

Contrast this with Theroux's 1978 vision of Central America, narrated from his hotel balcony:

Guatemala City, an extremely horizontal place, is like a city on its back. Its ugliness, which is a threatened look (the low morose houses have earthquake cracks in their facades; the buildings wince at you with bright lines) is ugliest on those streets where, just past the last toppling house, a blue volcano's cone bulges . . . [The volcano's] beauty was undeniable, but it was the beauty of witches. (Cited in Pratt 1982:149)

Rather than the colonial portrait of a cornucopic Eden, here "the task to be accomplished is a negative one of rejection, dissociation, and dismissal" (Pratt 1982:150), the landscape seen as degraded, polluted, used up. Postcolonial writers, who can no longer see themselves as engaged in either civilizing mission or easy appropriation of a country, draw a picture of incongruity, disorder, and ugliness.

A similar, if less dramatic, shift can be observed in *National Geographic* photography. From its inception at the beginning of the colonial era through the 1960s, the editorial commitment to portray the world in a positive light was rarely violated. Decisions to move to a more journalistic and balanced stance occurred in the postcolonial period and have resulted in a new picture of the world which is now both beautiful *and* ugly, ordered *and* disordered.

Two landscapes drawn from the pages of the *Geographic* make Pratt's point. In the first, taken in 1956, a white hiker on the island of Mauritius looks out from a mountaintop over a wide expanse of lush, bright-green forested valley. The sun is out, the landscape looks rich and unspoiled. Come forward to 1982 and a photograph taken from a rooftop in Khartoum, Africa. This is Pratt's postcolonial landscape view, with its muddy, dark colors, its depiction of low urban sprawl, its lack of a focal point. This picture does not celebrate what it sees. In the thirty-year space between the pictures, the white observer, while still at a height, has disappeared, resources have been used up, the sun has gone in.

The Naked Black Woman

Nothing defines the *National Geographic* for most older American readers more than its "naked" women. The widely shared cultural experience of viewing women's bodies in the magazine draws on and acculturates the audience's ideas about race, gender, and sexuality, with the marked subcategory in each case being black, female, and the unrepressed. This volatile trio will be examined in greater detail later. For now, it is enough to point out that the magazine's nudity forms a central part of the image of the non-West that it purveys.[12]

The first inclusion of a bare-breasted woman in the pages of the *Geographic* occurred in 1896, and was accompanied then, as now, by shameless editorial explanation. The pictures, Gilbert Grosvenor said in 1903, were included in the interest of science; to exclude them would have been to give an incomplete or misleading picture of how the people really live. This scientific goal is seen as the sole purpose of the photos, with the National Geographic Society taking, according to one observer, "vehement exception to comments about the sexual attraction or eroticism of the photographs" (Abramson 1986:141). The breast represents both a struggle against "prudery" (Bryan 1987:89) and the pursuit of truth rather than pleasure. The centrality of a race-gender code to decisions about whose breasts to depict cannot be denied, however. With some very recent exceptions (photographed discretely from behind), none of the hundreds of women whose breasts were photographed in the magazine were white-skinned. The struggle against prudery did not lead to documentation of the coming of nude sunbathing to Mediterranean beaches, and we recall the case of the photo of a bare-breasted Polynesian woman whose skin tones had been darkened in the production process (Abramson 1985:143). Moreover, genitals are rarely photographed, even where full nudity is customary. In the November 1962 issue a very young Vietnamese girl, bare-bottomed and facing the camera, has had her vulva airbrushed (p. 739).

The imputation of erotic qualities or even sexual license to non-Westerners (particularly women) is one likely result of *National Geographic* presentation of their bodies for close examination. In addition, the nakedness of the *Geographic's* subjects might be seen as continuous with the nude as a perennial theme in Western "fine arts." While some of these women are posed for surveillance and resemble the mug shot more than the oil canvas, many are rendered through pose and lighting so as to suggest artfulness. In Western cultural rhetoric, women are beautiful objects. Their photographs in the magazine can play a central role in allowing the art of photography to exist silently beneath a scientific agenda and thereby increase readership and further legitimate the _Geographic's_ project as one of both beauty and truth. All of this elaborate structure of signification, however, is built on a foundation of racial and gender subordination: in this context, one must first be black and female to do this kind of symbolic labor.

Conclusion

We have seen how _National Geographic_ presents a special view of the "people out there." This view—a world of happy, classless people outside of history but evolving into it, edged with exoticism and sexuality, but knowable to some degree as individuals—is both distinctive in comparison with other mass media representations and continuous with some prevailing cultural themes. The contrast in the magazine between the other as familiar, one of the family of man, and as exotic is played out in sharper relief when the magazine is compared with those media in which the master figures are Libyan terrorists and Iranian mobs, Ethiopian famine victims and Vietnamese communists. These representations, dripping with evil, threat, and hopeless social and economic disorganization, may be given at least part of their force by the background of unperturbed _National Geographic_ images which the viewer of nightly TV news has previously seen. These kinds of broader cultural systematics bear further examination.

The _National Geographic_ images are continuous, on the other hand, with a number of themes that have appeared and reappeared over the centuries of contact between West, South, and East. These include themes of the natural man, of societies with no historical dynamism of their own, of the evolutionary ladder of societies with Africa at the bottom rung and Asia at the middle and with all as aspirants for the top—a place equivalent to a modern, Western life style. They are continuous with other long-standing anxieties about the sexuality of the racially different and anxieties that result in a studied looking away from economic exploitation and resulting miseries of poverty and ill health.

This view can be evaluated in a variety of ways—as innocent/kindly/relativistic, as naive/out of touch, as a special kind of neocolonial discourse which ultimately degrades its subjects, or as humanistic/liberal. Ultimately, the evaluation should be based not on the intentions of the magazine's makers but on the consequences of its photographic rhetoric. In what ways do these photos change or reinforce ideas about others held by their readers? How might these photos influence the practices of readers—as voters, neighbors to new immigrants, as white male co-workers with blacks and women, as consumers of products marketed as exotic?

We can now ask how each of these general themes appears when the *Geographic* has looked at any one world area. These regions, which have highly distinctive personalities in American popular culture, each get somewhat distinctive treatment in the magazine's pages.

Notes

[1]   It is perhaps not surprising that much of the most insightful work on the relationship between images and society has been done in the two areas of advertising (among others, Ewen 1988; Goffman 1979; Williamson 1978) and "documentary" photography. In this latter area, the bulk of the work done has been on early documentary photos in the U.S. and Europe (Moeller 1989; Tagg 1988; Trachtenberg 1989) and of tribal peoples (Geary 1988; Green 1984; Graham-Brown 1988; Lyman 1982).

[2]   "Non-Western" countries were defined as all areas outside of North America and Europe (the latter including Greece and Turkey). While Canada, Alaska, and the Soviet Union were generally excluded from our consideration, we did include articles on indigenous people of these areas. Articles on native peoples in the United States were not included because they constitute a very special group of people for magazine producers and readers alike. In taking our sample, we used only photographs in which a person was visible (more than a dot in a distant landscape).

[3]   The coders were ourselves and a graduate student in anthropology. Extensive preliminary coding led to revision and expansion of initial versions of the code sheet. After a final code sheet was decided upon, initial agreement between coders occurred for 86 percent of all decisions. Discussion between coders was subsequently used to resolve disagreements. The photographic features coded are described in Appendix A

[4]   Of the 568 sample pictures containing non-Westerners, 65 are in black and white.

[5]   Ritual tends to be depicted in color ($x^2 = 3.008$, df = 1, p = .083); only three of fifty portraits are shown in black and white.

[6]   The portrait is a popular form of photography in all genres. The portrait in *National Geographic* is relatively *uncommon* in comparison with family and advertising photos, which prominently feature the face or full-body posed portrait. Further research might reveal whether and how these differences in portrait rates occur by subject and genre.

[7]   Those articles include, among many others, "The GI and the Kids of Korea" (May 1953), "The Mekong, River of Terror and Hope" (December 1968), "Along Afghanistan's War-Torn Frontier" (June 1985). Issues covering the Vietnam War include June 1955, October 1961, November 1962, September 1964, January 1965, June 1965, September 1965, February 1966, February 1967, April 1968, September 1968, and December 1968.

8   Similar photos can be found in the *National Geographic*'s (and *Life*'s) World War II coverage (e.g., Bryan 1987:248–49).

9   Moeller (1989) points out, however, that it has sometimes been in the interest of the state to have more rather than less graphic images of war published. Midway through World War II, government censors changed policy to allow photos of wounded or dead American soldiers in order to "help 'harden' the resolve of the public at home" (1989:227). During less popular wars and during losing wars or phases of wars, apparently, both the military and the press tread more carefully, trying to avoid offending the public with death images.

10   In the NORC-Roper Center 1986 survey, 90 percent of all those surveyed so identified themselves.

11   The figures are 65 percent focused on men, 24 percent focused on women, while the remainder (11 percent) are pictures with an evenly divided gender ratio. We refer here to the gender of adults in the picture. We do not know whether a pattern of male predominance also occurs in photos of children.

12   Of the 235 sample photographs containing women, 11 percent showed women in what, to most Western eyes, would be some degree of undress, the great majority showing the breasts. Of the 425 sample photos with men in them, 13 percent showed shirtless men, and less than half of those were also "bottomless" to some degree.

THE COLOR OF SEX: POSTWAR PHOTOGRAPHIC HISTORIES OF RACE AND GENDER

Again and again, when the negative space of the woman of color meets the Age of Mechanical Reproduction or, worse yet, Baudrillard's "simulations," the resulting effect is . . . a form larger than life, and yet a deformation powerless to speak.

(Wallace 1990:252)

R ace is, as Henry Gates has said, "a trope of ultimate, irreducible difference between cultures, linguistic groups, or adherents of specific belief systems which—more often than not—also have fundamentally opposed economic interests" (1985:5). It is a trope that is particularly dangerous because it "pretends to be an objective term of classification." Gates points to the profoundly social nature of racial classification. Social groups engaged in struggle define racial boundaries in the contexts of that struggle; powerful groups then invoke biology in a post-hoc justification of the boundaries they have drawn. Those in power elaborate observable physical differences—no matter how subtle—into explanations, affirmations, and justifications for inequality and oppression. Once this work is done, and the boundaries are intact, racist theory produces full-blown descriptions of culture and personality that juxtapose powerful ego and degraded/dangerous alter, "lending the sanction of God, biology, or the natural order to even presumably unbiased descriptions of cultural tendencies and differences" (Gates 1985:5).

As Gates and others have so eloquently pointed out, racial difference—and its supposed cultural concomitants—is thus not the *source* of the many contemporary conflicts where it is said to be at issue. It is never a simple matter of two groups in contact finding themselves so physically and culturally different that they just cannot get along. Rather, racial and cultural difference become coded ways of talking about other differences that matter, differences in power and in interests.[1] For this reason—however absolute and intransigent they may seem—racial/racist theories must retain flexibility and are frequently ambiguous. As Omi and Winant (1986:x) have said, race is an inherently unstable "complex of social meanings, constantly being transformed by political struggle." To work to uncover the social arrangements that give rise to and reproduce racism is to place its analysis in realms of human agency and to emphasize the specificity of its historical forms.

Tranquil Racial Spaces

Race theories form one of the most powerful and lethal systems in the world for communicating about difference. Zora Neale Hurston wrote, "Race consciousness is a deadly explosive on the tongues of men" (1984:326). It has justified the most heinous of social relations, including slavery, genocide, and apartheid. Yet, dangerous as they are, race theories have infiltrated the commonsense thinking of most people in the United States, profoundly influencing the ways they perceive and account for cultural difference. Like other forms of essentialist reasoning, racist thought has the appeal of simplicity, and it draws authority from invoking biology and nature. The hegemony of a theory of race that insists on two "bounded" human categories has been challenged in the 1970s and 1980s by new waves of immigration from Asia and Latin America, confronting white America with tremendous diversity in physical appearance and widely varying relationships between race and class, education and social standing.

National Geographic magazine is the product of a society deeply permeated with racism as a social practice and with racial understandings as ways of viewing the world. It sells itself to a reading public that, while they do not consider themselves racist, turn easily to race as an explanation for culture and for social outcome. The Geographic headquarters itself has had few black employees up to the present, despite the predominantly African-American citizenry of Washington, D.C. It is not surprising, therefore, that while race is rarely addressed directly in the magazine, American racial categories powerfully structure the images contained in its pages.

One of the most powerful and distinctive tenets of racism in the United States is that "blackness" is an all-or-nothing phenomenon. Racial law through the period of the Civil War, and after, held that any "black" ancestry was sufficient to define one as black. As recently as 1983, this type of reasoning was upheld by the State Supreme Court of Louisiana, when it refused to allow a woman descended from an eighteenth-century white planter and a black slave to change the classification on her birth certificate from "colored" to "white" (Omi and Winant 1986:57). The laws in question and the cultural preconceptions upon which they were based insistently denied the reality of interracial sexual relations or of the sexual exploitation that so frequently accompanied the master/slave relation. They insisted on pure and unequivocal categories with which to reason about difference. Such airtight categories were viewed as necessary to guard the privileges of "whites" as absolute and to justify the denial of equality to "blacks" as an impossibility.

Nevertheless, when Euramericans turned their eyes outside the borders of their own country, other forms of reasoning prevailed. Evolutionist thought dominated attempts to understand the human diversity of the non-European world. Such thinking needed a continuum, one that was grounded in nature. Skin color is obviously highly variable, only with some difficulty made to accommodate the simple binary classification "black"/"white" in the United States. A continuum of skin color was thus a perfect biological substratum on which to graft stories of human progress or cultural evolution.

Late nineteenth-century fairs and expositions frequently organized the world cultures they presented along an evolutionary scale. These almost always corresponded to a racial continuum, as Rydell (1984) has noted, from the "savagery" of the dark-skinned Dahomeyans, to the Javanese "Brownies," to the "nearly-white" Chinese and Japanese. As evolutionary trajectories were reproduced over the course of the twentieth century, in anthropological theory and in white popular consciousness, they were almost always connected to a scale of skin color, which was then construed, in many cases, as an independent form of verifying their correctness.

As we turned to *National Geographic* photographs, we hypothesized that it was this more differentiated scale—rather than the simple binary opposition called into play for analyzing American culture—that would inform the ways *National Geographic* would portray, and readers would interpret, images of the third world. Distinctions in popular stereotypes of the peoples of Northern and sub-Saharan Africa, or of Melanesia and Polynesia, indicated that Euramericans drew conclusions about others based on the *degree* of darkness of skin color. As we analyzed constructions of race in *National Geographic* photographs, we thus coded them in a way that would allow us to determine whether "bronze" peoples were portrayed differently from those who would be more commonly seen as "black"; to see, in other words, if simple binary constructions informed the images, or if more complex evolutionary schema structured their messages. . . . It was based solely on observable skin color (not cultural characteristics). We used a decision rule that deliberately maximized polarization of categories; that is, when it was difficult to decide whether an individual was "bronze" or white, we coded white. When it was difficult to decide between bronze and black, we coded black. We coded only individuals identifiable as native to the region portrayed, eliminating the few Westerners who appeared in the photographs.

The period for which we analyzed photographs—1950–86—encompassed times of great turmoil in racially defined relationships in the United States. The late 1950s and early sixties saw struggles to overturn racial codes that were more intense than any since the Civil War era. Participants in the civil rights movement sought to obtain basic civil liberties for African Americans; they used the egalitarian verbiage of federal law to challenge the restrictive laws and practices of states and municipalities. Such changes did not simply require a change in the legal codes and their implementation however; they also demanded, as Omi and Winant have argued, "a paradigm shift in established systems of racial meanings and identities" (1986:90).

Nonviolent tactics such as freedom rides, marches, attempts to desegregate key southern school districts and universities, and sit-ins at segregated lunchrooms characterized the period up until the passage of the 1964 Civil Rights Act and the voting rights legislation of 1965. By the mid-sixties, however, many who had worked and hoped for these changes were disillusioned.

Changes in legislation had profound symbolic value, and materially benefited a small number of middle-class African Americans. But they did not alter the economic circumstances of the vast majority of blacks living in poverty, and they did not adequately challenge the tremendous and continuing burden of institutional racism. This led to an increasing radicalization of key branches of the civil rights movement and to angry rioting in places like Watts and Newark (Harding 1981; Carson 1981).

The civil rights movement contested white privilege and its counterpart, the institutionalized oppression of black Americans. It also contested the very meaning of race in American culture. As white Americans were deprived of one of the master tropes explaining their privileged position in the world, race became an uncomfortable topic for them. This discomfort was reflected in the pages of *National Geographic*. Clearly the magazine did not cover the turmoil in American cities during the period. At the same time, it sought to ease anxieties in its portrayal of the third world. As late as the early 1950s, the Euramerican reading public could comfortably view Asian and African peoples attending white explorers and photographers—carrying them across rivers, pulling them in rickshaws, carrying their packs and bags. By the late sixties, however, these images were too disturbing, the possibility of rebellion and anger too present. White travelers simply disappeared from the pictures, removing the possibility of conflictual relationships.

With this action, third world spaces were cleared for fantasy. Black and bronze peoples of Africa, Asia, and Latin America were shown going about their daily lives—happy, poor but dignified, and attuned to basic human values. The photographs themselves were not much different from those of previous decades; however, in the racially charged context of the fifties and sixties their meaning had changed. The implicit contrast with Watts and Newark, or even with Selma and Montgomery, operated behind the scenes. The third world was constituted as a safe, comfortable space, where race was not an issue and where white people did not have to reevaluate the sources of their privilege.

Apparently, though, in the minds of *National Geographic* editors, too much of even a reassuring fantasy could be disturbing. Until 1961, the numbers of white, black, or bronze people appearing in any given issue of *National Geographic* was variable. In 1952, for example, only about 15 percent of people depicted in articles on the third world were dark-skinned; in 1958, the figure was about 46 percent. Beginning in 1961, however, a remarkably stable pattern began to appear. For the next twenty-five years the percentage of dark-skinned people in any issue held very constant at about 28 percent. People who could be categorized as bronze formed a fairly regular 60 percent of the total, with the remaining 12% constituted by light- or white-skinned third world peoples. The intense stability of this pattern, and particularly the almost invariant proportion of dark-skinned people represented, suggests that editorial attention may have been focused on the issue.

This is admittedly indirect evidence. We did not find anyone at *National Geographic* who was willing to say that skin color per se was a consideration in putting together issues (although conversations in planning meetings suggest that it may well be). We do know, however, that *National Geographic's* marketing department gathered significant amounts of data on the popularity of different kinds of articles and that Africa was by far the least popular world region. By marketing definitions, African peoples constituted a difficult topic; to the extent that market concerns drive content, one would thus expect some sort of regulation of their coverage.

In photographs where dark-skinned peoples were portrayed, there were interesting regularities—contributing to an overall image of contentment, industriousness, and simplicity. The activity level of individuals portrayed in the photographs, for example, clearly sorted out on an evolutionary scale marked by skin color. Individuals coded as black were most likely to be depicted in high levels of activity—engaged in strenuous work or athletics. People coded white were most likely to be engaged in low-level activity—seated or reclining, perhaps manipulating something with their hands, but rarely exerting themselves. Those coded bronze were most likely to be found engaged in activities that fell somewhere between the two extremes, such as walking or herding animals. In keeping with this pattern, people of color (both black and bronze) were most likely to be portrayed at work in the photographs we examined, while people with white skin were most likely to be found at rest.

The determinants of such a portrayal are complex, and the message it conveys is multifaceted. We cannot rule out the brute empiricist interpretation that what is portrayed is determined to some extent by events in the real world: that photographers found dark-skinned peoples at work more often than lighter-skinned peoples. Yet when we are dealing with sets of published photographs that are chosen out of a universe of tens of thousands that were taken, we are clearly dealing with a problem of representation as well.

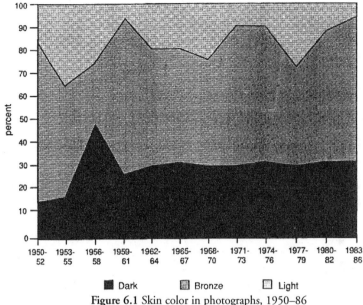

■ Dark ▨ Bronze ▢ Light

Figure 6.1 Skin color in photographs, 1950–86

Portraying people at work is in keeping with an editorial policy that demands a focus on the positive as construed in the United States, that is, the work ethic. It is possible to imagine that editors sought to counter images of the laziness of non-white peoples (in the Euramerican imagination) by deliberately presenting an alternative view. At the same time, in the contradictory manner characteristic of colonial/neocolonial mentality (see Bhabha 1983), it is also possible that deeply ingrained notions of racial hierarchy made it seem more "natural" for dark-skinned peoples to be at work and engaged in strenuous activity. White ambivalence toward the black male seems often to center on issues of strength: while vigor is good for the worker to have, it also has the threatening connotations of potential rebelliousness, and so some hobbling often follows the rendition of strength.

Few topics have occupied as much space in colonial discourse as the relationship of blacks to labor. As Euramericans sought to build wealth on the backs of colonized peoples and slaves, they sought to continually refine methods of maximizing the labor they were able to extract. Colonial administrators and plantation bosses continually reported on the success and failures of innovations in the process. The double mentality reflected in the reports was plain—while people of color were inherently suited to labor, they never wanted to work hard enough in the fields of their white masters. The image of a tremendous capacity for work, coupled with an unwillingness to actually work, gave rise to contradictory stereotypes. The heritage of these stereotypes and the labor relations that gave rise to them can be traced in the strenuously employed black bodies portrayed in the pages of *National Geographic*.

In equally regular ways, black and bronze peoples were more likely to be portrayed as poor and technologically backward. Individuals coded as white were more likely to be wealthy and less likely to be poor than other categories. Still, only 21 percent of black and 16 percent of bronze people were photographed in contexts of poverty. Fully 70 percent of the former and 72 percent of the latter were shown without any markers of wealth or poverty, and some of each group were portrayed as wealthy. There is clearly a tension at work in the photographs. The greater poverty of darker-skinned individuals may, in part, be empirically determined; it is also in keeping with popular Euramerican stereotypes of the degraded status of dark-skinned peoples. On the other hand, *National Geographic*'s policy of focusing on the positive and avoiding advocacy precludes too heavy an emphasis on impoverishment. Dark-skinned peoples have a somewhat greater tendency to be poor—one might construe the statistical weight of the photographs as saying—but in general, they live well.

Individuals coded white were most likely to be depicted with machines of one kind or another; black and bronze individuals were most likely to be shown with simple tools of local manufacture. Not surprisingly, people of color were more often depicted as engaged in ritual. This variable also sorted out along an evolutionary/skin color continuum: the darker the skin color, the more likely to engage in ritual practices. In classic evolutionist terms, superstition (represented by ritual) and science (represented by technology) were counterposed. Similarly, the darker the skin color of an individual, the less likely he or she was to be depicted in western-style clothing. The darker the skin of the people portrayed, the less they were associated with things European, and the more exotic they were rendered.

Given these trends, it was somewhat surprising to find that dark-skinned peoples were not photographed in natural settings (that is, in landscapes or greenery) more often than their lighter-skinned counterparts. They were, however, more likely to appear in settings where surroundings were not clearly discernible. Such portrayals tend to aestheticize the materials on which they focus. In this case, they force attention to the lines, shapes, and colors of the bodies themselves, rather than providing information about the context in which the bodies appear. Because such photos were relatively numerous, dark-skinned people consequently appeared in *social* surroundings less frequently.

People coded black or bronze were more likely to be photographed in large groups than those coded white. They were less likely to be portrayed alone or in small intimate groups. People of color were therefore less often the subject of individualized photographic accounts, attentive to "biographic" features and life circumstances. They were more often portrayed as part of a mass, perhaps thereby suggesting to readers that they had relatively undifferentiated feelings, hopes, or needs. Individuals coded black and bronze were far more likely to be photographed gazing into the camera than individuals coded white—a stance that, while complex and sometimes ambiguous—frequently suggests availability and compliance.

Despite some Euramerican stereotypes, dark skin was not associated with evidence of aggression in the pages of *National Geographic* through most of the period we have examined. . . . Aggression is generally taboo as a topic for *National Geographic* photographs, except in the highly specific case of depicting U.S. military power. Additionally, however, to retain its status as a place where white U.S. readers go to assuage their fears about race and cultural difference, *National Geographic* must studiously avoid photographs that might suggest a potential threat from colonized and formerly colonized peoples. To depict anger, violence, or the presence of weapons is to evoke the fear that they might be turned to retaliation. They serve as an uncomfortable reminder of a world given to struggles for independence, revolutions, and rebellions.

In the marketplace of images, *National Geographic* relies on two intertwined strategies. It relies on recognition—on offering readers what they already know and believe in new and appealing ways. Its reputation and sales also turn on the classic humanism with which it portrays the world. In its depictions of "non-white" peoples, the humanist mission—to portray all humans as basically the same "under the skin"[2]—comes into conflict with Western "commonsense knowledge" about the hierarchy of races.

The organization of photographs into stories about cultural evolution (couched in more "modern" terms of progress and development) provides the partial resolution of this contradiction. These stories tell the Euramerican public that their race prejudice is not so wrong; that at one point people of color *were* poor, dirty, technologically backward, and superstitious—and some still are. But this is not due to intrinsic or insuperable characteristics. With guidance and support from the West, they can in fact overcome these problems, acquire the characteristics of civilized peoples, and take their place alongside them in the world. In the context of this story, the fact that bronze peoples are portrayed as slightly less poor, more technologically adept, serves as proof that progress is possible—and fatalistically links progress to skin color.

At the same time, the "happy-speak" policies of *National Geographic* have meant that for people of color—as for others—the overall picture is one of tranquillity and well-being. We are seldom confronted with historical facts of racial or class violence, with hunger as it unequally affects black and white children, or with social movements that question established racial hierarchies. One photographer expressed this discrepancy poignantly, pointing to a photograph of an African family in a 1988 issue on population. "The story is about hunger," he said, "but look at these people. It's a romantic picture."

This is not to say that no one at the National Geographic Society is attentive to these issues. Dedicated photographers and editors worked hard in the 1970s to produce and push into print two deeply disturbing accounts of apartheid. And while this attempt engendered a repressive movement within the society's Board of Trustees, an article critical of South African black homelands appeared in February 1986.

The same strategies, however, pursued in different epochs, can have different meanings and consequences. The humanist side of *National Geographic* in the 1950s and 1960s denied social problems; it also provided images of people of color living their lives in relatively dignified ways. It gave short shrift to poverty and disharmony, but it permitted a certain amount of identification across racial boundaries. In a period when racial boundaries were highly visible and when African Americans were struggling for equal rights under the law, these images could be read, at least in part, as subtle arguments for social change.

The 1970s have been characterized as a period of "racial quiescence," when social movements waned and conflicts receded (Omi and Winant 1986:2). Racial oppression did not cease, but it was not as openly contested. In turn, the 1980s saw a backlash in undisguised attempts to dismantle legislation protecting civil rights and nondiscriminatory practices. These moves did not require and, in fact, assiduously avoided, an explicitly racial discourse. Busing, originally implemented to desegregate schools, was overturned under banners of "community control" and "parental involvement." Rejections of racially balanced textbooks were couched in terms of battles against "secular humanism" and "political correctness." And in the 1988 presidential campaign, movements of people of color were recast as "special interests" (Omi and Winant 1986:125).

In such a context, classic humanism takes on pernicious overtones. The denial of race as a *social* issue, in a society with a profoundly racist history and where institutional racism still exists, forecloses dialogue on the issues. *National Geographic* has not intentionally contributed to this foreclosure; it goes on producing pictures in much the same way it has for years. And yet the message that we are all alike under the skin takes on new meaning in a social context which denies that discrimination exists or that race has been used to consolidate the privilege of some and oppress others. The racism of the 1980s was not confrontational and defiant; it simply turned its back on the issues. The tranquil racial spaces of *National Geographic* can only contribute to this willed ignorance.

The Women of the World

National Geographic's photographs of the women of the world tell a story about the women of the United States in the post-World War II period. It is to issues of gender in white American readers' lives, such as debates over women's sexuality or whether women doing paid labor can mother their children adequately, that the pictures refer as much as to the lives of third-world women. Seen in this way, the *National Geographic's* women can be placed alongside the other women of American popular culture: the First Lady, the woman draped over an advertisement's red sports car, the Barbie doll, the woman to whom the Hallmark Mother's Day card is addressed. Rather than treating the photos as simply images of women, we can set them in the context of a more complex cultural history of the period, with the sometimes radical changes it brought to the lives of the women who are the readers (or known to the male readers) of the magazine.

Research on the visual representation of women makes clear that female images are abundant in some domains (advertising) and virtually absent in others (photojournalism of political subjects). The invisibility extends much further for women of color. In popular images as well as the dominant white imagination, as Hull, Scott and Smith (1982) have so eloquently told us, "All the women are white, all the blacks are men," and black women are simply invisible. The photographs of *National Geographic* are indispensable because it is one of the very few popular venues trafficking in large numbers of images of black women. While the photographs tell a story about cultural ideals of femininity, the narrative threads of gender and race are tightly bound up with each other. In the world at large, race and gender are clearly not separate systems, as Trinh (1989), Moore (1988), Sacks (1989), and others have reminded us.

For the overwhelmingly white readers of the *Geographic*, the dark-skinned women of distant regions serve as touchstones, giving lessons both positive and negative about what women are and should be (compare Botting 1988). Here as elsewhere, the magazine plays with possibilities of the other as a flexible reflection—even a sort of funhouse mirror—for the self. The women of the world are portrayed in sometimes striking parallel to popular images of American womanhood of the various periods of the magazine's production—for instance, as mothers and as beautiful objects. At certain times, with certain races of women, however, the *Geographic's* other women provide a contrast to stereotypes of white American women—they are presented as hard-working bread-winners in their communities. Primarily, however, the *Geographic's* idealization of the world's people extends to women in egalitarian fashion. To idealize "the other woman" is to present her as like, or aspiring to be like, her American counterpart. The other woman is exotic on the surface (she is dressed in an elaborate sari and has a golden nose ring) but her difference is erased at another, deeper level (she is really just a mother, and like the American woman, interested in making herself beautiful through fashion). The woman's sameness in difference allows us to avoid the sense of threat that confrontation with difference presents and allows us to pursue the illusory goal of wholeness.

As with American women in popular culture, third-world women are portrayed less frequently than men: one quarter of the pictures we looked at focus primarily on women.[3] The situation has traditionally not been much different in the anthropological literature covering the non-Western world, and it may be amplified in both genres where the focus is on cultural differences or exoticism. Given the association between women and the natural world, men and things cultural (Ortner 1974), a magazine that aspires to describe the distinctive achievements of civilizations can be expected to highlight the world of men. But like the people of nature in the fourth world, women have been treated as all the more precious for their nonutiitarian, nonrationalistic qualities. Photographs of women become one of the primary devices by which the magazine depicts "universal human values," and these include the values of family love and the appreciation of female beauty itself.[4] We turn to these issues now, noting that each of them has had a consistent cultural content through the postwar period, during historical changes that give the images different emphases and form through the decades.

The Motherhood of Man. There is no more romantic set of photographs in the *Geographic* than those depicting the mothers of the world with their children. There is the exuberant picture showing the delight of a Kurd mother holding her infant. Filling much space, as an unusually high percentage of the magazine's mother-child pictures do, the photograph covers two pages despite the relative lack of information in it. Its classical composition and crisp, uncluttered message are similar to those in many such photos. They often suggest the Western tradition of madonna painting and evoke the Mother's Day message: this relationship between mother and child, they say, is a timeless and sacred one, essentially and intensely loving regardless of social and historical context— the foundation of human social life rather than cultural difference. The family of man, these pictures might suggest, is first of all a mother-child unit, rather than a brotherhood of solidarity between adults.[5]

For the magazine staff and readers of the 1950s, there must have been even more power in these images than we see in them today. The impact of the photos would have come from the intense cultural and social pressures on middle-class women to see their most valuable role, often their only one, as that of mother (Margolis 1984). The unusually strong pressure of this period is often explained as motivated by desires to place returning World War II veterans (and men in general) in those jobs available and by anxieties about the recent holocaust of the war and the potential for a nuclear conflagration, which made the family seem a safe haven (May 1988). As a new cult of domesticity emerged, women were told—through both science and popular culture—that biology, morality, and the psychological health of the next generation required their commitment to full-time mothering. This ideological pressure persisted through the 1950s despite the rapid rise in female employment through the decade.

The idealization of the mother-child bond is seen in everything from the warm TV relationships of June Cleaver with Wally and the Beaver to the cover of a *Life* magazine issue of 1956 devoted to "The American Woman" showing a glowing portrait of a mother and daughter lovingly absorbed in each other; all of this is ultimately and dramatically reflected in the period's rapidly expanding birth rate. This idealization had its counterpoint in fear of the power women were being given in the domestic domain. In both science and popular culture, the mother was criticized for being smothering, controlling, oversexualized, and, a bit later, overly permissive (Ehrenreich and English 1978; May 1988).

The *National Geographic*'s treatment of children can be seen as an extension of these ideologies of motherhood and the family. As the "woman question" came to be asked more angrily in the late 1950s, there was a gradual erosion of faith in the innocence of the mother-infant bond and even in the intrinsic value of children (Ehrenreich and English 1978), centered around fears of juvenile delinquency and the later 1960s identification of a "generation gap." The *National Geographic*, however, continued to print significant numbers of photographs of children, perhaps responding to their increasingly sophisticated marketing information, which indicated that photographs of children and cute animals were among their most popular pictures.

As the magazine has moved into depicting social problems through the seventies and eighties, however, the child has become positioned to tell the most poignant part of the story. In a wrenching photograph that Wilbur Garrett took in Laos, a Hmong family sits on a bench, the mother breast-feeding a baby, the father holding a toddler who appears to be asleep (January 1974:100–101). No one is smiling. The caption lets us know that the older child is dead, the parents grieving. Only then do we comprehend that the mother's hand is touching her child's shroud rather than his blanket and read the parents' faces as mournful rather than simply solemn or strained. While the caption begins lyrically with the magazine's standard infrastructure of balance, "Milk of life, shroud of death," it goes on to give the grim statistics for these people of 50 percent infant mortality rate, 35-year life expectancy.

Throughout the 1950s and 1960s, however, there were few poignant pictures of children, and they remain relatively rare. The more prevalent, pleasant pictures still play a fundamental role in raising the comfort level of those readers for whom articles on nonwhite peoples are the most unpopular type. For them, the loving mother and smiling child are a quick fix. Indeed, the black mother may be the *most* valorized kind of dark-skinned person for magazine readers, as in the culture at large, where one finds the "mammy" figure of film and literature and the stoic, capable single mother on whom documentaries of American life have often focused (Collins 1991:67–90). Why has this woman been such an important figure? In part, it must be because the traditional maternal role is seen as teaching children to be polite, to be good citizens, to reproduce the status quo. If the most valued black person for white Americans will be the least threatening one, then the culturally constructed image of the black mother will fill the bill. The photo of a Bedouin mother and child can suggest, like a number of others, the mother's protectiveness as well as her own vulnerability or fear (December 1972:838–39). We might ask if the perceived danger of things foreign increases the power of the mother to be portrayed as especially protective. Given the kindly intentions in editorial policy, the sympathetic other will often be a mother, protecting both her infant and the reader.

In pictures of mother and child, it often appears that the nonwhite mother is backgrounded, with her gaze and the gaze of the reader focused on the infant. The infant may in fact be an even more important site for dealing with white racial anxieties, by virtue of constituting an acceptable black love object. A good number of pictures in the postwar period have the form of these two: one a Micronesian infant and the other an Iraqi infant, from 1974 and 1976 respectively, each peacefully asleep in a cradle with the mother visible behind. The peacefulness constitutes the antithesis of the potentially threatening differences of interest, dress, or ritual between the photographed adult and the reader.

Women and Their Breasts. The "nude" woman sits, stands, or lounges at the salient center of *National Geographic* photography of the non-Western world. Until the phenomenal growth of mass circulation pornography in the 1960s, the magazine was known as the only mass culture venue where Americans could see women's breasts. Part of the folklore of Euramerican men, stories about secret perusals of the magazine emerged time after time in our conversations with male *National Geographic* readers. People vary in how they portray the personal or cultural meaning, or both, of this nakedness, some noting it was an aid to masturbation, others claiming it failed to have the erotic quality they expected. When white men tell these stories about covertly viewing black women's bodies, they are clearly not recounting a story about a simple encounter with the facts of human anatomy or customs; they are (perhaps unsuspectingly) confessing a highly charged—but socially approved—experience in this dangerous territory of projected, forbidden desire and guilt. Such stories also exist (in a more charged, ironic mode) in the popular culture of African Americans—for example, in Richard Pryor's characterization, in his comedy routines, of *National Geographic* as the black man's *Playboy.*

The racial distribution of female nudity in the magazine conforms, in pernicious ways, to Euramerican myths about black women's sexuality. Lack of modesty in dress places black women closer to nature. Given the pervasive tendency to interpret skin color as a marker of evolutionary progress, it is assumed that white women have acquired modesty along with other characteristics of civilization. Black women remain backward on this scale, not conscious of the embarrassment they should feel at their nakedness (Gilman 1985:114–15, 193). Their very ease unclothed stigmatizes them.

In addition, black women have been portrayed in Western art and science as both exuberant and excessive in their sexuality. While their excess intrigues, it is also read as pathological and dangerous. In the texts produced within white culture, Haraway (1989:154) writes, "Colored women densely code sex, animal, dark, dangerous, fecund, pathological." Thus for the French surrealists of the 1930s, the exotic, unencumbered sexuality of non-Western peoples—and African women in particular—represented an implicit criticism of the repression and constraint of European sexuality. The Africanism of the 1930s, like an earlier Orientalism, evidenced both a longing for—and fear of—the characteristics attributed to non-Western peoples (Clifford 1988:61). The sexuality of black women that so entertained French artists and musicians in cafés and cabarets, however, had fueled earlier popular and scientific preoccupation with the Hottentot Venus and other pathologized renditions of black women's bodies and desires (Gilman 1985).

The *Geographic*'s distinctive brand of cultural relativism, however, meant that this aspect of black sexuality would be less written in by the institution than read in by readers, particularly in comparison with other visual venues such as Hollywood movies. Alloula (1986) gives the example of the sexualized early twentieth-century "harem" postcards of North African women. His thesis is that the veil fascinates a Western audience because it is read as a no-trespass message, and it is experienced by outside men as frustrating and attractive for this reason. It became an object of Western quest from a sense of the need to penetrate beyond it through, simultaneously, the light of photography, the reason of enlightened social change, the knowledge of science, and the desire of the flesh (compare Fanon 1965). One can also see the distinctive *Geographic* style in comparison with *Life* photography of non-Western women. We can see the stronger cultural viewpoint on race at work in a 1956 *Life* article on "other women," which ran next to an article on American women of various regions of the country. The two articles read as a kind of beauty pageant, with all the photographs emphasizing the sitter's appearance, sexuality, and passivity. Ultimately, the magazine's editors judged American women the better-looking set (many captions also noted the "natural," "healthy," wholesome—non-perverted?—quality of the American women), but the adjectives they used to caption the non-Western women described their sense of the more passive and sexually explicit stance of the other women. So they are variously praised for their "fragility," "great softness," "grace," "langorous" qualities, and eagerness "to please"; "the sensuous quality often seen in women of the tropics" was found in one Malayan woman. The hypersexual but passive woman here replicates the one found by many Westerners in their imaginary African travels throughout the last century (Hammond and Jablow 1977). In the *Life* article, all of the non-Western women except the one Chinese "working girl" (and many of the American women), touch themselves, their clothes, or fans in the usual pose for characterizing female self-involvement (Goffman 1979).

As in German photography at Barnum in central Africa, those who would communicate the message that non-Western others are enlightened felt the necessity to mute certain kinds of facts. Although King Nioya at Barnum had many wives, there is relatively little evidence of this in European photography of the court, and so, too, the *Geographic* rarely shows female or male sexuality in more explicit forms. Although emphasis on the veil has been strong throughout the *Geographic*'s history, it seems deployed more in a narrative about progress than one about sexuality, as we will see. The magazine and its readers are caught between the desire to play out the cultural fantasy of the oversexed native woman and the social controls of sexual morality, of science, and of cultural relativism.

If *National Geographic* trades on the sexuality of black women, it is less comfortable with that of black men. Men coded black were far more likely than those coded white to appear bare-chested in the pages of the magazine—often in poses that drew attention to musculature and strength. The *National Geographic* has apparently tried to include pictures of "handsome young men" (Abramson 1985:143). For American readers, male muscles take the place analogous to female breasts as signs of gendered sexuality (Canaan 1984). Many pictures visually or through their captions draw attention to the rippling muscles of photographed men. A picture of a man from the Nuba mountains in the Sudan (November 1966:699) fills the page, primarily with his torso rather than face or full body, accentuating his strongly defined musculature. The caption highlights his brawn and implicitly suggests that this physicality is at the expense of intelligence: "Muscles like iron, his leather arm amulet worn as insurance against disaster, a champion wrestler exudes confidence. In his world, a man's strength and agility count for much, and at festivals he earns the plaudits of his peers. But modern civilization—a force beyond his comprehension—threatens his primitive way of life."

The magazine has been extremely skittish, however, about portraying male genitals. As described earlier, a respect for the facts does not inhibit the careful erasure of all evidence of male penises from photographs. In cultures where men do not customarily wear pants, the magazine has relied on lengthening loincloths, drawing in shorts, or simply airbrushing offending body parts to avoid offending the white reading public. The fear of—and desire to erase—black male sexuality has a long tradition in Euramerican culture. It reached its fullest and most heinous development in the paranoid fantasies of organizations such as the Ku Klux Klan and in the castrations and lynchings of southern black men for real or imputed advances toward white women (Carby 1985:307–8). Haraway (1989) and Torgovnick (1990) offer vivid examples and analyses of the evidence of miscegenation and black abduction anxieties in American popular culture materials, such as the Tarzan stories and movies. Masquerading as taste or propriety, however, the underlying anxiety also finds its place in the pages of *National Geographic*.

Like the nude and its role in Western high art painting (Hess and Nochlin 1972; Betterton 1987; Nead 1990), nudity in *Geographic* photographs has had a potential sexual, even pornographic, interpretation. Such interpretations would obviously threaten the magazine's legitimacy and sales, achieved through its self-definition as a serious, relatively highbrow family magazine. Pornography represents just the opposite values: "disposability, trash," the deviant, the unrespectable, the low class (Nead 1990:325). Like fine art, science attempts to frame the nude female body as devoid of pornographic attributes. While art aestheticizes it, science dissects, fragments, and otherwise desexualizes it. The *National Geographic* nude has at times done both of these contradictory things.

The *Geographic* nude is first and foremost, in readers' attention, a set of breasts. This follows the culture at large, where the breast is made a fetish of, obsessed on. And the obsession is not just with any kind of breast. As Young (1990:191) has pointed out, breasts are "normalized," leaving women to feel themselves inadequate for not having the culturally dictated "one perfect shape and proportion for breasts": young, large, round, but not sagging. If the *Geographic* is identified with the female breast, then a cultural history of the *Geographic* must take account of changing attitudes towards women's breasts and bodies over that period.

Unfortunately, significant change has been hard to come by. From the pinup (which still had some currency at the beginning of the period) to the large-breasted model recently heralded by fashion magazines as "back for the nineties," the obsession has continued unabated but for the Twiggy and braless moment of the late sixties and early seventies. If anything, the objectification of the breast has increased; it is now so radical that breast enlargement surgery was undergone by nearly a hundred thousand women in 1986 alone. The *Geographic* may reflect this trend when it increasingly exposed women's breasts in the seventies and eighties, taking them out of the shadows where they were more often found in earlier periods. The now foregrounded breasts are also strikingly more often teenage. A taboo that remains in place throughout this culture is showing old women's sagging or dimpled breasts. The *Geographic* has included these breasts, in the interest of veracity, but bows to cultural pressures by almost invariably printing them in smaller or dimly lit formats.

Two important stylistic changes can be identified in photos of women's bodies in the magazine, one related to changes in commercial photography of women and the other to the growing tolerance of "aesthetic" pictures in the *Geographic* of the eighties. Beginning in the late fifties, certain changes in the way women were photographed in commercials began to be reflected in *National Geographic* images.[6] In early advertisements of the period, women are shown directly involved in the use of a product, as when a woman with a fur stole is shown being helped into her 1955 Chrysler by the doorman of an obviously upscale building. By contrast, a 1966 Chevrolet ad shows a woman lying on the roof of the car putting on lipstick, with a small inset photo that has her sitting on the roof being photographed by a man. The ads of the 1950s show women as domestic royalty; the later ads place them in more straightforwardly sexual roles and postures.

In *National Geographic* documentary images as well, we find a shift, coming some years after that in commercial photography; the naked woman moves from being just an ethnographic fact ("this is the way they dress as they go about living their lives") to being presented as in part an aesthetic and sexual object. After 1970, naked women are less often shown framed with men, less often mothering, more often dancing or lounging.[7] The erotic connotations of the horizontal woman, drawn on by advertisers (Goffman 1975), and of the woman absorbed in dance, combine with more romantic, aesthetic styles to create photos which follow the inflation of sexualized images of women in the culture at large (N. Wolf 1991). Contrast the 1986 highly aesthetic photo of a Micronesian teenager, whose direct gaze invites the reader to make contact and whose hazy green background suggests tropical romanticism, with the more clinical 1970 shot of two women buying herbs at a market in Ethiopia. The breasts of the women are clear and central to the photo's narrative, but focus is also on the twigs being passed between the seller of herbs and one of the women and on the camels in the near background. The picture's composition and straightforward realism, as well as the informative caption tell us something ethnographic—that is, about something more than women's beauty or women's bodies.

The development of commercial styles elsewhere in the culture amplifies an effect of photographs of women noted by Pollock (1987); the addition of a woman to a photographed scene often succeeds, given cultural ideologies and history, in changing the scene from a still life or object of contemplation to a purchasable commodity. This is because women have traditionally been seen as objects to be possessed, owned, or controlled, and as ornaments to the lives of men. In the case of the *Geographic*, that commodity is a potential tourist destination. Newly glossy images of women led the way in selling the third world to travelers.

A second explanation for changes in rendering the nude woman is found in the increasing tolerance of a more aesthetic rendering of all subjects in the *Geographic*. Aesthetic style, however, has special implications and nuances when the photos are of women. What arises after the fifties in the *Geographic* is not just a more self-consciously aesthetic style but a style whose uses elsewhere in the culture were centered on photography of women, as in fashion and other commercial work.

The cultural debate (however minor in scale and impact) over whether the nudity in the *Geographic* was or is appropriate follows shifting and conflicting definitions of acceptable portrayals of women's bodies (Nead 1990). At issue is not simply whether women's bodies are displayed, but what the cultural context of those images is (Myers 1982; Vance 1990); that context includes the sexualization of the breasts, the objectification of women, the racist understanding of black femininity, and the shame that inheres in American culture to sexuality itself.[8] Nonetheless, the still heavily white male photographic and editorial staff at the *Geographic* appears relatively unaffected by feminist critiques of the use of women's bodies or the critique of colonial looking-relations (Gaines 1988) that prompt both the frequent inclusion and a particular distorted reading by subscribers of the nude black woman's body. The African-American cabdriver who took one of us to *Geographic* headquarters was less sanguine, even angry, when he noted that the magazine's white women are well covered.

The Kitchen Debates in Africa: Woman's Place in the March of Progress.
In a subtly nuanced analysis of the genre of 1980s Hollywood success movies, Traube (1989) details the influence of the Reagan years and a particular moment of labor demography and consumer capitalism in the construction of the films' plots and styles. These films describe, among other things, the gender-specific dangers and possibilities of the world of managerial work for the middle-class youth who view these movies on their way to corporate work lives. Specifically, they include "warning of the feminizing effects of deference on men and, conversely, the masculinizing effects of ambition on women" (1989:291). The *National Geographic's* women do not provide as easy an identifying anchor for the magazine's readers as do these movies' characters, but their image, too, has responded to changes in the politics and rate of American women's labor force participation. They have also played a role in articulating longstanding cultural notions about the role of women in socioeconomic development overseas. We will now examine problems of the progress of women here and abroad.

Against the indolent native of colonialist discourse, the *Geographic's* industrious native toils in response to an editorial policy which calls for a sympathetic other. The way women's work is portrayed, however, shows some culturally predictable differences from that of men's. As in the wider culture, women's work is sometimes presented as less intellectually demanding, more toilsome. Take the Melanesian man and woman set up on opposite pages (April 1969:574–75). A male archer on the left is labeled "man, the hunter" and, on the right, a photo of a woman with child in a netbag carrying a large load of firewood, "woman, the laborer." The woman smiles under her burden, perhaps thereby evoking images long in circulation in Western culture: these are images that romanticize the hard-working black woman, often ignoring the difference between her enduring and enjoying (much less opposing) oppression (hooks 1981:6). In this latter cultural discourse, the black woman could endure what no lady could and therefore revealed her more natural, even animal nature (81–82). For many readers of the

Geographic, it may be an easy step from the celebration of the strong work-ing woman to her dehumanization as someone with less than human abili-ties to withstand those burdens.[9]

Cultural ambivalence toward women working outside the home has been profound during the postwar period, when employment for which women six-teen and older received wages grew from 25 percent in 1940 to 40 percent in 1960. More of this is accounted for by African-American women, half of whom were employed in 1950, with their wage-paying work continuing at high rates in the following decades. The ideological formulation of the meaning of women's work has changed. Working women in the fifties were defined as helpmates to their husbands. Only much later did women's work come to be seen as a means to goals of independence and self-realization (Chafe 1983), although even here, as Traube (1989) points out, messages were widely available that women's success in work was threatening to men. This ambivalence occasionally shows up in the *Geographic* when the laboring woman is presented as a drudge or when her fem-ininity, *despite her working*, is emphasized. An example of the latter is found in a photograph of a Burmese woman shown planting small green shoots in a garden row (June 1974). Retouching has been done both to her line of plants and to the flowers encircling her hair. The sharpening and coloring of these two items lets the picture tell much more clearly a narrative about her femininity and her pro-ductivity and about how those two things are not mutually exclusive.

More often, however, the labor of women as well as other aspects of their lives are presented by the *Geographic* as central to the march of progress in their respective countries. Women are constructed as the vanguard of progress in part through the feminizing of the developing nation-state itself (Kabbani 1986; compare Schaffer 1988) How does this work? In the first instance, those foreign states are contrasted, in some Western imaginations, with a deeply masculine American national identity (Krasniewicz 1990, Jeffords 1989), a gendering achieved through the equation of the West (*in the West*, of course) with strength, civilization, rationality, and freedom, its other with vulnerability, primitivity, superstition, and the constraints of tra-dition. Once the equation was made, articles can be titled as in the following instance, where progress is masculinized and the traditional nation femi-nized: "Beneath of Surge of Progress, old Mexico's Charm and Beauty Lie Undisturbed" (October 1961).

From the perspective of the colonial era, the symbolic femininity of the non-Western states would seem to have been solidly established, but this kind of rhetoric may have lost some of its power in the new world of social relations of the 1970s and 1980s. The more salient actors in U.S. media coverage of the third world seem now to be male terrorists in the Middle East and male economic competitors in Japan and Korea. Starving ungendered children have some representational space, but female workers are still not visible. How the *Geographic*'s recent coverage articulates with other media representations of the shifting gender of the foreign remains to be studied.

Fanon (1965:39) pointed out in his analysis of French colonial attitudes and strategies concerning the veil in Algeria that the colonialists' goal, here as elsewhere in the world, was "converting the woman, winning her over to the foreign values, wrenching her free from her status" as a means of "shaking up the [native] man" and gaining control of him. With this and other motives, those outsiders who would "develop" the third world have often seen the advancement of non-Western women as the first goal to be achieved, with their men's progress thought to follow rather than precede it. In the nineteenth century, evolutionary theory claimed that the move upward from savagery to barbarism to civilization was indexed by the treatment of women, in particular by their liberation "from the burdens of overwork, sexual abuse, and male violence" (Tiffany and Adams 1985:8). It "saw women in non-Western societies as oppressed and servile creatures, beasts of burden, chattels who could be bought and sold, eventually to be liberated by 'civilization' or 'progress,' thus attaining the enviable position of women in Western society" (Etienne and Leacock 1980:1), who were then expected to be happy with their place.[10] The *Geographic* has told a much more upbeat version of this story, mainly by presenting other women's labors positively.

The continuation of these ways of thinking into the present can be seen in how states defined as "progressive" have been rendered by both Western media like the *National Geographic* and the non-Western state bureaucracies concerned. Graham-Brown (1988) and Schick (1990) describe how photographic and other proof of the progress or modernity of states like Turkey and prerevolutionary Iran has often been found primarily in the lives of their women, particularly in their unveiling.[11] Indeed, as Schick points out, "a photograph of an unveiled woman was not much different from one of a tractor, an industrial complex, or a new railroad; it merely symbolized yet another one of men's achievements" (1990:369).

Take the example from the *Geographic*'s January 1985 article on Baghdad. Several photographs show veiled women walking through the city streets. One shot shows women in a narrow alley. The dark tones of the photograph are a function of the lack of sunlight reaching down into the alley, but they also reinforce the message of the caption. Playing with the associations between veil and the past that are evoked for most readers, it says, "In the shadows of antiquity, women in long black abayas walk in one of the older sections of the city." A few pages earlier, we learn about the high-rise building boom in the city and the changing roles of women in a two-page layout that shows a female electrical engineer in a hard hat and jeans organizing a building project with a male colleague. The caption introduces her by name and goes on: "Iraqi women, among the most progressive in the Arab world, constitute 25 percent of the country's work force and are guaranteed equality under Baath Party doctrine." On the opposite page, the modern buildings they have erected are captioned, "New York on the Tigris." The equation of the end point (Manhattan) with the unveiled woman is neatly laid out.

The goal of progress through women and of women's progress might have been inferred by many viewers from a 1968 photo from Ecuador (February: 271) showing a family of four in the park, sitting in front of the man's abstract painting. This thoroughly modern nuclear family enjoys the clean and cultivated leisure brought by that progress, with the woman most easily understood as housewife and mother. With the bifurcation of the frame into two halves, one side containing the man's artwork, and the other the mother and her children, the symbolic dualism familiar to Western audiences of women/child/nature and men/independent/art is achieved. This couple has no further to go on the Great March. The photo also shows that the kindly-light policy makes a critique of patriarchy as problematic as a critique of anything else.

This celebration of simultaneous women's liberation and national progress is not the whole story, of course. The magazine also communicates— in a more muted way through the fifties and into the sixties—a sense of the value of the natural, Gemeinschaft-based life of the people without progress. Progress can be construed as a socially corrosive process as it was in the late nineteenth century, when non-Western women were seen as superior to their Western counterparts because too much education had weakened the latter, sapping vitality from their reproductive organs (Ehrenreich and English 1978:114). The illiterate woman of the non-Western world still lives with this cultural inheritance, standing for the woman "unruined" by progress.

Another potential factor in the questioning of progress in gender roles is the feminization of natural landscapes. As Schaffer (1988) has shown for

Australian culture and Tiffany and Adams (1985) for the Americas, the landscape has been culturally construed as female over the entire period since discovery. The one who comes to exploit and change it is male, and so the undeveloped third world/feminine can be construed as a repository of timeless (not political) wisdom about the values of a simple life, family, and living in harmony with nature.

An example of the contradictory place of progress is found in two photographs that draw attention to housewives. In the first, an Inuit woman wearing a fur-trimmed parka stands in front of a washing machine: "Unfamiliar luxury," the caption says, "a washing machine draws a housewife to the new 'Tuk' laundromat, which also offers hot showers" (July 1968). This picture is deliberately structured around the contrast between the premodern and the modern, with the evaluative balance falling to the luxurious present. It might have still resonated for readers with the image from 1959 of Nixon and Khrushchev arguing over the benefits of capitalism next to a freshly minted washing machine and dryer at the American National Exhibition in Moscow. In those debates, Nixon could argue that the progress of American society under capitalism is found in its ability to provide labor-saving devices to women. "I think that this attitude toward women is universal. What we want is to make easier the life of our housewives," he said. In the gender stories told during the cold war, family life and commodities provided what security was to be found in the post-Hiroshima, post-holocaust world (May 1988). The non-Western woman, too, could be deployed as proof of capitalism's value, of the universal desire for these goods, and of the role of women in the evolution of society.

From January 1971, however, an article entitled "Housewife at the End of the World" documents the adventures of an Ohio woman settling in Tierra del Fuego, and congratulates her on adapting to local norms of self-sufficiency and simplicity. The last photo's caption articulates the theme of the whole article: "Life in this remote land spurs inventiveness. . . . My special interests keep me so busy I have little time to miss the conveniences I once knew." The North American woman chooses to forgo the benefits of progress, in search of an authentically simple place, as her "younger sister" climbs the ladder in the other direction.

In stories of progress and/or decline, Western and non-Western women have often been played off against each other in this way, one used to critique the other in line with different purposes and in the end leaving each feeling inadequate. The masculine writer/image maker/consumer thereby asserts his own strength, both through his right to evaluate and through his completeness in contrast to women. Although non-Western men cannot be said to fare well in these cultural schemes, they are used less frequently and in other ways (Honour 1989) to either critique or shore up white men's masculinity.

In sum, the women of the non-Western world represent a population aspiring to the full femininity achieved in Western cultures, and, in a more secondary way, they are a repository for the lost femininity of "liberated" Western women. Both an ideal and thus a critique of modern femininity, they are also a measure to tell the Western family how far it has advanced. They are shown working hard and as key to their country's progress toward some version of the Western-consumer family norm. The sometimes contradictory message these pictures can send to middle-class women is consistent with cultural ideologies in the United States that by turns condemn and affirm the woman who would be both mother and wage earner. We can see the women of the *National Geographic* playing a role within a social field where the cold war was being waged and where social changes in kinship structures and gender politics were precipitated by the entrance of white women into the paid labor force in larger and larger numbers.

Conclusion

We have focused here on the rendition of racial and gender difference in the *Geographic*. We can now step back and remind the reader that the color of sex in the magazine emerges first from the photographer's work. The *Geographic* photographer has always been and predominantly remains, both literally and symbolically, a white man. And not just any white man, but the whitest and most masculine version possible: the great hunter/adventurer (Bright 1990:137–38), free to roam the globe in search of visual treasure, flamboyantly virile in his freedom from observation and evaluation, and his bravery in entering the dangerous realms at the ends of the earth, in continents still dark for most of his audience.[12] While the photographs that we find in the magazine are often gentle, beautiful images of people construed as feminine, the image-maker—at least as many viewers imagine—looks out on this exotic world from that Marlboro Country where the jaws are all square with a tough growth of stubble and the Indians are all gone. . . .

Notes

[1]   This is not to deny that there are complex correspondences between culture and racial categories as socially deployed. Once race has been used to marginalize and isolate social

groups, shared experiences of oppression, coping, and resistance may give rise to shared cultural premises. The "culture" or "cultures" that result, however, are at least partly a consequence of the deployment of racial categories and not evidence of the validity of the categories themselves.

2   In part because of its focus on everyday life, *National Geographic* does not trade in the standardized images of black people that have been common in Western art—some of which have been characterized by Honour (1989) as "heroes and martyrs," "the benighted," "the defiant," and "the pacified."

3   This proportion is based on those photos in which adults of identifiable gender are shown (N = 510). Another 11 percent show women and men together in roughly equal numbers, leaving 65 percent of the photos depicting mainly men.

4   The popularity of this notion in American culture, which *National Geographic* relies on as much as feeds, is also one wellspring for American feminism's focus on universal sisterhood, that is, its insistence, particularly in the 1970s, that Western and non-Western women will easily see each other as similar or sharing similar experiences.

5   The popular Family of Man exhibition also included a substantial section devoted to mothers and infants, unfortunately nicknamed "Tits and Tots" by the staff of photographers who organized it (Meltzer 1978). This exhibit, immensely popular when it toured, became a best-selling book.

6   For an example of the connection between *Geographic* and commercial styles, see the similarity between women's fashion photography of the period and the galleries of Polynesian beauties remarked on in chapter 5 [of *Reading National Geographic*]. One Tahitian woman is posed for a side portrait with her head pushed forward, accentuating a long neck and paralleling the elegance of the model of high-fashion photography of the 1950s.

7   This is based on the twenty photos in our sample of 592 where women are shown without shirts on; half of that number occurred from 1950 to 1969 and the other half from 1970 to 1986 (one would, of course, expect there to be somewhat fewer such photos as urbanization and change in dress styles spread across the globe). Some of the same phenomena noted here have been found in advertising in American family magazines (that is, a decrease in images of married women shown in child care and an increase in those showing them at recreation), although in the latter ads the trends begin earlier, in the later 1940s (Brown 1981).

8   The *Geographic*'s breasts should be seen against the broader background of the social changes in the industrial West relating to sexuality. Foucault (1978) has noted that those changes have been mistakenly associated with a "liberation" of sexuality. In fact, he sug-

gests, with the emergence of the modern state and its regulatory needs has come an obsession with talking about and managing sex—through science, state policy, clinical medicine, and now photography.

[9] That step may have been taken by white feminism as well, hooks points out: "When the women's movement was at its peak and white women were rejecting the role of breeder, burden bearer, and sex object, black women were celebrated for their unique devotion to the task of mothering; for their 'innate' ability to bear tremendous burdens; and for their ever-increasing availability as sex object. We appeared to have been unanimously elected to take up where white women were leaving off" (1981:6). See Hammond and Jablow (1977) for an analysis of the particular strength of the notion of nonwhite women as beasts of burden in the case of African women; see also Collins (1991).

[10] Western feminism in the 1970s may have simply transformed rather than fundamentally challenged the terms of this argument as well when it argued that the women of the world were oppressed by men and were to be liberated by feminism as defined in the West (see Amos and Parmar 1984).

[11] Although feminist anthropology has analyzed and critiqued these kinds of assumptions, it has nonetheless often continued a basic evolutionary discourse in the assumption that Ong has identified: "Although a common past may be claimed by feminists, Third World women are often represented as mired in it, ever arriving at modernity when Western feminists are already adrift in postmodernism" (1988:87).

[12] The masculine part of this ethos is found in contemporary anthropology as well, as indicated by Okely (1975). The racially white part is noted by Said (1989).

AMERICAN DENIM: BLUE JEANS AND THEIR MULTIPLE LAYERS OF MEANING

Beverly Gordon

B lue jeans, the now-ubiquitous denim garments that almost constitute a uniform on high school and college campuses, have been an integral part of the American scene for about 130 years. In that time they have embodied many different messages, and functioned in different ways—as symbols of rebellion; outlets for personal creativity; emblems of up-to-date, fashionable awareness; and as evidence of generational longing and insecurity. Changes in jeans styling, embellishment, and marketing are closely tied to changes in the society as a whole, and these changes serve as a subtle but accurate barometer of trends in contemporary popular culture. The jeans phenomenon merits serious attention on the part of the popular culture scholar.

The Blue Jean as Laborer: The Wild West and the Farmer

Jeans first appeared in their now-familiar form in California in the second half of the 19th century. Levi Strauss, a Bavarian immigrant, came to San Francisco in 1850 with a supply of strong canvas cloth that he hoped to sell to people making tents and wagon covers, but when he saw the kind of hard wear the gold prospectors gave their clothes, he had it made into sturdy pants. "Levi's" were really born when Strauss switched to a heavy denim fabric a few years later. Copper rivets were added at the stress points in 1873 (Ratner 1–2; Shea 31; Brooks 64–5). Jeans first evolved, then, as practical rather than fashionable clothing, and were associated with hard-working physical laborers, especially those from the rough and rugged West. By the early twentieth century, when Levis competed with other brands such as Wrangler and Lee, jeans and related denimwear such as protective overalls were the modal garments for farmers. By 1902 the Sears and Roebuck catalogue offered five different denimwear styles (Rupp 83). Again, individuals who wore these garments were not "fashionable," they were not making a statement of any kind; they were simply choosing serviceable, affordable clothing.

The Blue Jean as Anti-Fashion: The First Association

Jeans were first adopted as a kind of anti-fashion—a conscious, pointed state-ment that goes against the fashion norm and says, "I am different, I am not like you"—by a group of artists in the Santa Fe area in the 1920s (Brooks 58). Generally well-educated individuals of both sexes took to wearing jeans as a badge of their own group identity and special status. They were identifying themselves with the ruggedness, the directness, and the earthiness of the laborer, and were placing themselves as a part of the Western scene. They also adopted a unisex look long before it was the norm.

This group of artists continued to sport jeans in the 1930s, but some-thing of the same impulse was also promulgated in the mainstream fashion world. Levi Strauss executives began encouraging Easterners who were taking the newly-popular "dude ranch" vacations to outfit themselves with jeans or overalls, and the garments even became available for the first time in upscale New York stores. Levi Strauss ran an ad in the April, 1935 *Vogue* that stated, "true Western chic was invented by cowboys" (Brooks 70; Berendt 24). Although the trend did not really take off at this time outside the dude ranch context, this was perhaps the first instance where fashionable consumers were encouraged to take on the aura of a particular lifestyle by wearing jeans.

The Blue Jean as War Hero: Widening the Base of Support

World War II was a turning point for blue jeans in America. Materials were scarce as resources were diverted to the war effort, but with the increasing number of workers in the factories and munitions plants, great quantities of durable work clothes were needed. Jeans were declared "essential commodi-ties," and to serve the needs of thousands of Rosie the Riveters, the Blue Bell company came out with a special Wrangler dungaree style dubbed "the Jeanie" (Brooks 71; Quinn 19; Shea 31). Once again, these were not really fashion-able garments—they were work clothes. They were still used only in a partic-ular context. Because factory war work was seen in a positive light, however, the garments were perceived as part of the patriotic, all-pitching-in spirit, and were thought of fondly. To women workers who had been used to wearing dresses and more constricting garments, they must have also seemed liberat-ing and refreshingly comfortable. Wartime fashion was changing, also, and taking much of its detailing from the rather unfashionable wartime scene. Head wraps or turbans, originally used in the factories to keep long hair out of the machinery, became part of acceptable evening wear. Shoulder pads, originally seen in military uniforms, became an indispensable part of women's civilian garments. Jeans were associated with a particular war-era lifestyle, and were poised somewhere in the middle on the fashion/anti-fashion continuum.

The Blue Jean Anti-Fashion: Tomboys, Bad Boys and Bohemians

After the war, jeans were no longer just unfashionable; they came to have widespread distinct anti-fashion associations. The hard-edged, square-shouldered female styles gave way in the high-style world to the ultra-feminine and very dressy "New Look," and the more rugged, unisex denim garments began to be associated with youth, freedom, and rebellion. One of the first things Western American servicemen stationed in Europe did when peace was declared was trade their uniforms for blue jeans. They were free, and they were finished with carrying the burdens of the world. Bennington College students, who were generally known as "artistic" and rather unconventional, adopted jeans as a "virtual uniform" on their Vermont campus (Brooks 58). They too used their clothing to symbolize freedom—freedom from the norms of conventional society.

Sometimes this freedom was simply the prerogative of youth, and was seen as innocent and harmless. Eddie Fisher crooned *Dungaree Doll* in the late 1940s (Rosenberg and Bordow xi), and evoked the image of a happy-go-lucky bobby soxer, a tomboy who would eventually, in the words of another post-war era song, "trade her bobby sox for stockings." Another type of freedom emerged in the early 1950s, however, which was seen as much more sinister. There was a group of disenfranchised individuals who could not find a place in the conformist climate of Cold War America and who reacted to it with alienation and disdain. These were the young people symbolized in Marlon Brando's *The Wild One* and James Dean's *Rebel Without a Cause*, the angry or confused or simply no-good "juvenile delinquents" who at their most extreme flashed switchblades and tire irons and terrorized neighborhoods. These young people, also, wore jeans: jeans and leather jackets were the anti-fashion wardrobe that symbolically flaunted the mores of the frightened society at large. Jeans were so strongly associated with these outcasts, in fact, that a 1959 movie about an unwed teenage mother was tellingly titled *Blue Denim* (Shea 30). The good-versus-bad connations were symbolized by a "dress right" campaign launched by the American Institute of Men's and Boy's Wear and aimed particularly at blue jeans (Brooks 72).

Associations with the wild west actually strengthened or reinforced the anti-fashion statement that jeans made in the 1950s. This was the era of the Gray Flannel Suit and the Organization Man;[1] it was a time permeated by what author Peter Beagle characterizes as "a strangled, constipated idea of a proper life" (Beagle 14). It was also the era of the Hollywood and TV Western. Good and bad cowboys were sometimes differentiated by the color of their hats, but they all wore jeans. The Western simultaneously replayed the good guys/bad guys scenario of the Cold War and represented an escape from it, a foray into a still wild or "untamed" past where people did not have to fit into such carefully prescribed niches. Baby-boom children who grew up with Western heroes grew up with images of jeans, and wore them for their creative play. They wore them when they wanted to step into a fantasy world that was outside the world of piano lessons, visiting relatives and other dutiful activities.

Anti-Fashion at its Peak: The "Jeaning of America" and the Personalized Jean

It was in the 1960s that the "jeaning of America" occurred, and jeans took on a new role. The first signs of the shift really began in the late 1950s, when another type of rebel, the bohemian or "beatnik," began to adopt them with black sweaters for everyday wear. Unlike the Brando/Dean "bad boy" rebel, this was a dissenter, an urban intellectual who came to an anti-fashion statement of this sort from a thought-out position about the materialistic, conformist society of the day. To wear plain jeans and dark colors was to reject the more-is-better, new-is-better mentality of the Organization Man world. 1962, according to Levi Strauss executive Alfred Sanguinetti, marked the "breakout" point in jeans sales, with sales figures doubling in just three years. They further quintupled between 1965 and 1970 (Brooks 73–74).[2] By 1967 the anti-fashion statement was screaming across the land, for jeans were one of the most visible symbols of the rapidly increasing numbers of disenfranchised youth. The late 1960s were, of course, the turbulent period in which there was a marked escalation of the undeclared war in Vietnam, a war that polarized the society and led to a widespread rejection of mainstream social norms on the part of the younger generation. The youth-dominated counter-culture, which was made up of the same baby-boomers who had worn jeans as play clothes and had grown up with James Dean and other such cultural icons, turned to jeans very naturally. Jeans were practical, long-lasting, and unchanging; they were the very antitheses of the mainstream "straight" world where fashion was by its very nature ever-changing and quickly obsolescent. They were cheap, comfortable, and associated with physicality; they represented freedom from dutifulness, and because they were simultaneously associated with work and play, came to stand for a society where there really was no distinction between the two. As Valerie Carnes put it in a 1977 article entitled "Icons of Popular Fashion,"

> Denim jeans became [in the 1960s] the ultimate no-fashion put-down style—a classless, cheap, unisex look that stood for, variously, frontier values, democracy, plain living, ecology and health, rebellion *a la* Brando or Dean, a new interest in the erotic import of the pelvis, or, as Charles Reich suggests in *The Greening of America*, a deliberate rejection of the "artificial plastic-coated look" of the affluent consumer society. (237)

Jeans may have been the common anti-fashion denominator among the young, but all jeans were not alike. Jeans wearers avoided the plastic veneer and the sameness and artificiality it represented by the very act of wearing their jeans. Jeans conformed more and more to their own particular body shapes as they were worn and washed (cotton denim shrinks and stretches each time it is washed and reworn). Over time jeans came to carry particular "scars"—stains, rips, frayed areas, patches—that could be associated with remembered events and experiences. A pair of jeans became intensely personal. If a small hole developed it might be left alone as a "badge" of experience, or great deliberation might go into the choice of an appropriate fabric with which to cover it. Soon, counter-culture youth were *glorifying* their jeans—decorating and embellishing them, making them colorful and celebratory, and making them into visible, vocal personal statements. Silk, velvet, leather, feathers, bells, beads, rivets, sequins, paint—anything that could be applied to denim fabric was applied to someone's jeans, jeans jackets, and related accessories. Men who had never learned to sew and who under most circumstances would think of embroidery as unmanly learned the necessary stitches to work on their own clothes. The unisex garment that symbolized the alternative youth culture was an appropriate vehicle for the breakdown of gender roles, and besides, one's jeans were too personal to trust to anyone else. By 1974 imaginatively adorned jeans were such a pervasive and interesting phenomenon that the Levi Strauss company sponsored a national "denim art" contest and was deluged with entries. Entrants repeatedly stated that they found it difficult to part with the garments long enough for them to be displayed in the exhibition; they felt they were giving up a part of themselves. "I feel most myself when I have my jeans on" was a typical comment from an entrant. "My jeans are an extension of me"; "my shorts [are] my autobiography on denim" (Beagle 14, 73).

The Blue Jean as Fashion: Absorbing the Counter-Culture with a Designer Label

In some ways it had by this time become almost necessary to dramatically personalize one's jeans in order to still make an anti-fashion statement. Many of the outward signs and even some of the underlying ideas of the counter-culture had been adopted (some might say usurped) by the mainstream culture at large. Blue jeans in and of themselves were so well accepted in the establishment that even such political figures as New York City mayor John Lindsay and presidential candidate Jimmy Carter were happy to be photographed wearing them. Anti-fashion had not only been absorbed by fashion, but had become part of its very essence. John Brooks, writing in *The New Yorker* in 1979, attributed the fashionable usurpation of the jeans phenomenon to the early 1970s "search for the fountain of youth" (Brooks 60), but it may have been as much a sign of an underlying widespread hunger for life-affirming values in what was a confused and dark time.

Jeans and other denim garments were also seen in the early 1970s as quintessentially *American.* Jeans had been developed in the United States, of course, and had long carried associations of the American West, but once they had filtered into the international fashion scene, they came to stand for the country as a whole. In 1973 the American Fashion Critics presented a special award to Levi Strauss for "a fundamental American fashion that . . . now influences the world." Nieman Marcus also gave Levi Strauss its Distinguished Service in Fashion Award that same year (Carnes, 236).[3] The popular press began to print rhetorical questions like, "after all, what's more American than denim?" ("Do It Up Denim!" 142) and in 1974 American Motors Corporation contracted with Levi Strauss to provide blue denim fabric for upholstery for its Gremlin and Hornet cars (Fehr 73). The Gremlin, which was promoted as America's answer to the Volkswagon beetle, was meant to be both upbeat and patriotic, and denim furnishings were thought to communicate both qualities.

Jeans sales continued to climb. By 1977 over 500 million pairs were sold in this country alone—more than twice the number of the total population (Brooks 58).

Fashion and anti-fashion came exceedingly close during this period, but there were continually two thrusts to the jeans craze. The counter-culture continued to thrive and maintained and fostered a do-your-own, personalize-your-clothing vision. Numerous instruction books were published between 1973 and 1977 that carried a power-to-the-people message and told people how to fashion and re-fashion their own denim clothing. Publications with such titles as *Clothing Liberation*, and *Make it in Denim*, *The Jeans Scene*, *The Jeans Book*, and *Native Funk and Flash* (Harlow; Jacopetti; Johnson; Rosenberg and Weiner; Todhunter; Torbet) continued to advocate inexpensive and comfortable clothing that made use of worn garments and other available materials. Cast-offs and odds and ends could not only be salvaged, but creatively used.

At the same time, there was a high-fashion version of this democratic, anti-fashion trend. Couturiers who saw these creative outfits on the streets and in such legitimizing exhibitions as Wesleyan University's "Smart Ass Art" (1973) and Levi Strauss' "Denim Art" at the Museum of Contemporary Crafts (1974) moved in and produced their own high-style versions of counter-culture styles. Givenchy designed an entire denim wardrobe for film star Audrey Hepburn, for example, and Giorgio outfitted Dyan Cannon and Ava Gardner (Fehr 55, 66; Shea 29). A $2,325 denim-lined mink jacket and mink-cuffed jeans were shown on the fashion runways in Paris in 1974, and professionally-designed embroidered, sequinned and nail-studded ensembles were going for about $500 in New York boutiques (Fehr 27, 45). Recycled and well-worn fabrics—hallmarks of the counter-culture look—were part of this style. Giorgio's jeans outfits that sold for $250 were made from already-used denim, for example, and designer shops in department stores like Lord and Taylor sold recycled jeans for three times the price of new ones (Fehr 46).

By the late 1970s, when the baby-boomer generation had been largely absorbed into the work force and the responsibilities of parenting, and the counter-culture vision had become diffused, the high-style fashion forces won out over the anti-fashion style. Couture denim filtered down into the ready-to-wear market. Designer labels became an obsession; "designer jeans" were "*the* pants in America," according to a Saks Fifth Avenue retailer. Calvin Klein, who drew attention to jeans sporting his label with an erotic advertising campaign, sold 125,000 pairs a week in 1979 (McCord 115). Designer jeans were in such demand that there was a thriving counterfeit trade, and by 1981 *Good Housekeeping* magazine ran a feature advising consumers how to make sure they were buying the "real thing." (202)[4]

Designer jeans were often based on anti-fashion prototypes (both Calvin Klein and Oscar de la Renta are known to have sent photographers out into the streets of New York to document what people were wearing) (Carnes 235–36), but they tended to be subtle: they did not, in the early Reagan era, generally sport embroidered patches and tattered fringe. Often nearly indistinguishable (except by the small designer label sewn on the back pocket), they offered ostentatious but restrained snob appeal. Jeans were no longer the "great American equalizer;"[5] homemade and recycled garments did not have a place in this less democratic age—or rather, they had a place, but it was back with the poor and have-nots. Designer jeans were made to fit and flatter the body, but they were made to be long lasting and uniform rather than to age and change with the individual. In 1984 several fabric manufacturers came out with new polyester/denim blends that were intended to stretch with the body and keep their shape. The Sydeco company introduced "Forever Blue," a new fade-resistant jeans fabric that was designed to "look new longer" ("Institute Report" 124).

The Blue Jean as Fashion: Pre-Packaged Experience

The Aged Jean. It seems fitting to begin the most recent chapter of the jeans saga in 1985, with the story of "The Authentic Stone." This was a product developed by Mr. Marshall Banks, who got the idea when he discovered a small piece of pumice stone in the pocket of his newly-purchased jeans. Banks learned that the stone was accidentally left behind from the "stone washing"—the preconditioning process—that the jeans had been subjected to. Small pieces of pumice, which is an abrasive material, had been added to a pre-market wash in order to soften the garment.[6] As the earlier description of innovative 1984 jeans fabrics makes clear, stone-washing and other preconditioning treatments were not yet *de rigueur*. Banks stated, presumably with his tongue in his cheek, that he hoped to appeal to the "do-it-yourselfer" with his Authentic [pumice] Stone packaged in its own "bed of denim." He felt his product blended "the whole 60s look with a status connotation"; it was a symbolic pre-packaging of experience, a fashionable way of referring to the anti-fashion of the past. One hundred thousand Authentic Stones had been sold to leading department stores by 1986 ("A Six Dollar Stone Wash" 77).

The 1960s anti-fashion style had indeed been a look of well-used, lived-in jeans. The Vietnam years were enormously intense—every day brought the promise of incredible revelation or impending apocalypse[7]—and experience was highly charged. The jeans one wore were part of the experience; they were faithful companions, they had been there. Even if they weren't heavily decorated, they were "encrusted" with memories (Fehr 11), and held the accumulated charge.[8] Small wonder that aged, faded, tattered jeans were treasured: they were not only comfortable, but were far richer and more meaningful than those that were new and unmarked.

The best jeans were those that had aged naturally, over the course of time and experience, but there were numerous home-grown or do-it-yourself methods to speed up the aging process in order to look presentable. Folk wisdom suggested the best way to soften and shape one's jeans was to repeatedly get them wet and wear them until they dried. This could be done by soaking in the bathtub, but the sun-and-salt-water of the ocean beach environment was much preferred.[9] New jeans were also home-treated by rubbing sandpaper and pumice stones across the fabric, by burying them, or by adding washing soda or bleach to a tubful of water (Beagle 39–40; Fehr 62–4). The bleach treatment was more controversial, largely because it weakened the fabric in the wrong places, and looked bleached rather than worn (Todhunter 26–7).

The faded look was commercially imitated in a pre-bleached fabric for the first time in 1969, presumably inspired by the sun-bleached denims seen on the Riviera, and the look was popular in France (Carnes 235; McCord 115). Some very high-priced customized jeans were pre-faded; items taken to "Robbie's Stud and Rhinestone Shop," an establishment that serviced fashion-conscious celebrities in Los Angeles, for example, were sent to a denim fading lab before the studding process began (Fehr 55). A few American laundry companies developed fading treatments in 1973 and jeans manufacturers like H. D. Lee contracted with them for several thousand faded garments (Fehr 64; Koshetz 47), but bleached fabrics were still not the norm. More and more "pre-washed" denims were on the market by the late 1970s, but the phenomenon crept in slowly. A 1981 *Mademoiselle* fashion column spoke of the "new, faded look," but disparaged it for its extra costliness. Readers were advised to use inexpensive commercial color removers or fading products on their jeans if they liked the look of prewashed fabric ("Denims: Here's How . . ." 258).

The prewashed look was characteristic of jeans manufactured by Guess, Inc., a company started in 1981, interestingly enough, by four brothers who had emigrated to the United States from France. Guess jeans achieved their well-worn look through a stonewashing process that took up to 12 hours, and by 1986 the company was already having trouble finding launderers with whom they could subcontract, as the treatments were breaking even the strongest washing machines (Ginsberg 4–5). Guess products, though expensive, began "flying off department store shelves" almost as soon as they were stocked (Slutsker 210), and Guess captured a significant piece of the youth market by the mid 1980s. Other companies quickly found ways to emulate the prewashed look. *Rolling Stone* magazine proclaimed in May of 1986 that the "best jeans available" were triple bleached and double stonewashed (Schecter 67–71), but the sentiment was still by no means universally accepted. One commentator writing in *Esquire* protested that hastening the aging process was a form of "faddish dishonesty." "To wear jeans is to create a life mold of oneself in denim," he exclaimed; pre-worn jeans are not a reflection of the "person within" (Berendt 25). Numerous "upscale" American designers were using denim in their new lines, but were concentrating on less casual items such as dresses and coats, and aging treatments were not part of their design process (Goodman 48–51; "Designing the Blues," 78–9; La Ferla 60; "Denim Rides Again" 76–8).

The Guess prototype and its "worn to death" look[10] continued to permeate the retail denim market, however, and it has effectively dominated the 1987–1988 fashion season. With fierce competition for the many dollars spent on jeans and other denim items (more than thirteen pairs of jeans were sold every second in 1986) ("Denim Rides Again" 76) it is not surprising that novelty would be at a premium, but there is another, more fundamental reason that such products caught on. The contemporary crop of worn and faded looking denimwear provides its primarily young customers with a costume that has *lived*. It carries a feeling or ambiance, an illusion of experience. It, even more seriously than the Authentic Stone, represents a pre-packaged kind of experience that is risk-free.[11]

The actual intense and heady experiences of the counter-culture Vietnam generation are not available to today's youth. "Free love" and easy sexuality have been tainted by the terrifying fear of AIDS, and optimistic faith in expanded consciousness through mind-altering drugs has been destroyed by the spectre of crack and other lethal substances. The world no longer seems full of unending promise. It is no longer possible to take to the road with the certainty that there will be "brothers" who will provide places to stay along the way; this is the age of the homeless, and people avert their eyes. The realities of child abuse, incest, alcoholism and family violence are ever-more evident. There is no groundswell of passionate feeling to tap into, no clear vision of a better future. Unlike the children of the 1960s, then, the children of the 1980s are cautious, and rightfully afraid. I maintain that they have taken to the washed-out tattered garments because they *imply* experience, adventure and drama, and offer a vicarious (though not really conscious) experience of it. These clothes provide the security of the most up-to-date fashion, but the fashion itself alludes to anti-fashion of an earlier time, and plays upon a longing for the (counter) culture that produced it.

Distressed Denim. The terms used to describe the new denimwear are quite telling. Denim is now subjected not only to stones, but to acid; it is "abused," "distressed," "sabotaged" and "blasted"; it has been "washed out." It is also cold and frigid: it is "frosted," "frozen out," and "iced"; and "glacier" or "polar-washed." At first these terms seemed reminiscent of the words used in the Vietnam era for the drug experience ("stoned," "wasted," "wiped out"), but in reality they have a much harder, more anguished edge. One was stoned or wiped out from an abundance of experience; now one has simply weathered the storm ("Storm Riders," and "White Lightening" are two contemporary jeans styles). Today's "Get Used" fashions echo the underlying desperation of the age.

Descriptive labels that come with this aged denimwear try to be comforting. "This garment is made to look used and soft," one states. "It is broken in just for you." Customers are reassured that the jeans are "inspired by the faded, comfortable character of well worn clothing," or by the "comfortable good looks and free-wheeling spirit of aviators and prairie hands." This is "authentic apparel," state the labels; these garments are "like three years old." The underlying message is that the world out there is a tough one, but the clothing has been through it and has already taken it. It is protective, for it acts as a foil and absorbs the shock so its owner doesn't have to. It is soothing: "worn denim is man's best friend."[12]

The 1988 season denimwear also borrows from the free-spirited, make-your-own, recycle-it trend of the mid 1970s. Couturiers were beginning to show this look about two years ago, but now increasing numbers of ready-to-wear garments are designed so as to look as if they were made from several pairs of cut-up and reused jeans. There are waistband details tucked into bodices or turned upside-down on the bottom of jackets; there are odd pockets and belt loops sewn in at jaunty diagonal angles. Contrasting color patches, particularly in mattress ticking prints, are also evident.

Sadly, all of these trendy looks are mere facades. Pre-washed jeans are not really made "just for" anyone; they hold no one's individual contours. Jackets may have extra waistbands and added pockets or patches, but they do not have the free-spirited spontaneity and freshness of the make-your-own era. Much of the tattered quality of contemporary denimwear, also, looks contrived and unnatural. Wear and tear that develops during consecutive hours of laundering does not necessarily occur in areas that would be naturally stressed or worn, and sewn-in fringed selvages look too regular to be real. When a whole line of jackets even bears a "rip" in the same place and the rip is always outlined with rows of stitches, the point is exceedingly forced. These clothes may at first allude to another era, and may offer the illusion of experience and comfort, but illusions are all they offer. They are in reality prepackaged, just like the Authentic Stone. They set up a facade for their wearers, a facade that makes them seem larger than they may be able to be. The look has struck a responsive chord, for it speaks to a yearning on the part of the young jeans customer, a yearning for a time when the world was not just tough, but exciting, and full of promise and imminent discovery.

Selling the Image. Photographs used in magazine advertisements for this denim clothing support the thesis developed above. Jeans manufacturers take it for granted at this point that their product is desirable, but struggle to create memorable images that prospective customers will identify with. Consequently, the photographs do not feature the garments as much as create a mood or tell a story. The stories are dreamy and "mythic" (Conant 64)[13] and full of implication. Sometimes they imply a free and uninhibited sexuality—Calvin Klein ads featuring photographs by Bruce Weber consist of ambiguous images such as one woman surrounded by four men, two of whom are shirtless, or an odd tangle of bodies on the grass. Guess advertisements often include unbuttoned and unbuckled garments, and glimpses of lacy underwear beneath. A recent Jordache ad was headlined, "I Can't Get No Satisfaction," and simulated a young man's internal monologue: "I don't know what's with you girls . . . Your body says yes but your lips say no . . . but you, Sandy, you're not like the rest. You wouldn't play with my head . . ." The story had a happy ending, for in the next frame Sandy and the young man are entwined together, and he is peering soulfully into her denim jacket. Even where there is no explicit sexuality, there is a sensual undertone. Characters in Guess ads are always positioned suggestively, leaning, stretching or slouching with studied ease.

Many of the vignettes include references to the adventurous past of the blue jean. There are couples leaning on motorcycles (Calvin Klein) and men in black leather gloves (Guess); rugged rodeo riders or freewheeling Western characters with bolo ties or bandana neckerchiefs (Guess, Levis); and even a young girl with a head kerchief that looks as if she just stepped off the wagon train (Guess). There are aviators and wavy-haired workers from the World War II era (Work Force—the Gap), and sullen bohemian-types dressed in black (Calvin Klein).

The characters in these advertisements are uniformly young and attractive, but they rarely seem full of vitality, joy or optimism. Often, they face completely away from the camera or have their faces totally or partially obscured by unkempt long hair (itself a reference to the 1960s) or by shadow. Where faces are visible, expressions tend to be enigmatic; dreamy or thoughtful, perhaps, or petulant, sad, or weary. This enigmatic quality is quite anonymous, and suitably enough it allows potential customers to project themselves into the scene and become one of the characters. The scenes hint, in a rather desultory way, of experience and adventure, and imply that the worn garments the characters wear will bring that experience within the reach of even the most unadventurous or inexperienced teenager.

Blue jeans and related denim garments have, in sum, come to stand not just for the Wild West or the rugged laborer or the hardworking farmer— they have become an integral part of the whole American (and perhaps the world-wide) scene. They have been bleached, ripped, washed with acid, washed with stones, patched, cut up, decorated, distressed, and "worn to death," but they are resilient, and seem to always be able to return in yet another guise and take on yet another layer of meaning. They have at different times seemed matter-of-fact and part of the scenery, and at other times have called out for notice and attention. They have served both as symbols of the culture at large and of subsets of that culture, and of rebellious, outspoken counter-culture groups; they have been fashionable, unfashionable, and hallmarks of anti-fashion. They have embodied many of the longings, beliefs and realities of the generations that have worn them. We must watch and try to understand them as they continue to evolve.

Notes

[1]   See Russell (48) for a discussion of the gray flannel suit imagery. The movie by that name came out in 1957. See also William Hollingsworth Whyte, *The Organization Man*. (New York: Simon & Shuster, 1956)

[2]   Brooks reports that the Levi Strauss company commissioned a survey in 1965 that indicated most people still associated the jeans with farmers, but the turning point in the popular association must have occurred very shortly thereafter.

3   Alison Lurie (87) later came to attribute the popularity of Levis in Europe to the belief among European teens that "the power and virtue of America" was contained in the jeans, and would rub off on anyone who wore them.

4   Counterfeiting of jeans had actually begun some time before this date, with the bulk of the bogus products going overseas. Thirty-five thousand pairs of forged Levis and Wrangler label jeans were confiscated in West Germany in 1977. See "West Germany: A Booming Market in Counterfeit Jeans" (38–9).

5   This epithet (and a similar one, the "great common denominator") had been bandied about considerably in the late 1960s and early 1970s. See Fehr 35, Shea 29.

6   Fehr claims (63) that the original derivation of the phrase "stone wash" comes from a pre-industrial era when garments were softened by a long exposure to running water. The garments were buried in streams, she says, and held down by rocks or stones. I have been unable to confirm this explanation, and rather suspect it is more likely related to the fact that fabric was long cleaned by rubbing over stones in the stream beds.

7   I speak from memory.

8   The thesis that clothing and other objects can hold a psychic charge has been developed at length by Mihaly Csikszentmihalyi and Eugene Rochberg-Halton in *The Meaning of Things: Domestic Symbols and the Self.* Although this feeling about jeans was probably at its strongest in the Vietnam era when the jeans were still symbolic of counter-culture beliefs, it has clearly not died out. In 1985 sculptor Bob Edlund offered to preserve the spirit of one's jeans forever by "freezing" them in characteristic poses with several coats of fiberglass resin. Edlund said he came up with this idea because jeans "are the hardest things in the world to part with." He even planned to coat children's overalls in this manner, much in the spirit of bronzed baby shoes. See *People* ("For A Mere $1,250" 79).

9   Brooks claims (80) he was given this advice when he bought his first pair of jeans in 1979; jeans "connoisseurs" had the benefit of years of experience when they told him what to do. Beagle also discusses this process at length (39–40).

10 This was the actual phrase used by *Rolling Stone* fashion editor Laurie Schecter (68).

11 It is somewhat outside the parameters of the jeans story, but another type of fashion that caught on in the mid 1980s was the safari-look, made up primarily of cotton khaki garments. The look was spurred on by such popular movies as the "Raiders of the Lost Ark" and "Out of Africa," but it was first marketed by an innovative company named Banana Republic. When it was a new company, Banana Republic bought up lots of used army and safari clothing and restyled them for its customers. (See feature program on specialty retailers, *Adam Smith's Moneyworld,* airing on P.B.S. network T.V., October, 1986). These safari-type clothes also provided a safe fantasy—a vicarious sense of adventure.

¹² These adjectives and statements were all copied from labels on denimwear found in a variety of department stores in Madison, Wisconsin in February, 1988.

¹³ There are even some jeans advertisements that are framed and titled, like slice-of-life or art photographs. *Seventeen* magazine carried an ad for Jeanjer denimwear in September, 1986, for example, that featured a snapshot-like image of a sensual girl in jeans and a denim jacket, outlined in black and clearly set off against the page. It was captioned, "'Desert Blues', 1986."

Works Cited

Beagle, Peter. *American Denim: A New Folk Art.* (Presented by Richard M. Owens and Tony Lane) New York: Harry N. Abrams, 1975.

Berendt. John. "Blue Jeans," *Esquire* September 1986: 24–6.

Brooks John. "Annals of Business: A Friendly Product," *New Yorker* 12 November 1979: 58–80.

Carnes, Valerie. "Icons of Popular Fashion," *Icons of America*, Ray N. Browne and Marshall Fishwick, eds. Bowling Green, Ohio: Bowling Green State University Popular Press, 1978: 228–240.

Conant, Jennet. "Sexy Does It," *Newsweek* 15 September 1986: 64.

Csikszentmihalyi, Mihaly and Eugene Rochberg-Halton. *The Meaning of Things: Domestic Symbols and the Self.* Cambridge: Cambridge University Press, 1981.

"Denim Rides Again," *Life* September 1986. 76–8.

"Denims: Here's How to Buy the Best and Fade Them Fast." *Mademoiselle* August 1981: 258.

"Designing the Blues," *New York* 17 November 1986: 78–9.

"Do it up Denim!" *Mademoiselle* February 1978: 140–44.

Fehr, Barbara. *Yankee Denim Dandies.* Blue Earth, Minn.: Piper Press, 1974.

"For a Mere $1,250, Sculptor Bob Edlund Will See to it that Your Jeans Never Wear Out," *People* 11 November 1985: 79.

Ginsburg, Steve. "Despite a Feud, Marcianos Make Guesswork Pay," *Women's Wear Daily* 25 November 1986: 4–5.

Good Housekeeping April 1981: 202.

Goodman, Wendy. "Upscale Blues," *New York* 10 February 1986: 48–51.

Harlow, Eve. *The Jeans Scene.* New York: Drake, 1973.

"Institute Report: Denim Update," *Good Housekeeping* September 1984: 124.

Jacopetti, Alexandra. *Native Funk and Flash*. San Francisco: Scrimshaw Press, 1974.

Johnson, Jann. *The Jeans Book*. New York: Ballantine Press, 1972.

Koshetz, Herbert. "Laundry Offers New Way to Age Jeans," *New York Times* 7 August, 1973: 47.

La Ferla, Ruth. "Singing the Blues," *New York Times Magazine*, 13 July 1986, Section 6: 60.

Lurie, Alison. *The Language of Clothes*. New York: Random House, 1981.

McCord, Jacqueline. "Blue Jean Country," *New York Times Magazine*, 29 April 1979: 115.

Quinn, Carin C. "The Jeaning of America—and the World." *American Heritage* April 1978: 14–21.

Ratner, Elaine, "Levi's," *Dress* 1 (1975): 1–5.

Riesman, David. *The Lonely Crowd: A Study of the Changing American Character*. Garden City: Doubleday, 1953.

Rosenberg, Sharon and Joan Wiener Bordow. *The Denim Book*. Englewood Cliffs, N.J.: Prentice Hall, 1978.

Rosenberg, Sharon and Joan Wiener. *The Illustrated Hassle-Free Make Your Own Clothes Book*. San Francisco: Straight Arrow Press, 1971.

Rupp, Becky. "In Praise of Bluejeans: The Denimization of America," *Blair Ketchum's Country Journal* December 1985: 82–6.

Russell, Douglas A. *Costume History and Style*. Englewood Cliffs, N.J.: Prentice-Hall, 1983.

Schecter, Laurie. "Red-Hot Blues," *Rolling Stone* 8 May 1986: 67–71.

Shea, Robert. "Yesterday's Leggings Are Today's Fashion Craze." *Today's Health* March 1975: 29.

"A Six Dollar Stone Wash," *Newsweek* 22 September 1986: 77.

Slutsker, Gary. "The Smoking Bun," *Forbes* 25 March 1985: 210.

Todhunter, Hazel. *Make it in Denim*. New York: Taplinger, 1977.

Torbet, Laura. *Clothing Liberation: Or Out of the Closet and Into the Streets*. New York: Ballantine Press. 1973.

"West Germany: A Booming Market in Counterfeit Jeans," *Business Week* 8 August 1977: 37–38.

WHY IS THE VEIL SUCH A CONTENTIOUS ISSUE?

Imtiaz Ahmad

Wearing of the veil among the Arabs, much after the spread of Islam, was more a matter of social status than a religious injunction. It was only later, when western colonial rhetoric began touting the veil as an expression of Muslim backwardness, that it began to be seen as a symbol of retaliation against colonial arrogance. Besides, is the opposition to it out of a concern for women's rights or is it a desire to conform to western thinking?

On the face of it, the controversy sparked off by Shabana Azmi calling for a debate on the veil would appear to be simply a controversy over the shariat and its interpretation. This is how it was represented by Muslim clerics who raised the objection that Azmi had no religious education and could not pronounce on the veil.

Are the shariat and its interpretation really crucial to this controversy? Or, are there other factors responsible for making the veil such a contentious question, not only in India but in other parts of the Muslim world as well? As far as the shariat is concerned, there exists clear theological and historical evidence that the veil is hardly demanded by the shariat and was not a common practice in Arab society which saw the emergence of Islam. The Quranic verse which the Muslim clerics cite as endorsing the veil amounts to no more than a recommendation that women should dress modestly and go about with circumspection in the public domain.

Veiling was not a common practice in Arab society for a long time after the advent of Islam. Veiling existed in pre-Islamic times and was not introduced by Muhammad. As among the Greeks, Romans, Jews and Assyrians, who too practised veiling, it was connected with social status. Only the women of the upper social strata wore the veil. Commoner Muslims neither wore nor were obliged to wear it. Even Muhammad's wives did not go about wearing the veil. Accounts of early Islamic period tell us about Aisha and another of Muhammad's wives carrying water to men in the battlefield, their garments tucked up and their anklets showing.

This freedom came to be curtailed for Muhammad's wives as he aged and his standing required that his wives should be distanced from commoners. A series of verses were revealed requiring his wives to wear the veil ('darabat al-hijab') which was interchangeably meant to denote both the veil and separation. In fact, in the 'hadith' literature the expression "she has taken the veil" meant she has become the wife of Muhammad, which goes to show that veiling was restricted to his wives and was not practised widely. It was only later, by which time Islam had travelled to territories where seclusion of women was an established practice, that the promotion of Muhammad's wives as models for other women to emulate and growing prosperity that veiling came to be practised more widely but was never an issue of public discourse.

Matter of Public Debate

It was in the 19th century that the veil became a matter of public debate. The peculiar practices of Islam with respect to women had always formed part of western rhetoric of the inferiority of Islam. With colonial penetration, this rhetoric became increasingly central through a fusion of the earlier rhetoric of inferiority of Islam with the language of newly emergent feminism in the west. Even though the European male establishment contested the claims of feminism back home, it redirected its language to cultures and people in the colonised societies. With respect to Islam, the construction was that Islam was inherently oppressive to women, that the veil epitomised this oppression, and that these practices constituted the principal reason for the general backwardness of Muslim societies. Veiling in the western eye became the symbol of both the oppression of women and the backwardness of Islam.

One of the consequences of the virulent colonial attack on native customs and practices, including the veil in the Muslim world, was that it provoked a strong reaction. Native thinkers argued that their cultural practices were not an expression of their backwardness. They were rather a sign of their civilisation and were not to be abandoned. They should be followed with greater vigour as a means of retaliation against the colonial attack on their culture. What was merely a form of apparel thus came to be vested with a symbolic significance. The veil came to symbolise in this resistance rhetoric the dignity of those customs that were under fierce colonial attack.

Colonial domination succeeded in producing, as Macaulay was to later articulate in the context of India, a class which had acquired attachment to colonial values and began to look at their own societies through colonial prisms. Qassim Amin, a 19th century Egyptian intellectual, called for the abandonment of the veil in Egypt and Kemal Ataturk administratively outlawed it in Turkey. Both came up against strong opposition because the local populations saw them as highly influenced by western culture and as being in line with the colonial attack on the veil and other practices which the colonial powers asserted reflected native backwardness.

The story has recurred many times in different Muslim societies and has always invoked a similar response. This has happened not because of what religion has to say on the issue of the veil. It has happened because any reference to the veil as being a sign of backwardness or oppression of women brings back memories of the earlier colonial attack and an attack on the veil is seen as coming from those who are culturally affiliated to the west and have no roots in their own societies and social milieu. This is as true of the reaction against Qassim Amin in Egypt, Kemal Ataturk in Turkey or Shabana Azmi and other feminists, whether Muslims or others, in India.

Two Questions

Essentially two questions lie at the root of the opposition to those who call for a debate on the veil or would like it to be abandoned. The first is the autonomy of women. No one can deny that as an item of dress, the veil can be relevant to women's rights. However, the substantive question to which many Muslim women, whether or not they don the veil, draw attention is: who has the right to decide whether or not the veil as an item of women's apparel is relevant to women's rights? Should this decision be made by Muslim men and women whose opposition to the veil is founded on western conceptions of what is appropriate for Muslim women? Or, should this decision rest with Muslim women themselves? Many Muslim women are prone to arguing that when items of dress—bloomers or bras—momentarily figured in the discourse of feminist women in the west, the decision to focus on them was that of women themselves. Why should the focus on the veil be decided by men or women who have already abandoned it?

Alongside this, an additional question often raised by Muslim women in this connection is whether those committed to the abandonment of the veil seriously believe in the liberation of women. Or, is what they are asking for merely substitution of an Islamic type of patriarchy with a western type of patriarchy without a radical alteration of gender relations. Since most Muslim reformers from Qassim Amin in Egypt, Kemal Ataturk in Turkey and Reza Shah in Iran have been themselves strongly patriarchal and somewhat misogynist, this question cannot be easily brushed aside. Many Muslim women, who are perfectly at ease taking cudgels with Muslim clerics for depriving them of rights guaranteed under Islam, ask whether the call for abandonment of the veil arises from genuine concern for women's equality or merely represent words and acts of those assimilating to western ways and smarting under the humiliation of being described as backward because "their" women wear the veil. Muslim reformers need to address these misgivings before they can hope to succeed.

UNIT THREE
CULTURE AND THE THINGS WE THINK

CULTURE AND THE THINGS WE THINK

The set of readings in this section examine the concept of *chi* in Ibo religious tradition, the prevalence and practice of Buddhism in Catholic Brazil and the practice and purpose of pilgrimage among the Hindus. The unit also includes the *Analects* of Confucius and comments of Mao Zedong on Communism and class struggle.

Ibo Religion

God and ghost. Life and death. In the Onitsha (Ibo) belief system, they are two sides of the same coin connected by the process of reincarnation. Central to this belief system is the concept of *chi*. Chi is the unique spiritual essence or personal god residing in each human being that guides and directs the course of his/her life. But, chi is not an autonomous entity. It is the spirit of the dead ancestor returning in the body of the newborn child. In the cycle of birth and death, chi provides the vital link. There are, of course, good and bad chi. The good dead—one who led a good life and was sent out of this world in a grand funeral is exhorted to return as the chi of the newborn. The bad dead are feared and seriously discouraged from being born again.

In the Ibo world, birth and death are desirable states for most of its members. *How does it contrast it with the Hindu and Buddhist concepts of karma and rebirth?*

Being a Zen Buddhist Brazilian: Juggling Multiple Religious Identities in the Land of Catholicism

Using the dispute over the control of the Buddhist temple as the starting point, the author examines the themes of authenticity of religious practices, the various pathways through which religious traditions travel to new places, the innovations and hybridization that old traditions undergo in new places and the construction of religious identities through selective appropriation of multiple religious traditions.

Buddhism was first introduced to Brazil via Japanese immigrants who came to work in the coffee plantations. The Japanese Buddhist considered their form of Buddhism, which consisted of forms of worship and funeral rites, the most authentic because they were the ones who brought Buddhism to Brazil. The second strand of Buddhism was developed by non-Japanese, U.S. educated, upper-middle-class Brazilians, which focused mainly on meditation as a way of experiencing enlightenment. While the Japanese Buddhists relied on missionaries from Japan to maintain and propagate their traditions, the Brazilian Buddhists' interest in the religion was imported from the U.S. through the internet, media, books on Zen, movies and travel. Though both strands had trans-national connections, for the Japanese in Brazil, religious identity was inextricably bound to their ethnic roots, whereas, for the Brazilians, Zen Buddhism was a marker of their cosmopolitanism, of their membership in the globalized *cyber-sangha* of like-minded cosmopolitan practitioners.

The attraction of Zen Buddhism for the Brazilians was that they could incorporate many of its precepts and practices such as belief in karma, meditation, healing practices and martial arts, into their daily life without totally abandoning their core Catholic faith. This blurring of religious boundaries was quite in keeping with the familiar Brazilian tendency to "creolize" foreign religious traditions and make it uniquely their own. It allowed them to move between diverse religious traditions, appropriating from each something that satisfied their spiritual needs.

The picture of Brazil that the author presents is quite different from the stereotypical image of it as a monolithic Roman Catholic country. The Brazil that we see is a pluralistic society with fluid religious borders that often crossed national boundaries. However, the election dispute at the Busshinji temple shows that this pluralism is yet to resolve the issues of ethnic identity, immigrant marginality and class status.

Image, Temple, and Pilgrimage

Fiona Bowie in *The Anthropology of Religion* (2005) characterizes pilgrimage as a specially constructed journey through time and space. Although pilgrimage is typically associated with the sacred, Morinis (*Sacred Journeys: the Anthropology of Pilgrimage*, 1992), in defining it as a "journey undertaken by a person in quest of a state he or she believes to embody a valued ideal" offers the possibility of including secular sites as well. It is a journey that is both intensely personal and experiential and, with a transformative potential that differentiates it from mere tourism. According to Bowie, there are five types of pilgrimage: (1) Pilgrimage to a sacred place (2) Pilgrimage to a sacred person (3) Pilgrimage related to a sacred object (4) Pilgrimage as a sacred text and (5) Pilgrimage as an allegorical journey. Hindu pilgrimage encompasses all of the above.

The central act of Hindu worship is *darsan* which means "seeing." The act of going to the temple is referred as seeking *darsan*—that is, "seeing" the image of the deity present in the temple. It is a reciprocal act because the worshiper is also seen and blessed by the deity. This act of seeing is extended to pilgrimage also. Pilgrimage travel is called *darsan* of a sacred place or a deity or a person. The pilgrimage sites are referred to as *tirthas* (sacred crossings), *dhams* (divine abodes) or *pithas* (divine seats). The map of Indian geography is dotted with thousands of sacred sites that include mountains (the *Himalayas*), the rivers (the Ganga), the oceans (the Indian Ocean), temples dedicated to special deities, places associated with divine deeds (Mathura, birthplace of Krishna), etc. Pilgrimage to places associated with saints or for the *darsan* of living saints is a common feature of Hindu spirituality.

The author provides a fascinating picture of the importance and popularity of pilgrimage among the Hindus in India. However, pilgrimage is an important theme in several world religious traditions. The *Haj*, the Islamic pilgrimage to Mecca, annually attracts several million Muslims and the Pope's annual Christmas Mass is attended by thousands of faithful from across the world. In trying to locate the meaning and the purpose of pilgrimage, we need to consider the expectations and the motivations of the pilgrims; their psychological and physical experiences; the religious and cultural meanings associated with a pilgrimage site; the reasons for its popularity and the social, political and economic impact on surrounding communities.

Confucius and Mao Zedong: Excerpts from the *Analects* and Mao's Selected Works

Confucius and Mao Zedong were two of the most influential men in Chinese history. In the *Analects*, Confucius offered a corrective to the political chaos and moral decay of his society. Two thousand years later, Mao Zedong found China similarly broken and defeated by the forces of feudalism and imperialism. Mao held Confucianism responsible for China's problems and rejected it as reactionary. Communist revolution based on the political ideology of Marx and Lenin was his solution. He argued that only Communism could liberate the country from its backwardness.

The question we might ask is how far did Mao go in breaking from the Confucian past? Mao had already modified the Marxist model to fit the Chinese reality: the backbone of the revolution was going be the vast masses of peasantry, not the industrial proletariat. Furthermore, in the Chinese context, the egalitarianism of a classless society was very much akin to the *jen* of

Confucian thought. Both strove to create conditions for harmonious living. In stating that the Communist Party's function was "working hard to create the conditions in which classes, state power, and political parties will die out very naturally and mankind will enter the realm of the Great harmony," Mao came very close to the Confucian view of government by personal virtue. Similarly, like Confucius, Mao saw education as a progressive force.

The reforms of Deng Xiao Ping has launched China in yet another new direction and has created a new interest in Confucian thought.

IBO RELIGION

Richard N. Henderson

[Although most of this chapter is written in the present tense for convenience of exposition, the time level reconstructed is just prior to 1880, but many of the patterns discussed remained in effect at the time of my research where I wish to emphasize that a pattern was strictly precolonial, the appropriate tense will be stated clearly.]

The major values of social life in Onitsha are rooted firmly in notions of filiation and descent. When Onitsha people assess the career of a person, their primary criterion is the number of children he has raised to support and survive him. Children are extolled in proverbs above any other good, even above the accumulation of wealth (*àku*); "children first, wealth follows" is a proverb affirming the route to success.[1] Onitsha people say that a wealthy person who has no children will reap a bad destiny, for his own relatives may conspire to seize his fortune. He may very likely die a "bad death" (*ájo ónwu*).

Onitsha proverbs make it quite clear that maintaining life is a justifiable end in itself only to the extent that it is productive or nurturant of more life. This overwhelming concern with the production and the continuity of life is basic to the fundamental concept of Onitsha philosophical and religious thought: the idea of *chi*.[2] Chi is "life" (*ñdu*), or life conceived as an animate self that guides the course of existence. The most directly important manifestation of this for any person is the "chi in me," which is thought of as a spiritual essence of the living self that guides and determines the course of that person's life from birth to death. It is believed that when an individual chooses "to enter the world" (*ínye-ùwa*), he makes a pact with a particular essential being (chi), selecting his length of life and his future activities; the choices so made are marked by the chi on his hand as his *àkàla-àka* ("marks of the hand"), or "destiny."

Any person is thought likely to be uncertain about the nature of putative life choices he has made (although some people are suspected, on the contrary, of knowing them and keeping them secret). Should anyone become anxious about this he can communicate with his chi to ascertain what these choices were. He can then affirm and adhere to these choices, or attempt to modify them if he regards them as undesirable. The chi is prominent when people consider making an overall assessment of the career of each individual, for a person is measured by the quality of the chi: for example, it is said that "one who dies without children, though he be rich, has a bad chi (*chí ójo*); a poor man who leaves many children behind him has a good chi (*chi óma*); and a man who dies wealthy and is properly buried by his many children has a very good chi indeed."

Since chi refers then to a single life acted out by each person, there are as many chi as there are living individuals. However, not only does chi have a more general and inclusive meaning as the essence of life, it is also projected as a life essence attributed to the entire universe, a universal self called *chi-ukwu* or *chukwu*, literally "great chi." The term chi-ukwu designates an ultimate self ordering the course and character of the universe as a whole, which in turn is conceived as a multiplicity of "worlds" (*ùwa*). This universal self is addressed in prayer as *chí-úkwu-òkike* "great chi the creator"; as *chì-nà-élu*, "chi in heaven"; and as *òlisa-èbúlu-ùwa*, "divinity who supports the world."[3] Chi-ukwu is said to have created all physical phenomena and endowed them; with force and direction: the sky (*ìgwe*), the heavenly bodies as his "messengers" and eyes, the earth (*ànì*) and the great river Niger (*òrumili*). Chi-ukwu sent trees to grow on the land, animals to roam it, men to occupy it, yams and other foods to feed people, and various objects as "medicines" (*ógwù*) to help them in the course of their lives. When a person dies, his chi ceases to exist as an independent entity, returning to the great ground of being in the sun or in the sky. Chi-ukwu exists as long as the universe which it personifies.

It is implicit in the logical structure of these terms that chi-ukwu is a subcategory of chi rather than the more general class within which chi may be categorized.[4] We may view the meaning of these concepts as a semantic structure, whose unmarked terms point to the general category within which the marked terms are a subcategory. It is reasonable to translate chi as "god," and chi-ukwu as "great god." However, Onitsha people also say that the great god is the source from which all particular gods of persons originate; it might therefore be equally valid to translate chi-ukwu as "god" and chi_2 as "personal god." We will hereafter use the terms "personal god" for chi_2, "great god" for chi-ukwu, and "god" without qualifier for chi_1 in the latter sense, the term also refers to daylight. (See Fig. 14.)

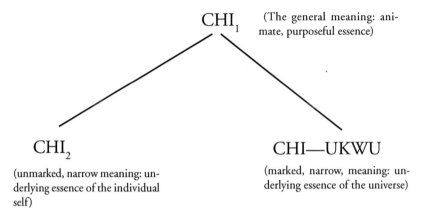

$$\text{CHI}_1 \quad \text{(The general meaning: ani-mate, purposeful essence)}$$

CHI_2
(unmarked, narrow meaning: underlying essence of the individual
self)

CHI—UKWU
(marked, narrow, meaning: underlying essence of the universe)

Fig. 14 The Semantic Structure of Chi

If the description of the Onitsha belief system thus far makes a concern with life and lifelike forces appear central, individual life itself is conceived not solely in opposition to the notion of death (*ónwu*), but partly as an imperfect approximation of it. Indeed, acts of attaining the heights of prestige by individuals in Onitsha are marked by identity-changing rituals that bring them closer and closer to death. The ultimate goal for every person is to lose his chi and thereby to become a "dead person" (*mmadù ónwu*), a "ghost" (*mmua*). The concepts of "god" and "ghost" form the major contrast pair in Onitsha religion, two forces in opposition which, however, interpenetrate through the process of reincarnation.

Onitsha belief postulates a multiplicity of worlds (*uwa*) in which existence occurs. The number of these worlds is indefinite (some say there are eight, some say seven, some four worlds) but from the viewpoint of men occupying this one, the other worlds are all "lands of the dead" (*anl mmuo*) into which all persons who die should subsequently be incarnated. On the other hand, these lands of the dead are also the sole sources of all new human beings in the empirical world. Men, wherever they are, are believed to be always "looking into" the other worlds, communicating with people there, and considering being incarnated there anew. All the dead are believed to take a continuous interest in this world. Indeed, some never leave it, and wander it in a state of perpetual, incorporeal unrest; these are "bad dead" (*ajo mmuo*) who have violated the world order. They belong nowhere and do little but make trouble. The dead viewed hopefully as sources of new human beings are those who lived lives of fulfillment here in the past, who were sent out of this world with glorious funerals which facilitated their subsequent establishment in other worlds, and who consequently look back here with pleasant memories and thoughts of returning. These dead are exhorted by the living to return as infants and, periodically, in other forms.

The worlds of the dead are conceived as located nearby, in the vicinity of the earth in which they were buried, and it is believed that the closer a person was buried to a house, the more likely he or she will choose to reincarnate there as an offspring of its occupants. Hence highly valued persons are buried within their own house to facilitate their return, while those whose life courses have been condemned are cast away into distant bush so that they will not return. Those buried in or near their houses also continue to observe and protect their living children; they may be periodically invoked to return physically to this world in the form of "incarnate dead" (*mmanwu*) to inspect and judge the community—to express their pleasure at the celebrations of their living kinsmen or to demand that laws they have helped to support be upheld. They may also be invoked to enter incorporeally into objects constructed in their name to be fed, venerated, prayed to, and thanked for their spiritual assistance in maintaining long lives for their children and in bringing more children into this world.

The notion of reincarnation (*à bìalu n'ùwa ázo*— "one comes to the world again") thus defines personal identity in terms of its relation to the dead. It is a dead person, or rnrnuo, who chooses to return to this world in the form of a newborn child. To do so, the ghost walks to a crossroads (*ába-úzo*) of the two worlds, where it meets a personal god and makes a destiny-defining pact with that personal god. Through a creative act of the personal god, the ghost enters the body of the infant at birth, becoming the "seeds of heart" (*'nkpulu-óbì*) which provide the motive force underlying life, and the body emerges into the world as a living infant whose personal god has marked the lines of his destiny enigmatically into his hand.

The production of new lives, at this conceptual level, is believed to require two elements which, together with the empirical beliefs about conception, constitute the three necessary and sufficient agencies of birth. The first is the development of the physical body. In Onitsha theory, this entails the implantation of the male's "child seed" (*ùré nwá*) into the female's womb (*akpa nwa*). Ure is regarded as a category of blood (*obala*) that possesses a seed which grows just as a yam will when planted in good soil. If a man's ure is good and a woman's womb in proper condition, conception is certain to follow repeated sexual intercourse.

But the formation of a human being as distinct from a mass of flesh or a monster depends upon the second and third agencies, the choices of a dead person or ghost, who becomes the motive force driving a life by making its pact with a personal god. Evidence of the character of this ghost is sought by the parents in the infant's physical appearance and in certain observed behaviors, for it is believed that the ghost determines physical characteristics and certain putatively intrinsic tendencies such as "hot temper" (*óbì óku*). It is hoped that the dead person is a revered ancestor returned, but often malicious beings from unknown worlds may capriciously decide to enter this world. Equally capriciously, they soon will choose to depart. Parents hope the infant is a returned ancestor who was buried nearby, i.e. one (or more) of the deceased fathers, mothers, father's mothers or other ancestor who had observed local community life from the nearby subterranean locality, found it good, and has chosen to return.

Among the Nri-Awka Ibo peoples around Onitsha, each individual tries to determine, at some stage of his life, which ancestor has formed that compact which has resulted in his identity. Once this ancestor has been determined by a diviner, the person makes an objectification of the personal god, in the form of a stick from an *égbò* tree (Newbouldia laevis) which is cut, placed in a bowl, and periodically "fed." This stick is called *ókposi* and symbolizes both a dead ancestor (*mmua*) and the individual's personal god (*chì*). When he dies, his personal god has departed and therefore, after funerary rituals have assisted him to reach the spirit land, this stick is discarded. His sons then fashion a new okposi stick, to represent him as a ghost (*mmua*) who still takes interest in his offspring. Thus in the object of the okposi, the notions of god and ghost are conceptually linked.

In Onitsha, however, the practice and belief are more complex for here a personal god is represented not by one wooden stick but by five sticks called "seeds of god" (*ñkpulu-chì*), which are kept in a wooden "vessel of god" (*ókwa-chì*). Hence the essence underlying an individual's life course is represented not as an undifferentiated particle, but rather as a compound of units which, taken together, determine his character and life. Four of these sticks also refer to ancestors; some Onitsha people say that they represent ghostly contributions from the ancestral worlds of the father, the mother, the father's mother, and the mother's mother. The fifth stick, however, represents dead who are not ancestral. It is called *ògbónùke* or *ògbò-nà-ùke*, which Onitsha people translate as "age-set and misfortune," and its link to other worlds is not to ancestors but to "one's comrades" (*ñdi-òtu-ya*), or ghostly contemporaries regardless of their ancestry. Attached to this age-set representation is a wooden image of a man with ram's horns on his head, usually holding a machete in his right hand. This image, called *ìkéngà*, represents the essence of a man's will to success; it is viewed as part of a man's personal god, more specifically part of his ogbonuke.[5]

In Onitsha, then, the structure of a personal god contains these five components, which are usually worshipped as a unit but, in the case of agb;'nuke, sometimes separately. Although the personal god is identified with the entire life course of a person, it is not thought to be strictly localized inside the human body with which it is identified (though there is some hint of its relation to the head). The ghostly components supposed to determine basic features and tendencies are thought to be located in the heart, but they are also often externalized in the wooden objects that represent them, and the whole personal god is said to reside in its vessel.

When a man dies, all his chi sticks are discarded, for the personal god has departed forever. But the senior son of the deceased person will then "bring his father into the house" by collecting four large egbo sticks, which are also called okposi and represent the ghosts, plus (sometimes) a fifth object, his father's ikenga. Thus the set of symbols of the dead that a man acquires after his father has departed is homologous to the set of objects that represent his own character and destiny, his personal god. If one were to quantify human character in Onitsha terms, four-fifths of a man's personal identity would appear (at this point) to depend upon the choices of ancestors, one-fifth upon a preincarnate pact made with his spiritual contemporaries. In this set of ideas, the social categories of kinship and age-set gain unitary religious foundation through the linking of a person's god with various kinds of ghosts of the dead.

Notes

[1] Proverbially, Onitsha people liken children to the tie-clothe that support a person's belly, helping him to walk the road of life. It is said that when one dies, his offspring should be as numerous as the grains of sand that bury a yam. The value of children is often affirmed in the personal names given them, for example, "Child surpasses money" (*Nwá-kà-égo*), "Child is shelter" (*Nwá-bù-ñdo*).

[2] My analysis of this subject is indebted to the work of Talbot (1926), Horton (1956, 1961, 1967), and Bradbury (1960).

[3] The latter term is clearly related to the Benin term for the high god: Osanobua. Olisa is a term often used by riverain Ibo as equivalent to chi-ukwu.

[4] This analysis differs somewhat from that of Horton (1956), but does nor contradict it. Onitsha people say that a person plagued by misfortune sometimes prays to chi-ukwu to give him a better chi in his next incarnation, and the chi returns to the sky after death. Talbot (1926:2:40-41) clearly perceived the central significance of the notion of chi and its relations to conceptions of self and universe.

[5] The term ogba means "age-set," and and the Onitsha people translate uke as "fortune," implying "misfortune." See Jones (1962:192), where uke clearly means an "association."

BEING A ZEN BUDDHIST BRAZILIAN: JUGGLING MULTIPLE RELIGIOUS IDENTITIES IN THE LAND OF CATHOLICISM

Cristina Rocha

Busshinji Temple, March 2000

The room is teeming with excitement. Folding chairs are arranged in rows. Japanese men wearing suits and ties are sitting in the front rows and Japanese women are at the back, as is appropriate in Japanese culture, where men take precedence. In the middle rows, there are many T-shirted non-Japanese Brazilians, men and women mixed, as befits their culture. This is the forty-seventh General Assembly of the Sōtō Zen Buddhist Community of South America (Comunidade Budista Sōtō Zenshū da América do Sul), and, as usual, it is taking place in the basement of Busshinji (Buddha Heart-Mind Temple) in São Paulo city. There are about 115 people present, most of them non-Japanese Brazilians and Japanese descendents; very few are part of the old, first-generation Japanese community.

Tension is in the air because this morning elections are taking place. Two congregations are vying to run Busshinji's administration—one composed of the old, traditional, Japanese board, the other composed of their descendents who align with the non-Japanese Brazilians. To aggravate matters, after a five-year hiatus, a new *sōkan* has just arrived from Japan.[1] In the interim, this position was filled by the missionary in charge of Busshinji, a non-Japanese Brazilian woman, Coen Souza, who trained under the Zen master (*rōshi*) Maezumi at the Zen Center of Los Angeles (ZCLA) for three years and then in Japan for a further twelve years.[2] Although Coen is a non-Japanese Brazilian nun, she had slowly gained acceptance among the Japanese community because she worked hard to preserve the rituals the Japanese community expects to be performed. Speaking both Japanese and Portuguese fluently, she was a successful intermediary between the Japanese and Brazilian communities. Paradoxically, her success was also the source of tension. From 1995 (the year she was appointed) until 2000 (the year she lost her position in the temple),

Coen increasingly attracted Brazilians of non-Japanese ancestry and began to conduct most of the temple's activities in Portuguese. On that very morning, she had reluctantly consented to run for the presidency of the Japanese descendents' faction. Because of the growth in the number of non-Japanese Brazilian adherents under Coen's missionary work, this congregation had succeeded in gaining control of the temple in 1998, when both groups disputed elections for the first time. Now, with the presence of an "authentic" Japanese missionary (the *sōkan*) to oversee the elections, would the coalition of non-Japanese Brazilian and young Japanese descendents still prevail?

The new *sōkan* starts his speech, and his tone is conciliatory: "In the past five years, when there was no *sōkan* in Latin America, the number of adherents of the Sōtō Zenshū increased, thanks to teacher (sensei) Coen's work. There are many Zen groups in the U.S.A., France, and Spain, and they speak many languages other than Japanese. Therefore, it is only natural that conflicts arise. But these conflicts are not necessarily negative. Let's think of conflicts as an opportunity for growth. . . ."

Yet the general mood is not one of appeasement and the old disputes for power are pervasive. Halfway through the assembly, following a series of speeches by former members of the 1998–2000 administration, a Japanese man suddenly stands up and bursts into Japanese. He is obviously upset. Many non-Japanese Brazilians call out angrily that he should be speaking Portuguese, but he resists. One Japanese descendent aligned with the non-Japanese Brazilian side shouts that they are in Brazil and should therefore speak Portuguese. Commotion takes over the room, only to be settled after some time, when a translator offers his services. It turns out that the Japanese was a member of the administration prior to 1998. He wanted to speak directly to the *sōkan* and to the fellow Japanese present so that his words would not be misinterpreted. His speech is cut short, and he goes back to his seat. The assembly proceeds with only minor incidents, and in the end a new board comprised of the Japanese descendents (aligned with the non-Japanese Brazilians) is elected. The morning is coming to a close, and everyone stands up to prepare the room for the big lunch that is ahead. *Feijoada* (a typical Brazilian dish purportedly originating from the food of slaves and consisting of black beans, meat, rice, oranges, and vegetables) is served alongside sushi and Japanese green tea. Forks, knives, and chopsticks rest on the table—an appropriate set of utensils for the ever-present contentions that Japanese, Japanese-Brazilians, and non-Japanese Brazilians undergo at Busshinji.

In this chapter, I will shed light on how these two distinct congregations have laid claim to Busshinji temple in São Paulo city. I shall argue that the conflicts over the "authenticity" of Zen stem from the different modes of religious practice. On the one hand, for the first-generation Japanese, religious identity is expressive of their ethnic identity; on the other hand, non-Japanese Brazilians use Zen Buddhism as a marker of social distinction.[3] After presenting an overview of the arrival of Zen in Brazil, identifying its demographics and adherents, I will proceed to map the Brazilian religious landscape in order to show how established religions in Brazil have creolized Zen Buddhism. I contend that converts use a Brazilian religious "grammar" as a matrix for new Buddhist "vocabulary," and that the process has facilitated the spread of Buddhism in the country.

Authenticity or Innovation?

An occasion such as an election is a very telling situation. It is a time when sides are clearly taken and decisions are made about who will hold power and for what purpose. Moreover, such an event works as a metaphor for what is really at stake—in this case, ethnic resistance against the surrounding society and the religious identity of both groups. For many Japanese (*issei*) and some second-generation Japanese-Brazilians (*nisei*), it is evident that theirs is the "authentic" Zen, since they were the ones who brought Zen Buddhism to Brazil. For them, "true" Zen is comprised of "masses" (as the members call the rituals, appropriating the Catholic word), namely, funerals and rites for the worship of ancestors. Ethnic boundaries are more clearly marked in situations where an individual or group is faced with the "other." For diasporic communities surrounded by a diverse population, these boundaries have to be constructed, policed, and reinforced, so that the ethnic identity of the community may be preserved.[4] Religion can provide a strong bond with the past and the homeland. The competition for authenticity described in the above narrative shows that, by preserving some Japanese cultural traits (among them language and religion), the Japanese-Brazilian immigrant community sought to maintain its ethnic identity as distinct from other Brazilians.[5]

On the other side of this dispute for authenticity are the non-Japanese Brazilians and some Japanese-Brazilians. For them, Zen Buddhism relies mainly on meditation (*zazen*) as a way of experiencing enlightenment. Invoking the Buddha Shakyamuni's meditation practice and subsequent enlightenment, as well as Dōgen's assertion that Zen is basically about meditation, they regard devotional practices and worship of ancestors as not authentic Zen Buddhism.[6] This kind of conflict between motivations, practice, and aspirations has occurred in other Buddhist centers in the West.[7]

The Arrival of Buddhism in Brazil

Buddhism was introduced into Brazil by Japanese immigrants who first arrived in 1908 at the port of Santos, in the state of São Paulo.[8] These immigrants worked mainly in coffee plantations and had hoped to return to Japan as soon as they accumulated enough savings. The maintenance of their culture, language, religion, and beliefs was considered crucial. However, with the Japanese defeat in World War II, the immigrants had to give up their dream of returning to their home country, prompting them to request missionaries from Japan to preach in their new homeland. Until then, apart from a few independent missionaries, there were no Japanese religious organizations in Brazil that would officiate at the death of an immigrant.[9]

Zengenji, the first Sōtō Zen Buddhist temple in Brazil, was built in the early 1950s in Moji das Cruzes, a town in the outskirts of São Paulo City. In 1955, Busshinji was established in São Paulo City as the headquarters of the Sōtō Zen School in South America. These two temples, along with a temple in Rolândia, in the state of Paraná, have catered for three hundred Japanese-Brazilian families over the past four decades.

Buddhism was also introduced to Brazil by non-Japanese Brazilian intellectuals who imported European literature on Buddhism at the beginning of the twentieth century. The Buddhist Society of Brazil (Sociedade Budista do Brasil) was founded in 1923 by Theosophists in Rio de Janeiro but was soon dissolved. In 1955, Murillo Nunes de Azevedo reestablished it. Azevedo was deeply influenced by the ideas of the Theosophical Society, where he had acted as president of the Brazilian chapter for nine years.[10] As professor at the Pontifical Catholic University in Rio de Janeiro, Azevedo taught philosophy of the Far East and organized a collection of translations called *Luz da Ásia* (Light of Asia) for Civilização Brasileira, a wellknown publishing house in Brazil. In this collection, he published twenty books dedicated to Eastern philosophies. Among them was D. T. Suzuki's *Introduction to Zen Buddhism*, which Azevedo had translated into Portuguese in 1961. This book was fundamental to the spread of Zen Buddhist ideas in Brazil and was frequently cited in the interviews that I conducted among Zen practitioners in the late 1990s in Brazil.

Azevedo and other intellectuals followed a similar path. Their initial encounter with Buddhism and Zen was through imported literature (European and North American), which then led them to seek a place to practice; they found it in Busshinji in São Paulo. In order to cater to the demands of Brazilians of non-Japanese origin, in 1961 Ryōhan Shingū, the *sōkan* in charge at the time, created a Zen meditation group (*zazenkai*) that met every Saturday. His interpreter was Ricardo Gonçalves, a history professor from the prestigious University of São Paulo. In making Zen accessible to Brazilians, Gonçalves helped to break down the language barrier that had been the main obstacle to the proselytization of Buddhism in Brazil.[11] Until very recently, when Brazilians of non-Japanese descent sought association with other Japanese Buddhist schools, they were redirected to Busshinji, because "they speak Portuguese there, and it is the place for non-Japanese Brazilians," as some non-Japanese adherents told me. The diminishing numbers of Japanese-Brazilian members (a similar phenomenon pointed out by Tanabe, Chap. 3), along with the growth in Buddhism in the past decade, have prompted many Japanese Buddhist schools to make room for non-Japanese Brazilians. Indeed, a Jōdo Shinshū temple in Brasília has introduced meditation sessions in order to attract this new clientele.[12]

Buddhism in Numbers

Since 1976, as many as twenty-six Zen centers have been established for and by non-Japanese Brazilians in Brazil. Unlike Busshinji, they do not have Japanese immigrant adherents and so their practice is based on meditation. Statistics available on religion from the 2000 census show that, at that time, the Brazilian population of 170 million people was comprised of 74 percent Roman Catholics (125 million), 15.5 percent Evangelicals (26 million, including traditional Evangelicals and Pentecostals), 7.3 percent of no religion (12.3 million), 1.4 percent Spiritists (2.3 million), 0.14 percent Buddhists (245,000), 0.06 percent Jews (101,000), 0.04 percent esoteric religions (67,200), 0.03 percent Afro-Brazilian religions (51,000), 0.01 percent Muslims (18,500), and, finally, 0.06 percent indigenous religions (10,700).[13] It is worth comparing these figures with those of the 1991 census. While those who identified as Catholics decreased by 10 percent since 1991 (83.8 percent in 1991), there was an increase in other categories: evangelicalism (9.1 percent in 1991), no religion (4.8 percent in 1991), and Spiritists (1.2 percent in 1991).

As the statistics show, the great majority of Brazilians still come from Catholic families. What these figures do not show is the movement from one religion to another, multiple religious affiliations, as well as the combination of elements of different traditions, which is commonplace in Brazil. Many Brazilians either practice more than one religion at the same time or convert from one religion to another. Indeed, according to the Brazilian sociologist Reginaldo Prandi, one-quarter of the Brazilian adult population has converted to a religion different from the one they were born into.[14]

A survey I conducted among Zen practitioners in the cities of São Paulo, Rio de Janeiro, Ouro Preto, and Porto Alegre in 1998 and 1999 corroborates this fact. Out of a total of eighty respondents, the majority (sixty-six) came from Catholic families. The remaining fourteen respondents were equally distributed among Jewish, Spiritist, Evangelical, Protestant, the Church of World Messianity (Sekkai Kyūsei Kyō, a Japanese New Religious Movement [NRM]), and nonreligious backgrounds.

Of the eighty respondents practicing Zen Buddhism, twenty had moved from the religion of their upbringing to other religions before adopting Zen Buddhism. Many (nine) had been affiliated with Spiritism, but the majority also combined the religion of their upbringing with other religions, such as Protestantism, Theosophy, Rosicrucianism, the Church of World Messianity, Daoism, Nichiren Buddhism, Tibetan Buddhism, and nonreligious backgrounds. Eleven of these twenty "migrants" still practiced other religions while regularly practicing Zen meditation at their Zen center or temple.

Finally, when asked if they considered themselves to be Buddhists, thirty-eight respondents said "yes," while eleven answered "not yet," "sort of," or "almost." This is a hard question for Brazilians, as they consider Zen Buddhism and Buddhism in general mostly as a philosophy rather than a religion (see Clarke, Chap. 5). One respondent gave a very revealing response: "If one who practices *zazen* is considered Buddhist, then I am a Buddhist." The "not yet" Buddhists could be classified as "sympathizers," a term Thomas Tweed has used for "those who have some sympathy for a religion but do not embrace it exclusively or fully. When asked, they would not identify themselves as Buddhists. They would say they are Methodists, or Jewish, or unaffiliated."[15]

Who Are These Cosmopolitan Zen Buddhist Brazilians?

The interviews I conducted with non-Japanese Brazilian practitioners showed that their interest in Zen Buddhism was mediated by the United States, through the media, books on Zen,[16] movies,[17] and travel. The word

"Zen" is fashionable in the West: one sees Zen perfume, shops, beauty parlors, restaurants, magazine articles, and architecture. In Brazil it is a common occurrence to call someone "Zen," meaning very peaceful, collected, and tranquil. The word "Zen" usually appears in the title of newspaper and magazine articles that report on a range of alternative religions and practices, such as other Buddhist schools, yoga, Tai Chi Tchuari, and meditation. Furthermore, Zen has a positive image in the country; it is associated with refinement, minimalism, nontension, nonanxiety, exquisite beauty, and exoticism. Indeed, the word "Zen" appears almost daily in the trendy social column of *Folha de São Paulo*, one of the leading newspapers in Brazil.

Moreover, all of the people interviewed described their first contact with Zen as being through books. The United States is an ample source of ideas on Zen for various reasons. First, English is more accessible to Brazilians than Japanese. Indeed, most of the books on Zen available in Portuguese had first been translated into English. Moreover, because these practitioners come from the intellectual upper-middle class and are educated liberal professionals, many of them are able to read the books in English before they are translated. Some buy books on Zen via the Internet and/or subscribe to American Buddhist magazines, such as *Tricycle*. This is a very different constituency from that of Sōka Gakkai, which appeals to lower-middle classes (Chap. 5).

In the late 1990s, web sites of Buddhist texts translated from English into Portuguese by Brazilian Buddhists began to appear. The two visits by His Holiness the Dalai Lama to Brazil (1992 and 1999) were highly publicized in the media, and translations into Portuguese of his talks are on web sites as well. His books have been translated into Portuguese, and *The Art of Happiness: A Handbook of Living* (1999) was number one on a best-sellers' list for many months after it was published in June 2000. This book alone had sold 185,000 copies by July 2001 and became the publishing company's best seller since its establishment in 1975.[18] In August 2000, a long article in the leading newspaper *Journal do Brasil* titled "The Soft and Sweet Eastern Invasion: The Interest in Eastern Philosophy Increases and Opens a Series of New Book Releases Heralded by new Dalai Lama's Book," commented on the boom of books on Eastern philosophy, particularly Buddhism, due to the demand of readers. In addition, it reported on the growing interest in Buddhist psychology among Rio de Janeiro and São Paulo's psychoanalysts, which was also boosted by this year's release of Mark Epstein's book *Going to Pieces without Falling Apart: A Buddhist Perspective on Wholeness* (New York: Broadway Books, 1998).

The increasing number of web pages and e-mail discussion lists about Buddhism on the Internet is noteworthy.[19] It is impossible to report the current number of web pages, for new ones appear very quickly. However, e-mail discussion lists are more stable. There are five lists in Brazil, three of them dedicated to three different Buddhist schools (Theravada, Zen, and Tibetan), a general one on Buddhism, and one for discussion of scriptures and translations. An average of ten to twenty messages are posted daily on each list, and the topics discussed include vegetarianism, Catholicism and Buddhism, new books on Buddhism, interfaith dialog, reincarnation or rebirth, neophytes' doubts on behavior and doctrine, koans, announcements of retreats in Brazil and abroad, translations of scriptures and poems, and biographies of important Buddhist masters.

It is a significant fact that whereas Evangelical, Pentecostal, neo-Pentecostal, and Catholic (particularly the Charismatic) churches proselytize to Brazilian disenfranchised classes through radio and television,[20] the urban upper-middle-class and intellectual elite who are interested in Buddhism interact through a highly literate medium,[21] the Internet, forming a "cyber-sangha."[22] In contrast to radio and television, where there is the authority figure of the priest and no direct contact among the viewers, the cybersangha is more participatory, allowing recipients to interact and communicate with each other by posting messages. Doubts on the teachings, appropriate behavior, the differences among Buddhist schools, the history of Buddhism, and so on are answered, not by authorities on Buddhism certified by a Buddhist institution, but by the sangha itself. Moreover, anyone can construct a web site and furnish it by translating anything—from scriptures, Buddhist poems, and koans, to stories of great masters—all according to one's own personal interpretation and understanding. This is increasingly common in Brazilian cyberspace. These cybersangha features are consonant with trends of religious modernity such as an emphasis on individual quest, privatization of religion, shunning authority, and relying on experience rather than faith.[23] These are precisely the values prized by my informants when asked about the reasons for their choice of Zen Buddhism. Thus while Japanese and non-Japanese Brazilian Buddhist monks and nuns have been fundamental to the institutionalization of Buddhism in Brazil, much of the propagation of Buddhist ideas is also the result of these self-appointed speakers on its behalf.

The study of urban elite Brazilian Zen also requires an understanding of the transnational linkages that enable the white urban upper class to forge a sense of connection with their peers overseas. Such a fact creates a feeling of belonging to a subculture group that extends beyond national borders.[24] By going to retreats abroad, translating scriptures, and publishing them independently on the web, Brazilian Buddhists feel that they are part of a much larger world. Moreover, the prestige Buddhism is enjoying in the developed world also confers cultural capital upon the Brazilian urban intellectual elite, who play the role of introducing new ideas and ways of behaving into Brazil. Accordingly, I argue that being Buddhist is a way of belonging to the developed world and detaching oneself from the rest of the "backward" Brazilian population. This is something Brazilians aspire to intensely, especially because they have in the past two decades suffered considerably from the country's economic crisis, endemic corruption, inflation, and rampant crime and violence. According to the Brazilian anthropologist José Jorge Carvalho:

> Some sects have originated more due to a modernizing movement in our society than due to religious matters. The identity issue is crucial: to adhere to a certain group is to adhere to what is up-to-date, it is to be able to do certain things which are currently prestigious. [It] is a way of connecting oneself to the meaning producing centers.[25]

In light of the transnational links between the Brazilian urban intellectual elite and their counterparts overseas through books, media, travel, movies, and the Internet, the diffusion of Zen Buddhism in Brazil could be seen as part of a "faculty club culture," a term coined by Peter Berger as one of four processes of cultural globalization. According to Berger: "[The 'faculty club culture'] is the internationalization of the Western intelligentsia, its values, and ideologies carried by foundations, academic networks, and non-governmental organizations.' Similar to 'non-Japanese Zen', the 'faculty culture club' is primarily an elite culture, which spreads its beliefs and values through some of the media of mass communication. Some examples of these values are feminism and environmentalism."[26] Indeed, many of the adherents I interviewed told me that the close relationship between Buddhism and the ecological movement, as opposed to the Catholic way of approaching nature, made them adhere to Buddhism.

Moreover, Peter Berger argues that English is the lingua franca of globalization.[27] As I mentioned before, most of the information on Zen in Brazil is conveyed through Portuguese translations of English material. For instance, when Coen sensei was the head nun of Busshinji, in her weekly lectures she used to translate passages from books in English, written either by Japanese monks while they lived in America or by American scholars. At that time, there was also a scripture study group, where one lay ordained follower translated, printed, and handed out parts of books originally written in English to be studied. In the Zen Center of Porto Alegre, many adherents are learning English to be able to speak to Moriyama rōshi without the need of a translator. Following this trend of globalization of North American Zen, some practitioners even choose to travel to Zen centers in the United States and feel that it is more in tune with their own practice than is Japanese Zen. As a result of such transnational links, developments in North American Zen are very influential in Brazilian Zen. However, the ways in which Brazilians localize Zen differ, as their own religious matrix differs from that of North Americans.

As noted earlier, the vast majority of the people interviewed were Catholics before starting to "shop around" in the religious marketplace and eventually finding Zen Buddhism. Adherents who left Catholicism and are studying Zen Buddhism explain their disenchantment with the former as based on its dogmatism, its separation from daily life, its hierarchical organization, its attitude toward nature, and its almighty God. Looking for an alternative, Catholic adherents seek their symbolic universe via something that they can construct by themselves in daily life. They are attracted to the freedom of the individual to interpret the scriptures and the possibility of practicing mindfulness in daily life, outside the temple. Notably, these are the same themes invoked by Buddhist and New Age practitioners in the United States and United Kingdom.[28]

Likewise, Zen Buddhism for Brazilians accepts pluralism and diversity. This approach to religious practice is justified through the Zen Buddhist idea of nonattachment. The famous Zen saying: "If you meet the Buddha on the road, kill the Buddha" is interpreted by practitioners as the impossibility of one religion being the permanent answer to their spiritual needs. From this perspective, a practitioner may participate in meditation both in a Tibetan Buddhist center and at a Japanese Zen center. An adherent may even become lay ordained *(ordenado leigo; jukai)*[29] and receive different Buddhist names from different lineages.[30]

Another characteristic of those who seek Zen Buddhism is that they are in search of relief from personal problems. They wish to learn about their "innerself." Very frequently, people I interviewed said they sought Zen meditation as a way to learn about themselves. Zen meditation worked in place of psychotherapy or in conjunction with it.[31] One can appreciate how meaningful Zen Buddhism is for its adherents when one realizes that many practitioners use their leisure moments, such as weekends and holidays, to go to meditation sessions and retreats *(sesshin)*. The consumption of goods is clearly evident in the sales of books, magazines, courses, retreats, seminars, clothes, and utensils for meditation, as if enlightenment (satori) itself could be reached through consumption. Carvalho has noted that

> Samadhi, enlightenment, satori appear now also as a fetish, almost as a commercial exhibition, as image of power, as merchandise. The possibility of a trance, of a touch of energy, of a hug of divine love is as desired in the present social context as the acquisition of a car, of an appliance, of a trip to a famous place. The religious advertisement [. . .] has already incorporated, as any other advertisement of consumption society, the mimetic desire of ownership.[32]

Creolizing Zen in the Brazilian Religious Field

The term "creolization" originates from the Spanish *criollo* and Portuguese *crioulo*, both derived from the Latin verb *creare* (to breed or to create). Until recently, the concept of a "creole culture" was deeply connected to the encounter of African and European culture in the Caribbean. As a result, the term was extended to encompass the language spoken by these so-called Creole people. Such languages were the result of the superimposition of the dominant language's lexicon upon the dominated language's own syntax, grammar, and morphology. The resulting new language revealed a twofold predicament: at the same time it demonstrated that colonial peoples had yielded and adopted the dominant language by using its lexicon, it also showed that they had clung to inner forms of their own language as a matrix for this lexicon, a sign of resistance.[33]

Furthermore, contemporary scholars have detached the trope "creolization" from its Caribbean and linguistic roots and applied the term more broadly to processes of cultural encounter and exchange. Many cultural and postcolonial theorists have used "creolization" as a synonym for hybridity.[34] "Hybridity," however, as a metaphor for cultural contact, carries with it the predicament of its origins in biological science, where it was juxtaposed to notions of racial purity.[35] Hybridity also derives from horticulture and animal-breeding practices, which in turn juxtapose it with ideas of sterility and passivity, since hybrid plants and animals do not reproduce.[36] Notwithstanding contemporary recuperation of hybridity as a subversive practice/agency within postcolonial and cultural theory, it still has to grapple with the dilemma of the discourse of race. Creolization as an analytical trope, on the other hand, although having originated during colonial contact, carries notions of creativity, agency, and innovation on the part of the colonized.[37] Furthermore, the concept of creolization, when inflected by its linguistic facet, highlights *how* the process of continuous contact and negotiation takes place.

Nevertheless, I should mention a caveat before employing the term "creolization" to analyze Brazilian Zen. As previously mentioned, the word "creole" derives from the Portuguese *crioulo*, which even today is a derogatory term for Afro-Brazilians in Brazil. Furthermore, the use of this concept may lead some readers to think that the history of Brazilian society is deeply connected with that of the Caribbean. Nothing could be further from the truth. In spite of these drawbacks, I believe that, in the context of an analysis of Zen Buddhism in Brazil, the trope of creolization is meaningful because it sheds light on *how* Japanese Zen has been superimposed on a Brazilian religious syntax upon arrival in the country. Unlike the Jōdo Shinshu temple in Hawai'i, where the membership is dropping due to lack of "hybridization" (see Tanabe, Chap. 3), Busshinji temple thrived in the 1990s due to Zen's popular appeal and Moriyama rōshi's and Coen sensei's flexibility in negotiating with Brazilian culture. During this time, even "immigrant" Zen practices such as funeral and ancestor rites became more visible, and some non-Japanese Brazilians have taken part in them. While for Payne Shingon Buddhism's invisibility in the United States derives from Americanization and lack of exoticism (Chap. 4), Busshinji is visible because it has undergone renewal, introducing Japanese architectural features that invoke exoticism while making room for non-Japanese Brazilian practices. The Brazilian media, however, is just as obsessed with "convert" Buddhism as its U.S. counterpart (as pointed out by Payne). Although it is still too early to see the results of such creolization, I would like to explore *how* this process is taking place.

Although Brazil is well known by the epithet "the world's largest Catholic nation," such a description ignores the presence of many other religions and religious practices that have been introduced and creolized in Brazil since the Portuguese arrived in 1500. During the colonial period (1500-1822), Catholicism went through a process of creolization when it encountered Afro-Brazilian traditions and indigenous religions. Popular Catholicism was created from such a convergence, adding indigenous beliefs, rituals, and devotion to saints to the formal Catholicism of the clergy and upper classes.[38]

In the nineteenth century, immigration brought German Lutherans and other traditional Protestants to Brazil. By the beginning of the twentieth century, North American Protestant missionaries were sent to Brazil and started to preach outside of the ethnic enclave. Furthermore, still in the nineteenth century, French Spiritism—which would become one of the main religions in Brazil[39]—was introduced by the Brazilian elite who were quick to adopt the then new French fashion. Spiritism or Kardecism, as it is known in Brazil due to its founder Hyppolyte Rivail's pen name, Allan Kardec (1804–1869), was itself a synthesis of many religious practices such as Catholicism, Protestantism, and occult philosophies that flourished in eighteenth- and nineteenth-century Europe, such as Swedenborgianism, Mesmerism, Rosicrucianism, Freemasonry, and Theosophy.[40] Along with Spiritism, other esoteric traditions arrived at the turn of the century to pave the way for the diffusion of Eastern philosophies in Brazil. *Círculo Esotérico da Comunhão do Pensamento* (Esoteric Association for the Communion of Thought), an association that studied and disseminated Hindu philosophy, was founded in São Paulo in 1908. Later it established a leading publishing company for esoteric and Eastern philosophical books (Editora Pensamento). In addition, the Theosophical Society was established in São Paulo City in 1919, and in Rio de Janeiro in 1923.[41]

In the early twentieth century, Umbanda emerged—a quintessential Brazilian religious creation that deployed elements of the main religious traditions of the country (Catholicism, Kardecism, Afro-Brazilian, and indigenous religions). Umbanda was created by white middle-class Spiritists attracted by the possession rituals of the Afro-Brazilian religions.[42] Since it relies on Kardecist literature, Umbanda also draws ideas from Hinduism and Buddhism (derived from the Theosophical Society), which are reinterpreted to fit the demands of Umbanda's adherents.[43]

The main contributors to the wide acceptance of the concepts of karma and reincarnation in Brazil were Kardecist Spiritism and Umbanda. At the core of Spiritist doctrine is the idea of spiritual evolution through reincarnation. Karma, and its corollary, the law of cause and effect, determine reincarnation: if one's actions in a past life were negative, one reincarnates into a life of suffering (through poverty, disease, unhappiness). By contrast, if one practiced charity in a past life (a concept Kardec drew from Christianity), one reincarnates into a life of happiness. In this context, free will plays a key role, as human beings may choose what path to take in their lives. This means that the evolution of the spirit depends solely on its own efforts.[44]

Through interviews with practitioners, reading newspaper and magazine stories on Zen, and discussions on e-mail lists, I realized that the Zen ideas of karma, rebirth, and the individual's responsibility for his own enlightenment were creolized with Spiritist concepts to bridge the gap between Brazilian culture and Zen Buddhism. However, the apparent similarity of concepts disguises deep differences, particularly in relation to key terms such as "karma" and "reincarnation" or rebirth. However, because the adherents of Spiritism are mainly white upper-middle class, which is also the main segment of society that follows Zen Buddhism, the Spiritist connotation of these concepts is very much part of how Buddhism is understood in Brazil. Here I quote two dialogs of the ubiquitous discussions that take place on the Buddhist e-mail lists on these concepts.[45] The questions exemplify how Brazilians creolize their Christian and Spiritist ideas with the novelty that Buddhism presents. The answers are given by Brazilian Buddhist students who have been studying Buddhism much longer and can therefore clarify such confusion of concepts.

Q: Can somebody explain this to me? There is no individual soul that survives death, ok, I can believe that, but then what to do with the theory of reincarnation? (*Buddhismo-L*, July 15, 2000)

A: The Buddhist doctrine is very different from the Kardecist one. It is impossible to reconcile the belief in spirits and Buddhist teachings. According to the *dharma*, body and mind are a unity which is undone at the time of death; hence there isn't an individual being that survives. Life continues in other beings; life is regarded as a process, not as a chain of individuals. These are seen as mere illusions. As such, there is no reincarnation in Buddhism, but there is rebirth. (*Buddhismo-L*, July 17, 2000)

Q: In Judaism and Christianity there is guilt. Isn't it the same as negative karma? I keep hearing people telling me not to do this or that because of bad karma; this conditioning of bad and good, isn't it the same as in Judaism and Christianity? (*Zen Chung Tao*, November 9, 2000)

A: No, because in Judaism and Christianity one believes there is free will; in Buddhism we think that people act impelled by conditions (cultural, your parents, family, country) as well. Hence, there isn't an individual guilt. Karma is a much larger concept. No karma is completely individual; all actions influence the whole world. Changing karma is like steering a large ship: we need to hold the rudder for a long time until the ship's direction changes. That's why the training is long and hard. (*Zen Chung Tao*, November 10, 2000)

Another meaningful creolization takes place with Umbanda. Since Umbanda is itself an appropriation by Kardecist white Brazilians of Afro-Brazilian religions of possession, the theory of karma and reincarnation as a way of returning to earth to evolve spiritually is an essential part of it. Spirits are seen as needing to assist human beings to develop their own karma so that they too will have a better incarnation in the next life. In order to do that, they descend through mediums to help human beings, who usually seek their services to solve problems of love, work, illness, and legal difficulties.[46] There are seven lines of spirits with which to communicate. One of them is significantly called "Line of the East" or "Esoteric Umbanda."[47] Whereas in other lines mediums are possessed by indigenous, Afro-Brazilian, and African entities, in this line, Eastern entities such as "The Hindu/The Indian," "The Turk," "The Jew," "The Gypsy," "The Chinese," "The Goddess of Fortune" (sometimes interpreted as *Lakshmi*), and "Brahma" descend on mediums. Also associated with these figures is "The Buddha" who, in contrast to the other entities, is not incorporated by mediums but is exclusively associated with bringing in good fortune, happiness, and wealth. However, the images of Buddha that I found in Umbanda centers and in shops that cater for Afro-Brazilian traditions are, in fact, those of Hotei. Although originally regarded in China as the future Buddha (Maitreya), Hotei is known in Japan as one of the Seven Gods of Fortune. In Brazil, Hotei is thought of as the historical Buddha, and one can easily find small images of this fat-bellied, happy-faced Buddha in commercial outlets, coffee shops, and some homes. An informant told me that every Umbanda altar has a Buddha/Hotei, and if these altars are more elaborate, they also bear the Seven Gods of Fortune. India and the mythic "Orient" have always fascinated Umbanda practitioners. The same informant mentioned that books by Blavatsky and Lobsang Rampa were mandatory reads for Umbanda practitioners in the 1950s and 1960s: "all these authors were a huge success. Everyone wanted to open *chakras*, talked about vibrations and so forth" (personal communication).

These examples illustrate the fact that when the first Zen texts were introduced into the country in the 1960s, Buddhist concepts had long been in the Brazilian *imaginaire*, carried by Spiritists, Umbandists, and a host of Eastern and Occultist traditions that arrived in the country from the nineteenth century onward.

Zen and the New Age Boom

In the past two decades, so many New Age practices have become conspicuously present in Brazil that David Hess described the Californian New Age reality as bland compared to the Brazilian one.[48] Brazil is experiencing an expansion of alternative spiritualities among urban middle classes and elites.[49] The trend became evident in the late 1980s, when there was a remarkable increase in sales of esoteric books. By the 1990s, there was an extensive network of shops, seminars, therapies, and bookstores that catered to the demands of people who were interested in a vast range of practices and religions, such as New Age spirituality, yoga, and world religions such as Buddhism, Hinduism, and Japanese NRMs. Indeed, Robert Carpenter describes the Brazilian religious marketplace in such terms:

> [Brazil] is the home of the world's largest Catholic population, as well as to more Pentecostals, Spiritists, and adherents of traditions derived from African religions than can be found in any other country in the world. Moreover, there are more followers of the cluster of traditions known as Japanese New Religions in Brazil than in any other country outside Japan. Brazil's religious economy is unquestionably the most diversified in all of Latin America.[50]

New Age religions, such as the Rajneesh movement, are a common source of Zen adherents. The Rajneesh movement, a NRM that began in India in the early 1970s, drew on both Western and Eastern sources to form a synthesis of New Age spirituality. Bhagwan Rajneesh wrote a series of books where he analyzes and interprets Zen teachings. Most of them have been translated into Portuguese. Many adherents interviewed had been or still are his followers. Particularly in Porto Alegre, some adherents had a Buddhist name, which had been given at their lay ordination, and a Rajneesh name. The New Age boom is also responsible for a New Age University (Unipaz), which was established in Brasília, the nation's capital. Zen is taught at Unipaz, and the monastery of Morro da Vargem (in Espírito Santo state) is one of the recommended sites for students to conduct their last semester research.

Paulo Coelho, the Brazilian best-selling author who writes New Age, self-empowering and pilgrimage books, has a weekly column in *Folha de São Paulo*, where he usually writes about popular occultism, mysticism, and Buddhism. He particularly writes on Zen masters and their koans, spreading these tales to mainstream society. Likewise, the *Folha de São Paulo* web site has a link called "Tudo Bem, Tudo Zen" (Everything's alright, Everything's Zen, http://www.uol.com.br/bemzen), adopting the common usage of the word "Zen" as a synonym of peace and tranquility. In this site, many alternative practices and world religions are discussed.

The people I interviewed identified several New Age practices that they frequently associated with Zen Buddhism—practices of healing (yoga, shiatsu, *do in*, tai chi chuan, and acupuncture), eating habits (vegetarianism and macrobiotics), practices of self-understanding (many kinds of psychotherapy and astrology), martial arts (aikido, karate, and kendo), and other religions (Spiritism, African religions, Mahikari, and Rajneesh).

Let us start with healing practices. Many Brazilian adherents are first interested in shiatsu, a massage based on acupressure before getting in contact with Zen. Furthermore, meditation is closely associated with healing by the Brazilian media, particularly as a way of eschewing urban stress. For instance, the cover report of the national weekly magazine *Isto É* featured an article entitled "Meditation: How to Use This Ancient Technique to Overcome the Economic Crisis, Escape Daily Stress, Improve Your Concentration, and Make Difficult Decisions." The story reported that meditation as a technique has entered mainstream society, where instructors go to corporations, usually at lunchtime, to improve productivity.[51]

As for eating habits, there has always been a dilemma in Brazil: should Japanese food or organic, vegetarian, macrobiotic food be used in retreats (*sesshin*)? Urban Brazilians asked such a question in the 1960s and 1970s, when they started practicing Zen at Busshinji, the only temple that was open to Brazilians at the time. Because it catered mainly to the Japanese community, some Brazilian adherents got to the point of bringing their own food when going to retreats. Nowadays, after the establishment of Zen centers by non-Japanese Brazilians, fruit, brown rice, and vegetarian food are served most of the time. Vegetarianism is closely connected with Buddhism in the West. For instance, Jan Nattier describes how her Asian-American Buddhist friends felt ill at ease at a lecture by a famous Vietnamese monk because of the "not altogether friendly stares of the mostly Caucasian (and overwhelmingly vegetarian) crowd as they tried to enjoy their hot dogs and potato chips."[52] Similarly, one of the most popular topics discussed on Brazilian Buddhist e-mail lists is whether one should be vegetarian if converted to Buddhism. The same is true for the United States, as reports Richard Hayes, the moderator of *Buddha-L*, an international e-mail list.[53]

Martial arts are also very much a part of the Zen milieu. At Porto Alegre Zen Center, many adherents came from aikido classes, because their teacher has a close connection with Zen and Moriyama rōshi. Conversely, some Zen adherents started to study this martial art after meeting these aikido practitioners. Furthermore, many martial art halls (dojo) conduct Zen meditation before classes. Conversely, Busshinji temple also holds karate and kendo classes attended mainly by non-Japanese Brazilians.

Adding to such pluralization of faiths in the Brazilian religious field, Japanese NRMs such as Seichō-no-ie, Sekai Kyūsei Kyō, Brazil Sōka Gakkai International, Ōmoto, Tenrikyō, Risshō-kōseikai, Perfect Liberty Kyōdan (PL), and Seikai Mahikari Bumei Kyōdan arrived in Brazil in the 1960s and became highly successful among non-Japanese Brazilians in the following decades. For instance, in 1990, 90 percent of the followers of Seichō-no-ie, PL, and Sekai Kyūseikyō were non-Japanese Brazilians.[54]

As for the Buddhist traditions, Japanese, Tibetan, Korean, Chinese, Thai, and Singhalese Buddhist monks were increasingly present in Brazil in the 1990s. Dharma Centers (Buddhist centers managed by non-Japanese Brazilians) bring their spiritual mentors from abroad to give workshops, promote spiritual retreats, and disseminate their teachings. Many followers undertake trips to the centers where their mentors live.

I have already mentioned the conspicuous "religious migration" of Brazilians among these diverse religious traditions, and the consequent blurring of their boundaries. According to Brazilian anthropologist Roberto da Matta, Brazilians see these religious traditions as complementary, not mutually exclusive.[55] For instance, a survey conducted in 1988 showed that when Catholics who attended church once a week were asked if they believed in reincarnation, 45.9 percent said they did.[56] Since reincarnation is not part of the Catholic doctrine, one can see how permeable the borders of the Catholic world are in Brazil. Conversely, the survey also showed that 89.7 percent of the people classified as of "no religion" declared they believed in God, 55.9 percent declared they believed in heaven, and 44.1 percent believed in hell. It is clear that, the Catholic worldview has spread beyond its borders, carrying its influence even to groups that are distant from that worldview. A survey conducted by the agency Vox Populi in 1996 revealed that 59 percent of the Brazilian population believes in the existence of spirits, a concept accepted only by Spiritism and Afro-Brazilian religions such as Umbanda and Candomblé.[57] Undoubtedly, while the Catholic worldview has spread beyond its borders, the same is true for other religions in relation to Catholicism.

Conclusion

While the Japanese community in Brazil had to leave Buddhism behind, adopting Catholicism as a means of being accepted in the new country (much like the Japanese immigrants to the United States who converted to Christianity; Chaps. 3 and 4), many non-Japanese descent Brazilians have been adhering to Buddhism in the past years. These Zen adherents are part of the intellectual, cosmopolitan, urban elite who import Western discourse on Zen Buddhism through books, media, movies, travel, and, more recently, through the Internet. These cultural flows promote a subcultural group of Brazilian Zen adherents, who relate more easily with their peers in North America or Europe than to their fellow citizens of disenfranchised classes. Class differentiation is influential in choosing Zen—a highly literate choice indeed, as Zen literature is fundamental to their initial and sustained interest in Zen Buddhism.

While importing Buddhist concepts from metropolitan cultures overseas, Brazilians creolize it with an already pluralistic religious matrix and then propagate their interpretation of Buddhist teachings. Catholicism, Kardecist Spiritism, Afro-Brazilian religions, Japanese NRMs, and the New Age movement offer a profusion of faiths and beliefs onto which overseas Buddhist ideas can be superimposed and creolized. On the whole, already existing native religious matrices facilitated the acceptance of Buddhist concepts. Although such concepts do not necessarily have the same meaning in Brazilian culture, the slippages bridged the gap and helped to establish an understanding between the meaning-producing centers and interested Brazilians.

As a result of the diverse sources of knowledge on Zen, conflicts like the one I depicted in the opening of this chapter are ever-present. As a later development of that story, Coen sensei was dismissed from Busshinji in January 2001 and went on to establish a new temple in São Paulo City. The Japanese *sōkan* is presently the only authority at Busshinji, the Sōtō School's headquarters for South America. As a last point, I would like to note that creolization occurs also between Japanese and non-Japanese Brazilian practices. In my fieldwork I found that, whereas the Japanese superimpose Catholic terms and festivities on their Zen matrix, non-Japanese Brazilians and younger Japanese-Brazilians may ask Zen monks/nuns to conduct funerals, memorials, baby namings, and weddings. Religious boundaries are indeed very porous in Brazil.

Notes

I would like to thank Martin Baumann for giving me insightful suggestions on this essay, which is based on fieldwork conducted in Brazil in the years of 1998–1999 and 2001–2002. I used participant observation, in-depth interviews, and a survey of adherents in São Paulo, Rio de Janeiro, Pôrto Alegre, Ouro Preto, and Espírito Santo.

1 Superintendent for South America, or "bishop" as his position is referred to, the title being clear evidence of the Catholic influence that permeates Brazilian society.

2 Coen is the Portuguese spelling of her Buddhist name,

3 Pierre Bourdieu, *Distinction: A Social Critique of the Judgement of Taste* (Cambridge, Mass.: Harvard University Press, 1984).

4 Frederik Barth, *Ethnic Groups and Boundaries: The Social Organization of Cultural Difference* (London: Allen and Unwin, 1969).

5 Cristina Rocha, "Identity and Tea Ceremony in Brazil," *Japanese Studies* 19, no. 3 (1999): 287–295.

6 The Japanese monk Dōgen (1200–1253) brought the Sōtō Zen Buddhist school to Japan from China.

7 See, for example, Martin Baumann, "Creating a European Path to Nirvāna: Historical and Contemporary Developments of Buddhism in Europe," *Journal of Contemporary Religion* 10, no. 1(1995): 55–70; Rick Fields, "Divided Dharma: White Buddhists, Ethnic Buddhists, and Racism," in *The Faces of Buddhism in America*, ed. Kenneth Tanaka and Charles Prebish (Berkeley: University of California Press, 1998), 196–206; Paul Numrich, *Old Wisdom in the New World: Americanization of Two Immigrant Theravada Buddhist Temples* (Knoxville: University of Tennessee Press, 1996); Charles Prebish, "Two Buddhisms Reconsidered," *Buddhist Studies Review* 10, no. 2 (1993): 187–206.

8 For a more detailed history of Japanese and Zen Buddhism in Brazil, see Cristina Rocha, "Zen Buddhism in Brazil: Japanese or Brazilian?" *Journal of Global Buddhism* 1(2000): 31–55.

9 Jeffrey Lesser, *Negotiating National Identity: Immigrants, Minorities, and the Struggle for Ethnicity in Brazil* (Durham, N.C.: Duke University Press, 1999); Koichi Mori, "Vida Religiosa dos Japoneses e seus Descendentes Residentes no Brasil e Religiões de Origem Japonesa," in *Uma Epopéia Moderna: 80 Anos do Imigração Japonesa no Brasil*, ed. K. Wakisaka (São Paulo: Sociedade Brasileira de Cultura Japonesa, 1992), 559–601.

10 Murilo Nunes Azevedo, *O Caminho de Cada Um: O Budismo da Terra Pura* (Rio de Janeiro: Bertrand Brasil, 1996).

11 Ricardo M. Gonçalves, "O Budismo Japonês no Brasil: Reflexões de um Observador Participante," in *Sinais dos Tempos: Diversidade Religiosa no Brasil*, ed. Leila Landim (Rio de Janeiro: Instituto de Estudos da Religião, 1990), 177.

12 Regina Matsue, "O Paraíso de Amida: Três Escolas Budistas em Brasília" (M.A. thesis, University of Brasília, 1998).

13 *IBGE*, the Brazilian Institute of Geography and Statistics.

14 Reginaldo Prandi, "Religião Paga, Conversão e Serviço," in *A Realidade Social das Religiões no Brasil: Religião Sociedade e Política*, ed. Antônio Pierucci and Reginaldo Prandi (São Paulo: Hucitec, 1996), 257.

15 Thomas Tweed, "Nightstand Buddhists and Other Creatures: Sympathizers, Adherents, and the Study of Religion," in *American Buddhism, Methods and Findings in Recent Scholarship*, ed. Duncan Williams and Christopher Queen (Richmond, Eng.: Curzon, 1999), 74.

16 Many books have been translated; some of the titles are: D. T. Suzuki's *The Zen Doctrine of No Mind* and *Introduction to Zen Buddhism*; Shunryū Suzuki's *Zen Mind, Beginners' Mind*; Phillip Kapleau's *The Three Pillars of Zen*; Charlotte Joko Beck, *Nothing Special, Living Zen*; and most of the books by Thich Nhat Hanh. On the Internet site of a Brazilian bookstore in July 2002 the word "Zen" was used in forty-eight titles of books in Portuguese (http://www.livcultura.com.br).

17 The Hollywood movies *The Little Buddha, Seven Years in Tibet*, and *Kundun*, and non-Hollywood ones such as *The Cup* and *Samsāra* were very successful in Brazil. Even though they dealt with Tibetan Buddhism, they are directly associated with Buddhism itself and not specifically Tibet. Practitioners may attend various Buddhist schools at once.

18 Roberto Oliveira, "Fé de Pernas Cruzadas," *Revista da Folha*, July 15, 2001, 8–13.

19 For a bibliography on Buddhism in Brazil and a web directory of Brazilian Buddhist temples, monasteries, centers and e-mail lists, see http://sites.uol.com.br/cmrocha.

20 H. Assmann, *A Igreja Eletrônica e Seu Impacto na América Latina* (Petrópolis: Vozes, 1986).

21 The 2000 census shows that one-third of the Brazilians over ten years of age may be regarded as illiterate or "semi-illiterate," as they have not completed four years of schooling.

22 "Cybersangha" is a term coined in 1991 by Gary Ray to describe the Buddhist community online. For more on this, see Charles Prebish, *Luminous Passage: The Practice and Study of Buddhism in America* (Berkeley and Los Angeles: University of California Press, 1999).

23   Wade C. Roof, *Spiritual Supermarket: Baby Boomers and the Remaking of American Religion* (Princeton, N.J.: Princeton University Press, 1999), 46–110.

24   Ulf Hannerz, "The World in Creolisation," *Africa* 57, no. 4 (1987): 546–559.

25   José J. Carvalho, "O Encontro de Veihas e Novas Religiões: Esboço de uma Teoria dos Estilos de Espiritualidade," in *Misticismo e Novas Religiões*, ed. Alberto Moreira and Renée Zicman (Petrópolis: Vozes/UFS/IFAN, 1994), 77.

26   Peter Berger, "Four Faces of Global Culture," *The National Interest* 49 (1997): 23–29.

27   Ibid., 28–29.

28   Robert Bellah, "New Religious Consciousness and the Crisis in Modernity," in *The New Religious Consciousness*, ed. C. Glock and R. Bellah (Berkeley: University of California Press, 1976); Denise Cush, "British Buddhism and the New Age," *Journal of Contemporary Religion* 11, no. 2 (1996): 195–208.

29   *Jukai*: "granting (*ju*) the precepts (*kai*), the ceremonial initiation into Buddhism. In this ceremony one commits oneself to be completely devoted to the three jewels and the ten main precepts." Michael Diener, Ingrid Fischer-Schreiber, and Franz-Karl Ehrhard, *The Shambhala Dictionary of Buddhism and Zen*, trans. Michael Kohn (Boston: Shambhala, 1991), s.v. *Jukai*.

30   Wilson Paranhos, *Nuvens Cristalinas em Luar de Prata* (RJ: FEEU, 1994), 155.

31   Cristina Rocha, "Zen Buddhism in Brazil."

32   José J. Carvalho, "Características do Fenômeno Religioso na Sociedade Contemporânea," in *O Impacto Da Modernidade Sobre a Religião*, ed. Maria Clara Bingemer (São Paulo: Loyola, 1992), 153.

33   E. Stoddard and G. Cornwell, "Cosmopolitan or Mongrel? Créolité, Hybridity and 'Douglarisation' in Trinidad," *European Journal of Cultural Studies* 2, no. 3 (1999): 331–353.

34   Robert Young, *Colonial Desire: Hybridity in Theory, Culture and Race* (London: Routledge, 1995); Pnina Werbner and Tariq Modood, eds., *Debating Cultural Hybridity: Multi-cultural Identities and the Politics of Anti-Racism* (London: Zed Books, 1997).

35   Young, *Colonial Desire.*

36   For an account of hybridity that foregrounds the possibilities of agency and reproduction of culture in the context of an analysis of Buddhism in Hawai'i see Tanabe, Chapter 3.

37   Edward Brathwaite, *The Development of Creole Society in Jamaica 1770–1820* (Oxford: Clarendon, 1971).

38   Carvalho, "O Encontro de Velhas e Novas Religiões," 74; Christian Smith and Joshua Prokopy, *Latin American Religion in Motion*, 3.

39   According to J. Carvalho, "In many aspects, the Spiritist world-view became part of the national ethos, as much as Catholicism, and more recently Protestantism"; "O Encontro de Velhas e Novas Religiões," 74.

40   David Hess, *Samba in the Night: Spiritism in Brazil* (New York: Columbia University Press, 1994); Maria Laura Viveiros de Castro Cavalcanti, "O Espiritismo," in *Sinais dos Tempos*, 147–155.

41   Carvalho, "O Encontro de Velhas e Novas Religiões," 75.

42   Lísias Negrão, "Umbanda: Entre a Cruz e a Encruzilhada," *Tempo Social, Revista de Sociologia* 5, nos. 1–2 (1994): 113–122.

43   Renato Ortiz, *A Morte Branca do Feiticeiro Negro: Umbanda e Sociedade Brasileira* (São Paulo: Brasiliense, 1999), 16–17, 69–86.

44   Cavalcanti, "O Espiritismo."

45   *Buddhismo-L* (http://www.dharmanet.com.br/listas), October 2000 and April 2001.

46   Carmen Macedo, *A Imagem do Eterno: Religiões no Brasil* (São Paulo: Moderna, 1989), 47; Negrão, "Umbanda," 116.

47   Diane Brown, *Umbanda Religion and Politics in Urban Brazil* (New York: Columbia University Press, 1994), 55–77; Macedo, *A Imagem do Eterno*, 44–46.

48   As quoted in Robert Carpenter, "Esoteric Literature as a Microcosmic Mirror of Brazil's Religious Marketplace," in *Latin American Religion in Motion*, ed. Christian Smith and Joshua Prokopy (New York: Routledge, 1999), 242.

49   Ibid., 235; José G. Magnani, *O Brasil da Nova Era* (São Paulo: Edusp, 2000); Luis Soares, "Religioso por Natureza: Cultura Alternativa e Misticismo Ecológico no Brasil," in *Sinais dos Tempos*.

50   Carpenter, "Esoteric Literature," 243.

51   *Isto É* magazine (September 1998): 87–94.

52   Jan Nattier, "Buddhism Comes to Main Street," *Wilson Quarterly* 21(1997): 72.

53   Richard Hayes, "The Internet as a Window onto American Buddhism," in *American Buddhism: Methods and Findings in Recent Scholarship*, 174–175.

54   Robert Carpenter and Wade Roof, "The Transplanting of Seichō-no-ie from Japan to Brazil: Moving beyond the Ethnic Enclave," *Journal of Contemporary Religion* 10, no. 1 (1995): 41–53; Hideaki Matsuoka, "'Messianity Makes a Person Useful': Describing

Differences in a Japanese Religion in Brazil," *Japanese Journal of Religious Studies* 28, nos. 1–2 (2001).

55 Roberto da Matta, *O Que Faz o Brazil, Brasil?* (Rio de Janeiro: Rocco, 1994), 115–116.

56 Carlos Rodrigues Brandão, "A Crise das Instituições Tradicionais Produtoras de Sentido," in *Misticismo e Novas Religiões*, 40–41.

57 *Veja* (magazine), July 26, 2000.

IMAGE, TEMPLE, AND PILGRIMAGE

Diana Eck

A. The Temple and the Image

The construction and consecration of a temple, according to the architectural portions of the *śilpaśāstras*, is very much like the shaping and consecration of an image. For example, the ground on which the temple is to be constructed is carefully selected on the basis of its auspicious situation and seeded for the auspicious sign of germination. Then the local *genii loci* who dwell in that ground are invited to leave and take up residence elsewhere: "Let spirits (*bhūta*), gods (*deva*), and demons (*rākṣasa*) depart and seek other habitations. From now on this place belongs to the divinity whose temples will be built here."[1] Finally, at the very end of the construction process, the "eyes" of the temple are opened by the master architect and the priestly architect, who ascend to the top of the temple in the middle of the night and pierce open the eyes of the temple with a golden needle. Is the temple also a divine image, as well as the abode of a divine image?

In building a temple, the universe in microcosm is reconstructed. The divine ground-plan is called a *maṇḍala*, a geometric map of the cosmos. At its center is the sanctum, where the image will be installed. Its eight directions are guarded by the cosmic regents called the *lokapālas*. Various planetary deities, world guardians, and gods are set in their appropriate quadrant. The temple is an architectural pantheon, with each portion of the structure inhabited by the gods.

The particular *maṇḍala* of the Hindu temple is called the *vāstupuruṣa maṇḍala*. The Puruṣa is the cosmic "Person," from the sacrifice of whose giant body the entire universe was created, as told in Ṛg Veda X.90:

> From his mind the moon was born,
> and from his eye the sun,
> From his mouth Indra and the fire,
> From his breath the wind was born.

From his navel arose the atmosphere,
And from his head the sky evolved,
From his feet the earth, and from his ear
The cardinal points of the compass:
So did they fashion forth these worlds.[2]

The body, as an organic whole diverse in the function of its parts and limbs, is here the image appropriated for the cosmos. The symbolic parallel between body and cosmos is articulated ritually in the construction of the Vedic fire altar, in which the body of Puruṣa (also called Prajāpati) is reconstructed from the various parts of the cosmos. A similar reconstruction of the body-cosmos occurs in the construction of the Hindu temple. The temple is the condensed image of the cosmos.

Stella Kramrisch, in explaining the meaning of the *vāstupuruṣa maṇḍala,* writes: "Puruṣa is the Universal Essence, the Principle of all things, the Prime Person whence all originates. Vāstu is the Site; in it Vāstu, bodily existence, abides; from it Vāstu derives its name. In bodily existence, Puruṣa, the Essence, becomes the Form. . . . Puruṣa himself has no substance. He gives it his impress. The substance is of wood, brick or stone in the temple."[3]

The building of a temple, like the shaping of an image, is not left to the creativity of the architect or craftsmen. It carefully follows canons of building and is, from beginning to end, a ritual activity. "From the stretching of the cord, or the drawing of the lines of the *maṇḍala,* every one of the movements is a rite and sustains, in its own sphere of effectiveness, the sacred building, to the same extent as the actual foundation supports its weight."[4]

A classical north India temple in the *nagara* style[5] is striking to the eyes of the Western observer in two ways: first, its exterior is teeming with intricately carved ornamentation and bas relief figures and, second, its interior sanctum is dark and usually windowless. The temple is said to be the architectural likeness of a mountain. Indeed, the various names of temple styles are the names of those great Himālayan peaks which are the home of the gods: Meru, Kailāsa, and Mandara. Both its lush exterior and its cavelike sanctum point to the symbolic linking of temple and mountain.

The exterior of the temple, such as the temple of Kandarīya Mahādeva at Khajurāho, is a series of progressively higher porches or *maṇḍapas* culminating in the *śikhara,* the highest spire of the temple, situated directly over the inner sanctum. The word *śikhara* also means "mountain peak," and this temple-peak resembles a series of "foothills," the smaller *śikharas* massing, rising, one upon the other, toward their final culmination in the sun-disc, the *āmalaka*, the crowning cogged ring-stone at the very top of the temple.[6] Like the mountain, the temple links heaven and earth, and the sun-disc of the *āmalaka* is "the architectural symbol of the celestial world."[7]

The prolixity of the cosmic mountain, covered with all forms of vegetative, animal, human, and divine life, is also replicated in the temple. As the sunlight changes through the day, the figures of every niche of the temple come alive. There are women applying cosmetics, warriors preparing for battle, gods and goddesses, serpent hooded *nāgas*, lions and elephants. The directional guardians stand forth in relief to protect this *maṇḍala*.

If the exterior of the temple is the articulation of the plenum of life, the interior of the temple directs our attention toward the center, the seed, the source of it all. The sanctum, approached through increasingly dim-lit porches, is the symbolic equivalent of the cave, deep within the mountain. The Kandarīya is literally the temple "Of the Cave."[8]

The sanctum of the temple is called the *garbhagṛha*, the "womb chamber." In this room, as the temple is being constructed, a rite called *garbhadhāna*, the "implanting of the seed," takes place. In the middle of the night, the priest plants the "seed" of the temple, in the form of a small casket which is set into the foundation.[9] It is this seed which symbolically germinates and grows directly upward, through the vertical shaft of the temple to the sky. The *garbhagṛha*, with its cave atmosphere, reminds us that there is a mystery, a secret, at the heart of this exuberant tradition of spirituality. The deep interior of the tradition is not flooded by the light of cathedral windows, but is deep within.

The journey of the worshiper to such a temple-mountain is a pilgrimage. Approaching the temple, one circumambulates it, symbolically attending to the entire visible world of name and form. Having seen all there is to see on the intricate exterior, one journeys to the interior, to the very center of the world. Often there is another circumambulatory passage around the *garbhagṛha*. Having made this final circumambulation, one receives the *darśan* of the deity at the center.

The temple is covered with artistic images, and it contains a primary consecrated image in its inner sanctum. In a larger sense, however, the temple *is* an image. It is not any particular deity, but the sacred *maṇḍala* of the cosmos as a whole. Kramrisch writes, "The temple is the concrete shape (*mūrti*) of the Essence; as such it is the residence and vesture of God. . . . The devotee who comes to the temple, to look at it, does so as a 'seer,' not as a spectator.[10]

B. Image and Pilgrimage

The same impulse for the *darśan* of the image which is at the center of the temple cultus also provides the impetus for pilgrimage. People go to "take the *darśan*" of the place and its deities, and to receive the *prasād* from its temples.

The most common term for such pilgrimage places is *tīrtha*, literally a "crossing place" or a "ford." The term originally referred to the ford in a river, where one could safely cross to the other shore. Through the centuries some of India's most important places of pilgrimage have indeed been located along the banks of her great rivers and have been "fords" in this geographical sense. As pilgrimage places, however, they are also symbolic and spiritual fords, where one may cross the flood of *saṁsāra*. Just as the "far shore" has become the predominant Indian image of the final spiritual destination of the soul's pilgrimage, so the "crossing place" has become an important image of the means of getting there.

The practice of pilgrimage, *tīrthayātrā*, has long been an important part of India's religious life. As early as the time of the epic Mahābhārata in the first two centuries C.E., *tīrthayātrā* was compared to the Vedic sacrifice in its benefits and, unlike the sacrifice, was a ritual activity accessible to all, not only to the very rich.[11]

In India today, the advent of modern means of transportation has served to stimulate the zeal for pilgrim travel. Pilgrimage is as popular and important a religious and cultural phenomenon as it was in the height of the Middle ages in Europe. The organization of pilgrim tours is a thriving business, and these *tīrthayātrās* in "deluxe" buses are advertised to include dozens of sacred sites on their itineraries.

Pilgrimage and Landscape

The entire land of India is, to the eyes of Hindu pilgrims, a sacred geography—from the Himālayas in the north to the tip of India at Cape Comorin in the south. As pilgrims circumambulate a temple, so do some pilgrims circumambulate the whole of this sacred land, including on their route the four *dhāms* or "abodes" of the divine at the four compass points: Badrīnāth in the north, Purī in the east, Rāmeśvaram in the south, and Dvārakā in the west.

The names of the great mountain ranges, such as the Himālayas and the Vindhyas, and the names of the great rivers, such as the Gaṅgā, the Yamunā, the Narmadā, the Godāvarī, and the Kāverī—all are names that ring with mythological associations for Hindus. They are part of a very important symbolic geography which constitutes what Hindus mean by "India."

The Himālayas, for example, the "Abode of Snows," are also called *devālaya*, the "abode of the gods." Pilgrims have journeyed into the Himālayas for the *darśan* of great mountain peaks, such as Meru, the center of the world, Kailāsa, the home of Śiva, and Mandara, said to have been used as a churn to churn the Sea of Milk. They also seek the *darśan* of great Himālayan shrines, such as the Śaiva Kedārnāth, the Vaiṣṇava Badrīnāth, and the ice-*liṅga* at Amarnāth. The trek into the mountains has traditionally required great discipline and endurance and was often compared to the difficult austerities of ascetics and yogis.

The great Indian rivers, especially the Gaṅgā, have also been of symbolic importance. Himālayan pilgrims climb to the source of the River Gaṅgā Gaṅgotrī, where the river emerges from under a glacier. The Gaṅgā is called the River of Heaven and is said to have flowed in heaven alone before she agreed to come to earth. Śiva caught her in his tangled ascetic's hair to break the force of her fall, and from his head she flowed down through the Himālayas, leaving the mountains at Hardvār, also called Gaṅgādvār, "Door of the Gaṅgā," and from there flowing out upon the plains of India, past such great *tīrthas* as Prayāg and Vārānasī Kāśī, reaching the sea at Gaṅgā Sāgar on the Bay of Bengal. In Hindu hymns, the Gaṅgā is praised as a liquid form of Śiva's divine energy, Śaktī. Bathing in the Gaṅgā is said to wash away all one's sins. The other sacred rivers of India are likened to the Gaṅgā in their purity and are often said to *be* the Gaṅgā, diverted miraculously to the various regions of India. All water used in ritual is symbolically transformed into sacred water by invoking the presence of the Gaṅgā and the other sacred rivers.

While the Himālayas and the Gaṅgā are famous throughout India, there are hills, rivers, and mountains in the various regions of India which have their own sacred traditions. Regional pilgrimage—whether in Bengal, Mahārāṣṭra, or the Tamil south—has given a sense of unity and shared landscape to people of particular areas, language groups, or sectarian traditions. For example, the Śaiva *bhakti* tradition of Tamilnād has its own network of sacred shrines which link Tamil geography with the great deeds of Śiva

Mahādeva. These places are praised in various *sthalapurāṇas,* "place-legends," as well as in the hymns of the Tamil *bhakti* poet-saints, the *nāyanmārs,* who flourished in the sixth to ninth centuries.[12] These saints were themselves perpetual pilgrims, wandering from place to place in Tamilnād and singing the praises of the various shrines of Śiva. Their poems praise Śiva as he dwells in each of these shrines: ". . . the God of Tōṇipuram where the sea has many beaches," or ". . . the coral-hued Lord who dwells in Kānūr of the fragrant groves."[13] The love of nature and the intimate knowledge of the particular hills, seashores, and fields of Tamilnād is evident in these poems, which inspire pilgrims not only to the love of Śiva, but to the love of the landscape where he lives.

Pilgrimage and Myth

In addition to pilgrimage places of geographical beauty, there are the many *tīrthas* associated with great events of the mythological tradition. India's myths are living in the geography of the land, and conversely India's geography is alive with mythology. The *tīrtha* is conceptually the counterpart of the *avatāra,* the word used to describe the divine "descents" of the gods. *Avatāra* comes from a variation of the *tīrtha* verbal root (*ava* + *tṛ*) meaning to "cross down," and precisely at those countless places where the gods have "crossed down" into this world as *avatāras* are the *tīrthas* where earthly pilgrims can make their spiritual crossings.

Some of the places especially famous for the mighty events which happened there include Kurukṣetra, the site of the great war of the Mahābhārata; Ayodhyā, the ancient capital of Lord Rāma; and Rāmeśvaram, where Rāma established a Śiva *liṅga* after crossing the sea to Laṅkā to rescue Sītā. Great centers, like Kāśī, seem to collect mythological traditions, to the extent that virtually all the great mythic events are associated with the city. Perhaps the best example of the direct linking of place and myth is in the area around Mathurā, the birthplace of Kṛṣṇa in central North India.

The land of Kṛṣṇa, called Vraj, covers an area of some sixty-four square miles in the area around Mathurā. Its spiritual center is in the village of Vṛndāvan. The area is filled with sites which mark the mythic events of the life of Kṛṣṇa, from his birthplace in Mathurā, to the home of the baby Kṛṣṇa's foster parents in Gokul and the later childhood home of Kṛṣṇa in Vṛndāvan. The places of Kṛṣṇa's divine "play" (*līlā*) amidst the pastoral cowherding folk of Vraj are called *līlāsthalas,* the "places of the Lord's play."[14] There is the holy hill of Govardhan, which young Kṛṣṇa is said to have lifted with one finger;

there is the pool where his beloved Rādhā is said to have bathed; there is the tree by the river where Kṛṣṇa hung the clothes he stole from the milkmaids, the *gopīs*, as they bathed; and there is the grove where Kṛṣṇa and the *gopīs* danced in the middle of the night. Countless such *līlāsthalas*, associated with even the most minute details of Kṛṣṇa's life, have created a sacred landscape as intricate as that of medieval Palestine, where such sites as the place where Mary nursed Jesus, the place where Mary washed Jesus' clothes, and the place where the food was cooked to be served at the Last Supper, were located with imaginative precision.[15] In Vraj, these many places are said to bear the "traces" (*cihna*) of Kṛṣṇa, and they bid the pilgrim to constant remembrance of him and his miraculous life. While the pilgrim to Vraj may visit the temples of Vṛndāvan and Mathurā for the *darśan* of the various images of Kṛṣṇa, the real power of Vraj pilgrimage is in the land of Vraj itself. Pilgrims undertake a special pilgrimage through the rural countryside of Vraj, visiting the groves, the pools, and the hillocks where Kṛṣṇa's "traces" may be found. The earth itself is said to be holy here. The "dust of Vraj," (*Vraj kī raj*) is considered sanctified by the feet of Kṛṣṇa, and pilgrims touch it reverently to their foreheads.

Pilgrimage and the Sacred Image

There are other *tīrthas* in which primary importance is attached to the particular *image* of the deity which is found there, and not so much to the place itself or to its mythological associations. For example, pilgrims go to the sacred hill of Tirupati in Andhra Pradesh especially for the *darśan* of Śrī Veṅkaṭeśvara, an ancient icon said to be a form of Viṣṇu.[16] In Mahārāṣṭra, the twice-yearly pilgrimage of the Vārkarī sect to Paṇḍharpur is also oriented toward the *darśan* of a particular deity, Viṭhobā, who is said to be a form of Kṛṣṇa.[17] According to legend, the Lord came to bless a particular devotee who was faithful in his duties toward his parents. The devotee did not even take time from his filial duties to greet the Lord properly, but simply threw him a brick to stand on. Kṛṣṇa, impressed with such devotion, has remained standing there ever since.

Another icon of great renown is the cultic image of Kṛṣṇa as the Lord of Mt. Govardhan in Vraj. The image is not even in Vraj, however, but is in Nāthdvārā in Rājasthān. According to the Vallabhite sectarian tradition, the Lord appeared out of Govardhan in a spontaneously formed image called Śrīnāth-jī.[18] They served this icon of Kṛṣṇa in Vraj, and when Muslim persecution forced them to abandon Vraj, they took the icon westward and ultimately built a temple to house it in the Arāvalli Hills. The place, called Nāthdvārā, is visited by Vallabhite pilgrims solely for the purpose of having Śrīnāth-jī's *darśan*.

Finally, we should again mention the unique wooden images of Kṛṣṇa Jagannāth, Balarāma, and Subhadrā housed in the great temple complex at Purī. The cultus of Jagannāth, like that of all of the above mentioned images, has an antiquity which extends deep into the regional folk traditions.[19] Since the specifically Vaiṣṇava identity of these images is attached to a more ancient cultus, it is little wonder that the stories of Kṛṣṇa have little importance in Purī. The myths associated with this place are, rather, those which concern the appearance of these images, which are said to have been carved by the craftsman of the gods, Viśvakarman, from a log washed ashore in the time of the legendary king Indradyumna.[20] Here, as in many Indian temples with a strong regional affiliation, the day to day service of the deities in the temple is parallel in structure to the honor and service which the king used to receive.

Pilgrimage and the Saints

When the Tamil pilgrims walk to a distant Śiva shrine singing the songs composed by one of the *nāyanmār* poets over one thousand years ago, they join in a tradition which links them with the saints as well as with the sacred shrines. All over India, the *bhakti* movements emphasized the direct, devotional love of God. For some, such as Kabīr in the north and Basavanna in the south, this direct love meant a diminished regard for the elaborate brahmanical temple cult and for the great ritual centers of pilgrimage. God, after all, is close within the heart. For most of the *bhakti* saints, however, especially those who saw the Lord as intensely personal and endowed with qualities (*saguṇa*), the image-incarnations of the Lord were of great importance and became the focal point of their devotion. The saints sang their hymns at the doors of the temples, and so did the pilgrims who followed them. The Śrī Vaiṣṇavas went to Tirupati and Śrī Raṅgam. The Śaiva Siddhāntins went to Kāñcī and Cidambaram. The Gaudīya Vaiṣṇavas went to Vṛndāvan.

The saints themselves were often great pilgrims and wanderers. Many took up a life of homelessness, becoming itinerant minstrels and poets. The people of the *bhakti* movements which these saints launched have followed the footsteps of the saints in pilgrimage. In Mahārāṣṭra, for example, the Vārkarī pilgrims who journey to Paṇḍharpur bring the great Mahārāṣṭrian saints along on pilgrimage with them. Traveling in processional groups from their own districts, the pilgrims follow after a cart which carries the *pādukās*, "footprints," of one of the great saints, such as Tukārām, Eknāth, or Jñāneśvara. The most famous of these processions follows the *pādukās* of Jñāneśvara, starting from a village near Poona and traveling over 150 miles to Paṇḍharpur. On the way, they sing the songs of the Mahārāṣṭrian saints, who made this journey many times:

> I should like to become the small pebbles
> or the big stones, or the dust
> of the road which leads to Paṇḍharpur.
> Thus would I be under the feet of the Saints.[21]

While the pilgrims to Paṇḍharpur travel with the saints, they also travel *to* the saints, for two of the beloved Mahārāṣṭrian saints, Nāmdev and Cokhāmela, are interred right at the doorstep of Vithobā's temple. Worshiping the saints is part of the pilgrimage to Paṇḍharpur.[22] Elsewhere in India, pilgrimage to places associated with the saints, especially their tombs or *samādhis*, is not uncommon. A striking example is the annual pilgrimage to the tomb of the Rājput hero-saint Rāmdev, which attracts thousands of pilgrims from Rājasthān, Mahārāṣṭra, and Gujarāt each year.

The saints (*sants*) are not the same as the *sādhus*, the "holy men." Perhaps the most notable distinction between them is that the saints of the *bhakti* movements were, to a great extent, antiestablishment figures who often championed the downtrodden and the untouchables and despised brahmanical ritualism, while the *sādhus* and *sannyāsins* represent the brahmanical establishment, even in transcending it by casting off their worldly *dharma*. Nonetheless, the notion that there is something to be gained from the presence and *darśan* of a holy person is equally relevant to both saints and *sādhus*. Just as pilgrims follow the saints, so do they follow the *sādhus*.

Hindus seek the *darśan* of *sādhus* and *sannyāsins* who tend to congregate at the great *tīrthas*, such as Kāśī, Hardvār, and Badrīnāth. In a sense, these renouncers are the patrons of *tīrthas* and serve to enhance the popularity and power of the *tīrtha* by their very presence.[23] In the Bhāgavata Purāṇa, King Yudhiṣṭhira emphasizes this point in speaking to a sage who has just returned from a pilgrimage: "Devotees like you, who have become *tīrthas* themselves, are the ones who make the *tīrthas* into crossing places by embodying the presence of God there."[24]

The term *tīrtha* refers not only to places, but may also refer to people—holy people who have themselves become "crossings." In the ancient Jain tradition, the spiritual pathfinders were called *tīrthāṅkaras,* "ford-makers." Much later, one of the orders of *sādhus* organized by Śaṅkara took the name *tīrtha* as a title. The point is clear enough: holy men can also help one reach the "far shore." Thus, in going to geographical *tīrthas,* Hindus have had a special preference for those places where the walking-*tīrthas* congregate.

Pilgrimage Place as Divine Image

Just as the temple may become an image of the sacred whole of the cosmos, so do some *tīrthas* become images of the cosmos. The place becomes an icon.

A direct parallel to the structure of a temple may be seen in the city of Madurai in Tamilnād, where the city is laid out in the shape of a *maṇḍala.* At the center is the temple compound of Mīnākṣī and Sundareśvara, with its tall, elaborately carved gateways, called *gopurams,* in the four directions. Around the temple are three concentric square processional streets. Here an entire city has been built according to the plan of the *śilpaśātras,* and the plan is precisely that of the *vāstupuruṣa maṇḍala* which delimits the sacred space of a temple.[25] The city is the cosmos, bounded from forces of disorder by the boundaries of order which the *maṇḍala* establishes. Each year, in the Chittarai festival, the Goddess Mīnākṣī reestablishes the sacred order by conquering the lords of the eight directions and by establishing the sovereignty of herself and Śiva Sundareśvara at the center of this cosmos.

The city of Vārāṇasī, acknowledged by Hindus as a whole to be the most sacred of the *tīrthas,* is also a sacred image of the cosmos. The city is said to be the permanent earthly home of Lord Śiva, and it is often called Avimukta, the "Never-Forsaken," the place Śiva never leaves. According to myth, Śiva upholds this city on the tip of his trident even during the *pralaya* when the universal flood destroys the earth.[26] And from this place the world is created again. The city is also called Kāśī, the "City of Light." It is here, according to myth, that Śiva's fiery *liṅga* of light burst up from the netherworlds, split open the earth, and rose to pierce through the top of the highest heavens— a luminous, fathomless, *axis mundi.* Moreover, Kāśī is not only the location of that mythic episode, but is said to *be* that *liṅga* itself. The entire city, a sacred circle or *maṇḍala* with a radius of ten miles, is said to be a *liṅga*—the very embodiment of Śiva.

With its three thousand years of continuous habitation, Kāśī's *maṇḍala* is hardly as ordered as that of Madurai. Nonetheless, the elements of the whole are here. The eight directions are said to have originated in Kāśī, receiving their respective realms of sovereignty by establishing Śiva *liṅgas* in Kāśī. Similarly the heavenly deities who govern time are said to have received jurisdiction over time in Kāśī. The temples of all these deities, in addition to the temples of Viṣṇu, Durgā, Bhairava, Gaṇeśa, and all the gods, have their places within the patterns of Kāśī's sacred geography. At the center is the famous *liṅga* of Viśvanāth—Śiva as "Lord of the Universe." The whole of the city is protected by a grid of fifty-six Gaṇeśas, who sit at the eight compass points in seven concentric circles spreading outward from Viśvanāth.

As a microcosm, Kāśī is said to contain all the *tīrthas* of India's sacred geography within her borders. Thus, in the city of Kāśī there are temples, tanks, lakes, and rivulets which represent the symbolic presence of such places as Kedārnāth and Badrīnāth in the Himālayas, Kāñcī and Rāmeśvaram in the Tamil south, Purī in the east, Dvārakā in the west, the old cities of Mathurā, Ayodhyā, and Ujjain, the Narmadā and Godāvarī rivers, the Vindhya and Himālaya mountains.

In Kāśī, the whole of the sacred world is gathered together into one place. The sacred landscape of India is here. The great myths of the tradition are said to have happened here. There is a great density of images and *liṅgas* here. And there has always been a great congregation of saints, *sādhus*, and *sannyāsins* here.

Although Kāśī condenses the entire universe in its microcosm, it is also said to transcend the entire universe. It is well known as that *tīrtha* which enables those who die within its borders to make the final "crossing" from this shore of birth and death to the "far shore" of *mokṣa*. It is believed that to die in Kāśī is to gain liberation. Thus, while ordinary pilgrims may come to Kāśī with many of the same vows and desires they bring to other *tīrthas*, there is another group of pilgrims who come to Kāśī to stay and to live out their years until they die. For them, this is the destination at the end of the pilgrim road. It brings to an end not only the circuit of pilgrimage in India, but the long soul's pilgrimage through life after life.

Notes

[1]   Kramrisch, *The Hindu Temple*, p. 13.

[2]   R. C. Zaehner, trans. *Hindu Scriptures* (London: J. M. Dent & Sons, Ltd., 1966), pp. 8–10.

3   Kramrisch, *The Hindu Temple*, pp. 6–7. Kramrisch's work, which is certainly the major work on the Hindu temple, is in its entirety an exploration of the temple as *vāstupuruṣa maṇḍala.*

4   Kramrisch, *The Hindu Temple*, p. 39.

5   Rowland, pp. 276, 280 explains the *nagara* style of temple, as distinguished from the *drāviḍa* and *vesara* styles. Essentially, the *nagara* is the north Indian, post-Gupta temple, with the distinctive *śikhara* over the sanctum.

6   Kramrisch, *The Hindu Temple*, pp. 348–356, ("The Āmalaka").

7   Kramrisch, *The Hindu Temple*, p. 351.

8   Kramrisch, *The Hindu Temple*, p. 365.

9   Kramrisch, *The Hindu Temple*, p. 165.

10   Kramrisch, *The Hindu Temple*, p. 165.

11   Vishnu S. Sukthankar (and others), editors, *Mahābhārata,* 19 vols. (Poona: Bhandarkar Oriental Research Institute, 1933–1959), 3.80. 34–38.

12   See George W. Spencer, "The Sacred Geography of the Tamil Shaivite Hymns," *Numen*, Vol. XVII.3 (December 1970), pp. 232–244. There is also an excellent unpublished paper by Indira Peterson, "Singing of a Place: Pilgrimage as Metaphor and Motif in the *Tēvāram* Songs of the Tamil Saivite Saints," presented at the Southern Asian Institute, Columbia University, March 4, 1980. I am indebted to Indira Peterson for sending me a copy of this paper.

13   These verses, respectively by Appar and Campantar, are cited in Indira Peterson, "Singing of a Place . . .," p. 7.

14   For the *līlāsthalas* of Vraj, see Charlotte Vaudeville, "Braj, Lost and Found."

15   Perhaps the most entrancing of the medieval pilgrim narratives on the *līlāsthalas* of Palestine is Felix Fabri, *The Book of the Wanderings of Brother Felix Fabri*, tr. A. Stewart, (London: Palestine Pilgrims Text Society, Vol. X, 1887–97).

16   See P. Sitapati, *Śrī Veṅkaṭeśvara, The Lord of the Seven Hills, Tirupati* (Bombay: Bharatiya Vidya Bhavan, 1972).

17   See Charlotte Vaudeville, "Paṇḍharpūr, The City of Saints," in H. Buck and G. Yocum, eds. *Structural Approaches to South India Studies* (Chambersburg, PA: Anima Publications, 1973). There is also a monograph on Paṇḍharpūr by G. A. Deleury, *The Cult of Viṭhobā* (Poona: Deccan College, 1960). Vaudeville's article, although shorter, gives a clearer picture of the complex layering of folk traditions in Paṇḍharpūr.

18   See Charlotte Vaudeville, "The Govardhan Myth in North India," part II, "The Manifestation of Śrī Govardhannāthjī in the Vallabhite Tradition," *Indo-Iranian Journal* 22 (1980).

19   See Anncharlott Eschmann, "Hinduization of Tribal Deities in Orissa: The Śākta and Śaiva Typology," and "The Vaiṣṇava Typology of Hinduization and the Origin of Jagannātha" in Eschmann, et al., eds., *The Cult of Jagannāth and the Regional Tradition of Orissa.*

20   The story of Indradyumna is told in the *Skanda Purāṇa, Vaiṣṇava Khanda, Puruṣottama Māhātmya*, chapters 18 and 19.

21   Deleury, p. 76. This particular *abhaṅga* is Tukārām's.

22   Vaudeville, " Paṇḍharpūr: City of Saints," pp. 158–159.

23   A. Bharati, "Pilgrimage Sites and Indian Civilization," in J. W. Elder, ed., *Chapters in Indian Civilization*, Vol. I (Dubuque: Kendall Hunt Publishing Company, 1970), p. 90.

24   Bhāgavata Purāṇa I.13.10. C. L. Goswami, tr., *Śrīmad Bhāgavata Mahāpurāṇa* [With Sanskrit text and English translation], (Gorakhpur: The Gita Press, 1971).

25   Julian S. Smith, *Madurai, India: The Architecture of a City* (Cambridge: M.I.T. Master of Architecture Thesis, 1976).

26   See Diana L. Eck, *Banāras, City of Light* (New York: Alfred A. Knopf, 1982), Chapter 7, "City of All India."

CONFUCIUS

I f we were to characterize in one word the Chinese way of life for the last two thousand years, the word would be "Confucian." No other individual in Chinese history has so deeply influenced the life and thought of his people, as a transmitter, teacher, and creative interpreter of the ancient culture and literature, and as a molder of the Chinese mind and character. The other ancient philosophies, the religious systems of Taoism and Buddhism, all have known their days of glory and neglect; but the doctrines of Confucianism, since their general recognition in the first century before Christ, have never ceased to exert a vital influence on the nation down to our own century. Many Chinese have professed themselves to be Taoists, Buddhists, even Christians, but seldom have they ceased at the same time to be Confucianists. For Confucianism since the time of its general acceptance has been more than a creed to be professed or rejected; it has become an inseparable part of the society and thought of the nation as a whole, of what it means to be a Chinese, as the Confucian Classics are not the canon of a particular sect but the literary heritage of a whole people.

Considering his tremendous influence and importance, the life of Confucius is peculiarly human and undramatic. He was born in 551 B.C. in the small feudal state of Lu in modern Shantung province. His family name was K'ung, his personal name Ch'iu. "Confucius" is the Latinized form of "K'ung Fu-tzu" or "Master K'ung," the title commonly used in referring to him in Chinese. It is probable that his ancestors were members of the lesser aristocracy who had, however, sunk to a position of poverty and insignificance by the time of his birth. His father died when he was very young, leaving him to struggle alone with the problem of securing an education and making his way in the world.

The world he faced was not a bright one. China was divided into a number of small feudal states which were constantly bickering or making war upon each other or upon the barbarian tribes that pressed the Chinese people on all sides. The kings of the central court of the Chou dynasty, who had once given peace and stability to the nation, were weak and ineffective before the might of the more powerful feudal lords. Kings were ordered about by their vassals, rulers deposed or assassinated by their ministers, fathers slain by their sons. All was violence and disorder among the ruling class and there seemed to be no higher power, temporal or spiritual, to which men might appeal.

With energy and utter selflessness, Confucius set about to bring order and peace to his age. He believed that his place was in the world of politics and with almost pathetic persistence he sought through the states of China for a ruler who would be willing to employ him and his ideas in the government. He managed to find employment for a while in his native state of Lu and, according to tradition, rose to a fairly high position. But his success was short-lived; on the whole his political career was a failure, and more and more he turned his attention to the teaching of young men who, he hoped, might succeed in public life where he had failed. Judging from all accounts he was a teacher of rare enthusiasm and art; he was said to have had some three thousand students, of whom seventy-two were close personal disciples or known for their virtue. In his old age he retired to devote himself, so tradition says, to the editing of the texts of the Confucian Classics. He died in 479 B.C.

What was the solution which Confucius offered for the ills and evil of his day? It was the same solution which the philosophers and prophets of so many ages and cultures have offered: a return to virtue. Unless men individually embraced the ideal of jen—humanity, benevolence, or perfect virtue—there was no hope that society could be spared the evil, cruelty, and violence that was destroying it.

If there is nothing unique or arresting about this solution urged by Confucius, the reasons he used to persuade men of its aptness deserve close attention. First of all, he held out no utilitarian persuasions to attract men to the practice of perfect virtue. He knew too well from his own experience that virtue is often despised and persecuted, and he cautioned his disciples that they must be prepared to face frequent poverty and distress. The pursuit of material profit did not coincide, but more often directly conflicted with the dictates of virtue; it was the concern only of the small and unenlightened mind. The gentleman, mindless of comfort and safety, must fix his attention upon higher things.

Again, he was very sparing in the invocation of divine or supernatural sanction for his teachings. Confucius seems to have been a man of deep personal piety and reverence. But he lived in an age that was still dominated by a primitive fear of the supernatural and marred by gross and cruel superstitions. The rulers of his time firmly believed in the prophetic nature of dreams, the efficacy of the arts of divination, the baleful power of the spirits of the dead, and all manner of weird and unnatural portents and prodigies. Men still cowered before the eclipse and the age when human sacrifices were carried out on the death of a ruler was less than a century past. In such an atmosphere, Confucius chose to direct attention away from the supernatural and toward the vital problems of human society and the ordering of the state. Viewing so much of the history of this period through the pages of the literature of the Confucian school itself, it is difficult to realize how very rare this humanism and rationalism of Confucius and his disciples must have been in their own time.

Confucius had a strong belief in a natural order that was also a moral order. Heaven for him was a guiding Providence, and one's fulfillment as a man came from acting in accordance with the will of Heaven. This will, however, could be best understood through the study of history. In the traditions, customs, and literature of the past, in the collective experience of mankind, there was objective confirmation of the moral law written in the heart of man. From the ancient legends Confucius selected the figures of the sage-kings Yao and Shun, King T'ang, the wise founder of the Shang dynasty, and above all the great ancestors of the ruling house of the Chou, Kings Wen and Wu and the Duke of Chou, to be his ideals. These men had embodied the humanity and perfect virtue that he advocated, and their deeds and their reigns represented all that was wise and good in Chinese history and society. In particular Confucius looked back to an age of peace and order at the beginning of the Chou when its founding fathers, in the depth of their wisdom and virtue, had set up the institutions and organized the complex feudal hierarchy of the new dynasty, and created solemn rites and music for its leaders and people. These rites and music-dance compositions of the old feudal society, the *li* and *yüeh* which figure so prominently in Confucian literature, were regarded by Confucius with the utmost gravity. For they were the outward embodiment of the wisdom and virtue of their creators, the expression of reverence and perfect hierarchical order in society. And by the careful observance of these rites, the thoughtful contemplation of this music and its meaning, one could recreate in oneself the wisdom and virtue of the ancients and discipline oneself to the perfect order which they had intended. All the ills of his day Confucius attributed to the fact that the leaders of society had neglected the old rites, were performing them incorrectly, or usurping rites and ceremonies to which they were not entitled. For as a correct observance of the rites was a sign of perfect social order and the source of all spiritual enlightenment, so their neglect and abuse must be no more than the reflection of a deeper moral chaos and the beginning of spiritual darkness. To abuse the forms of the rites was to abuse the reality, the moral order which they represented. It was this abuse of the rites and titles of the social order, and the inner spiritual disorder which it represented, that Confucius deplored. Hence his call for a "rectification of names," that men might be in reality what they claimed to be in title, and his insistence upon a careful and reverent attention to the spirit and letter of the rites.

This emphasis upon ritual—an insistence upon it sometimes even when its original meaning was lost—must strike us as excessively conservative and formalistic, as indeed Confucianism in its later days often became. Yet implicit in this view was an idealization of the past that set a high standard for the present, and provided more of an impetus to reform, than to maintain, the status quo. Confucius' own life is sufficient evidence of his reformist spirit. He sought to conserve or restore what was good, while changing what was bad. Thus more fundamental to him than either conservatism or reformism in itself was a clear sense of moral values, expressed in his warm humanity, optimism, humility, and good sense. Confucius lived in a feudal society and conceived of society in terms of the feudal hierarchy. The common people were to be led, cared for, cherished, even taught, by the rulers; but their position at the base of the social hierarchy should not be modified, indeed, could not be without upsetting the whole vertical order.

Confucius' teachings were for the *chün-tzu,* the gentleman, the potential or actual ruler of society who alone possessed the vision to see beyond personal profit and material interest to the broader interests of the state and mankind. Yet he insisted that it was not mere birth or social position, but precisely this power of vision, this keener and more profound moral sense, which distinguished the gentleman, the true ruler. Like Plato he would have the kings be sages, for only a truly wise and virtuous ruler could fittingly head the hierarchy of society and lead all men, by the example and suasion of his own goodness, to perfect order and a practice of similar virtue. Because of this belief in the importance of character over birth, he gave himself to the teaching of promising young men regardless of their origins. He and his school are responsible for the pedagogic tradition which characterizes all of later Chinese history, for the optimistic belief in the perfectibility of man through learning, and for the reverence for the scholar and the man of letters so pronounced in Chinese society. And it is to a large extent the teachings and example of Confucius and his school which have convinced so many of the great men of later Chinese history that the highest career in life is that of the statesman, that the highest concern of the gentleman-scholar is politics and the proper ordering of the state.

Confucius and his teachings were little respected and less practiced by the men of his day, and for centuries the Confucian school remained only one among many rival schools of philosophy with its greatest strength in the area of Confucius' native state of Lu. But gradually Confucius' humanism began to triumph over the superstition and mysticism of other doctrines, his idealistic emphasis on virtue, kindness, and learning to attract more men than the harsh and cynical philosophies of other states. At last, in the second century B.C., Confucianism was declared the official creed of the nation and the Classics became the principal, if not the sole, study of all scholars and statesmen. Through the centuries the teachings of Confucius continued not only to be revered in China, but also to exert a tremendous influence in Korea, Japan and Annam. Confucius was given the title "Supreme Sage and Foremost Teacher" and his tomb and temple in Ch'ü-fu in Shantung became a kind of Mecca for all educated Chinese, while a Confucian temple on less elaborate scale was established in every county seat throughout the land. Under the Nationalist regime his birthday was (and still is on Taiwan) observed as Teachers' Day, a national holiday.

There is a large body of literature in Chinese, of varying degrees of reliability, on the life and teachings of Confucius. Among this the most important work is the record of the Master's activities and conversations compiled probably by his disciples' disciples, the *Analects*. This work is in twenty chapters and 497 verses, some consisting of the briefest aphorisms. From the time when Confucianism became widely accepted, the laconic and provocative sentences of this work, difficult though they often are to interpret, have exercised a profound influence upon the thought and language of the peoples of East Asia, while for the last eight hundred years it has been a basic text in Chinese education known to every schoolboy. We have selected and translated the more important passages and arranged them under a few significant topics.

Selections from the ANALECTS

Confucius the Man

Personality and Character

1. In his leisure hours, Confucius was easy in his manner and cheerful in his expression. [VII:4]

2. Confucius was gentle yet firm, dignified but not harsh, respectful yet well at ease. [VII:37]

3. Confucius fished but not with a net; he shot but not at a roosting bird. [He did not take unfair advantage of inferior creatures.] [VII:26]

4. When the stables were burned down, on returning from court, Confucius asked: "Was anyone hurt?" He did not ask about the horses. [X:12]

5. When Confucius was pleased with the singing of someone he was with, he would always ask to have the song repeated and would join in himself. [VII:31]

6. The Duke of She asked Tzu Lu about Confucius, and Tzu Lu gave him no answer. Confucius said: "Why didn't you tell him that I am a person who forgets to eat when he is enthusiastic about something, forgets all his worries in his enjoyment of it, and is not aware that old age is coming on?" [VII:18]

7. Confucius said: "Having only coarse food to eat, plain water to drink, and a bent arm for a pillow, one can still find happiness therein. Riches and honor acquired by unrighteous means are to me as drifting clouds." [VII:15]

8. Once when Tzu Lu, Tseng Hsi, Jan Yu, and Kung-hsi Hua were seated in attendance upon him, Confucius said: "You no doubt consider me a day or so your senior, but let us not mind that. When out of office you say among yourselves that your merits are not recognized. Now suppose some prince were to recognize your merits, what would be your wishes?" Tzu Lu without hesitation replied: "Take a kingdom of a thousand chariots, hemmed in by great powers, oppressed by invading troops, and suffering from famine in addition—I should like to take charge of it. In three years' time I could make it brave and make it understand the right course to

150

pursue." Confucius smiled at him. "And how about you, Ch'iu [Jan Yu]?" "Take a district of sixty or seventy *li* square,"¹ answered Jan Yu, "or say, one of fifty or sixty *li* square. I should like to take charge of it. In three years' time I could make its people live in abundance; but as for the promotion of rites (*li*) and music, I should have to leave that to a real gentleman." "And how about you, Ch'ih [Kung-hsi Hua]?" "Not that I say I could do it," he answered, "but I should like to be trained for it. At the ceremonies in the Ancestral Temple [of the Imperial House] or at the conferences of the princes, I should like to wear the ceremonial cap and gown, and be a minor assisting in the ceremony." "And how about you, Tien [Tseng Hsi]?" Tseng Hsi paused in his playing of the zither. Putting it aside he rose and replied: "I am afraid my wishes are entirely different from those cherished by these three gentlemen." "What harm is there in that?" said Confucius. "We are just trying to let each express his desire." Then he said: "In the latter days of spring, when the light spring garments are made, I would like to take along five or six grown-ups and six or seven youths to bathe in the River Yi, and after the bath go to enjoy the breeze in the woods among the altars of Wu-yi, and then return home, loitering and singing on our way." Confucius heaved a deep sigh and said: "You are the man after my own heart." [XI:25]

His Sense of Mission

9. Confucius said: "Were any prince to employ me, even in a single year a good deal could be done, and in three years everything could be accomplished." [XIII:10]

10. Confucius said: "Ah! There is no one who knows me!" Tzu Kung asked: "Why do you say, sir, that no one knows you?" Confucius said: "I make no complaint against Heaven, nor do I lay the blame on men. Though my studies are lowly, they penetrate the sublime on high. Perhaps after all I am known—by Heaven." [XIV:37]

11. When Confucius was in jeopardy in K'uang, he said: "Since the death of King Wen [founder of the Chou dynasty], does not the mission of culture rest here with us? If Heaven were going to destroy this culture, a mortal like me would not have been given such a place in it. And if Heaven is not going to destroy this culture, what can the men of K'uang do to me?" [IX:5]

12. When [Confucius' most worthy disciple] Yen Hui died, Confucius exclaimed: "Alas, Heaven has destroyed me! Heaven has destroyed me!" [XI:8]

13. Ch'ang-chü and Chieh-ni were cultivating their fields together. Confucius was passing that way and told Tzu Lu to go and ask them where the river

could be forded. Ch'ang-chü said: "Who is that holding the reins in the carriage?" Tzu Lu said: "It is K'ung Ch'iu [Confucius]." He said: "You mean K'ung Ch'iu of the state of Lu?" "Yes," Tzu Lu replied. Ch'ang-chü said: "If it is he, then he already knows where the ford is." Tzu Lu then turned to Chieh-ni. Chieh-ni asked: "Who are you, sir?" Tzu Lu said: "Chung-yu is my name." Chieh-ni said: "You are a follower of K'ung Ch'iu of Lu, are you not?" He said: "That is so." Chieh-ni said: "The whole world is swept as by a torrential flood, and who can change it? As for you, instead of following one who flees from this man and that, you would do better to follow one who flees the whole world." And with that he went on covering the seed without stopping. Tzu Lu went and told Confucius, who said ruefully: "One cannot herd together with birds and beasts. If I am not to be a man among other men, then what am I to be? If the Way (*Tao*) prevailed in the world, I should not be trying to alter things." [XVIII:6]

His Love of Learning

16. Confucius said: "At fifteen, I set my heart on learning. At thirty, I was firmly established. At forty, I had no more doubts. At fifty, I knew the will of Heaven. At sixty, I was ready to listen to it. At seventy, I could follow my heart's desire without transgressing what was right."[II:4]

18. When Confucius was in Ch'i, he heard the Shao music² and for three months he forgot the taste of meat, saying: "I never thought music could be so beautiful." [VII:13]

14. Confucius said: "When walking in a party of three, I always have teachers. I can select the good qualities of the one for imitation, and the bad ones of the other and correct them in myself." [VII:21]

17. Confucius said: "I am a transmitter and not a creator. I believe in and I have a passion for the ancients. I venture to compare myself with our old P'eng [China's Methuselah]." [VII:1]

15. Confucius said: "Sometimes I have gone a whole day without food and a whole night without sleep, giving myself to thought. It was no use. It is better to learn." [XV:30]

19. There were four things that Confucius was determined to eradicate: a biased mind, arbitrary judgments, obstinacy, and egotism. [IX:4]

20. Confucius said: "Those who know the truth are not up to those who love it; those who love the truth are not up to those who delight in it." [VI:18]

21. Confucius said: "Having heard the Way (*Tao*) in the morning, one may die content in the evening." [IV:8]

Confucius as a Teacher

23. Confucius said: "By nature men are pretty much alike; it is learning and practice that set them apart."[3] [XVII:2]

22. Confucius said: "In education there are no class distinctions."[4] [XV:38]

24. Confucius said: "The young are to be respected. How do we know that the next generation will not measure up to the present one? But if a man has reached forty or fifty and nothing has been heard of him, then I grant that he is not worthy of respect." [IX:22]

25. Confucius said: "When it comes to acquiring perfect virtue (*jen*), a man should not defer even to his own teacher." [XV:35]

26. Confucius said: "Those who are born wise are the highest type of people; those who become wise through learning come next; those who learn by overcoming dullness come after that. Those who are dull but still won't learn are the lowest type of people." [XVI:9]

27. Confucius said: "I won't teach a man who is not anxious to learn, and will not explain to one who is not trying to make things clear to himself. If I hold up one corner of a square and a man cannot come back to me with the other three, I won't bother to go over the point again." [VII:8]

28. Confucius said: "Learning without thinking is labor lost; thinking without learning is perilous." [II:15]

29. Confucius said: "Yu, shall I teach you what knowledge is? When you know a thing, say that you know it; when you do not know a thing, admit that you do not know it. That is knowledge." [II:17]

30. Confucius said: "Worthy indeed was Hui! A single bamboo bowl of millet to eat, a gourdful of water to drink, living in a back alley—others would have found it unendurably depressing, but Hui's cheerfulness was not affected at all. Worthy indeed was Hui!" [VI:9]

31. When Yen Hui died Confucius bewailed him with exceeding grief. His followers thereupon said to him: "Sir! You are carrying your grief to excess." Confucius said: "Have I gone to excess? But if I may not grieve exceedingly over this man, for whom shall I grieve?" [XI:9]

32. Confucius said: "A young man's duty is to be filial to his parents at home and respectful to his elders abroad, to be circumspect and truthful, and, while overflowing with love for all men, to associate himself with humanity (*jen*). If, when all that is done, he has any energy to spare, then let him study the polite arts." [I:6]

33. These were the subjects on which Confucius often discoursed: poetry, history, and the performance of ceremonies—all these were what he often discoursed on. [VII:17]

34. Confucius said: "Personal cultivation begins with poetry, is made firm by rules of decorum (*li*), and is perfected by music." [VIII:8]

35. Confucius took four subjects for his teaching—literature, conduct, loyalty, and truthfulness. [VII:24]

36. Yen Hui heaved a sigh and said: "You look up to it and it seems so high. You try to drill through it and it seems so hard. You seem to see it in front of you, and all of a sudden it appears behind you. The Master is very good at gently leading a man along and teaching him. He has broadened me with culture, restrained me with ritual (*li*). I just could not stop myself. But after I have exhausted every resource, there still remains something standing distinct and apart from me. Do what I can to reach his position, I cannot find the way." [IX:10]

37. Shu-sun Wu-shu said to the officials at court: "Tzu Kung is a better man than Confucius." Tzu-fu Ching-po told this to Tzu Kung, and Tzu Kung said: "It is like the matter of house walls. My house wall comes up only to the shoulder, and the people outside are therefore able to see my handsome dwelling, whereas the wall of Confucius rises fathoms high, and unless one is let in by the gate, one does not see the palatial beauty of the ancestral temple and the grandeur of the hundred ministrants inside. But few are they who have found the gate. What Shu-sun says is therefore perfectly easy to understand." [XIX:23]

The Teachings of Confucius

The Unitary Principle: Reciprocity or Humanity

38. Confucius said: "Tz'u, do you suppose that I merely learned a great deal and tried to remember it all?" The disciple replied: "Yes, is it not so?" Confucius said: "No, I have one principle that runs through it all." [XV:2]

39. Confucius said: "Shen! My teaching contains one principle that runs through it all." "Yes," replied Tseng Tzu. When Confucius had left the room the disciples asked: "What did he mean?" Tseng Tzu replied: "Our Master's teaching is simply this: loyalty and reciprocity." [IV:15]

40. Tzu Kung asked: "Is there any one word that can serve as a principle for the conduct of life?" Confucius said: "Perhaps the word 'reciprocity': Do not do to others what you would not want others to do to you." [XV:23]

41. Confucius said: "Perfect indeed is the virtue which is according to the Mean. For long people have seldom had the capacity for it." [VI :27]

42. Confucius said: "It is man that can make the Way great, not the Way that can make man great." [XV:28]

43. Chung-kung asked about humanity. Confucius said: "Behave when away from home as though you were in the presence of an important guest. Deal with the common people as though you were officiating at an important sacrifice. Do not do to others what you would not want others to do to you. Then there will be no dissatisfaction either in the state or at home." [XII:2]

44. Confucius said: . . . "The humane man, desiring to be established himself, seeks to establish others; desiring himself to succeed, he helps others to succeed. To judge others by what one knows of oneself is the method of achieving humanity." [VI:28]

Humanity (jen)

As the reader will already have judged from its frequent occurrence, *jen* is a key term in Confucius' thought. Sometimes rendered "goodness," "benevolence," or "love," it is the supreme excellence in man or perfect virtue. In later Confucian thought the concept was expanded greatly to suggest a cosmic power. To retain its basically and unmistakably humanistic sense, we have used "humanity" for *jen*, or, when some alternative rendering was clearly called for by the context, have added the romanized original in parentheses (*jen*). By observing the various uses of the same term in different texts, the reader should acquire a sense of both its centrality in Chinese thought and its breadth of meaning.

45. Fan Ch'ih asked about humanity. Confucius said: "Love men." [XII:22]

46. Tzu Chang asked Confucius about humanity. Confucius said: "To be able to practice five virtues everywhere in the world constitutes humanity." Tzu Chang begged to know what these were. Confucius said: "Courtesy, magnanimity, good faith, diligence, and kindness. He who is courteous is not humiliated, he who is magnanimous wins the multitude, he who is of good faith is trusted by the people, he who is diligent attains his objective, and he who is kind can get service from the people." [XVII:6]

47. Confucius said: "Without humanity a man cannot long endure adversity, nor can he long enjoy prosperity. The humane rest in humanity; the wise find it beneficial." [IV:2]

48. Confucius said: "Only the humane man can love men and can hate men." [IV:3]

49. Someone inquired: "What do you think of 'requiting injury with kindness'?" Confucius said: "How will you then requite kindness? Requite injury with justice, and kindness with kindness." [XIV:36]

50. Confucius said: "Is humanity something remote? If I want to be humane, behold, humanity has arrived." [VII:29]

51. Confucius said: . . . "Is there anyone who exerts himself even for a single day to achieve humanity? I have not seen any who had not the strength to achieve it." [IV:6]

52. Confucius said: "As to Hui, for three months his mind did not deviate from humanity. The others can do so, some for a day, some even for a month, but that is all." [VI:5]

53. Confucius said: "Riches and honor are what every man desires, but if they can be obtained only by transgressing the right way, they must not be held. Poverty and lowliness are what every man detests, but if they can be avoided only by transgressing the right way, they must not be evaded. If a gentleman departs from humanity, how can he bear the name? Not even for the lapse of a single meal does a gentleman ignore humanity. In moments of haste he cleaves to it: in seasons of peril he cleaves to it." [IV:5]

54. Confucius said: "The resolute scholar and the humane person will under no circumstance seek life at the expense of humanity. On occasion they will sacrifice their lives to preserve their humanity." [XV:8]

55. Ssu-ma Niu, worrying, said: "All people have brothers, but I alone have none." Tzu Hsia said: "I have heard it said [by Confucius] that death and life rest with Heaven's mandate and that wealth and honor depend on Heaven. Let the gentleman be reverent and make no mistake in conduct, and let him be respectful to others and observant of propriety. Then all within the four seas are brothers." [XII:5]

Filial Piety

56. Tzu Yu asked about filial piety. Confucius said: "Nowadays a filial son is just a man who keeps his parents in food. But even dogs or horses are given food. If there is no feeling of reverence, wherein lies the difference?" [II:7]

57. Tzu Hsia asked about filial piety. Confucius said: "The manner is the really difficult thing. When anything has to be done the young people undertake it; when there is wine and food the elders are served —is this all there is to filial piety?" [II:8]

58. Confucius said: "In serving his parents, a son may gently remonstrate with them. If he sees that they are not inclined to follow his suggestion, he

should resume his reverential attitude but not abandon his purpose. If he is belabored, he will not complain." [IV:18]

59. The Duke of She observed to Confucius: "Among us there was an upright man called Kung who was so upright that when his father appropriated a sheep, he bore witness against him." Confucius said: "The upright men among us are not like that. A father will screen his son and a son his father—yet uprightness is to be found in that." [XIII:18]

60. Tsai Wo questioned the three years' mourning and thought one year was long enough: "If the gentlemen for three years abstain from the practice of ritual, ritual will decay; if for three years they make no music, music will go to ruin. In one year the old crops are exhausted and the new crops have come up, the friction-sticks have made the several seasonal fires— one year should be enough." Confucius said: "Would you then feel at ease in eating polished rice and wearing fineries?" "Quite at ease," was the reply. Confucius continued: "If you would really feel at ease, then do so. When a gentleman is in mourning, he does not relish good food if he eats it, does not enjoy music if he hears it, and does not feel at ease in a comfortable dwelling. Hence he abstains from these things. But now since you would feel at ease, then you can have them." When Tsai Wo had gone out, Confucius said: "What lack of humanity in Yü [Tsai Wo]! Only when a child is three years old does it leave its parents' arms. The three years' mourning is the universal observance in the world. And Yü—did he not enjoy the loving care of his parents for three years?" [XVII:21]

Rites and Music

For Confucius the term *li*, which basically means "rites," embraced all those traditional forms which provided an objective standard of conduct. Thus, while *li* may in given instances refer to "rites," "ceremonial," or "rules of conduct," it has the general meaning of "good form" or "decorum." Confucius insisted, however, that the observance of *li* should be neither perfunctory nor rigid and inflexible, but should be in keeping with circumstances and also with that spirit of reverence and respect for others which the ceremonies or rules of conduct were meant to embody. By showing their intrinsic significance, he attempted to reassert the value of these traditional forms at a time when they were increasingly neglected or performed as mere pretense. Where the external form is indicated by *li* we shall render it "rites"; where the inward spirit, "decorum."

61. Tzu Kung proposed to do away with the sacrificial lamb offering at the announcement of each new moon. Confucius said: "Tz'u! You love the lamb, but I love the rite." [III:17]

62. Confucius said: "Courtesy without decorum becomes tiresome. Cautiousness without decorum becomes timidity, daring becomes insubordination, frankness becomes effrontery." [VIII:2]

63. Confucius said: "Rites, rites! Does it mean no more than jades and silks? Music, music! Does it mean no more than bells and drums?" [XVII:11]

64. Confucius said: "A man who is not humane, what has he to do with rites? A man who is not humane, what has he to do with music?" [III:3]

65. Lin Fang asked about the fundamental principle of rites. Confucius replied: "You are asking an important question! In rites at large, it is always better to be too simple rather than too lavish. In funeral rites, it is more important to have the real sentiment of sorrow than minute attention to observances." [III:4]

66. Confucius said: "If a ruler can administer his state with decorum (*li*) and courtesy—then what difficulty will he have? If he cannot administer it with decorum and courtesy, what has he to do with rites (*li*)?" [IV:13]

Religious Sentiment

67. Tzu Lu asked about the worship of ghosts and spirits. Confucius said: "We don't know yet how to serve men, how can we know about serving the spirits?" "What about death," was the next question. Confucius said: "We don't know yet about life, how can we know about death?" [XI:11]

68. Fan Ch'ih asked about wisdom. Confucius said: "Devote yourself to the proper demands of the people, respect the ghosts and spirits but keep them at a distance—this may be called wisdom." [VI:20]

69. Po-niu was ill and Confucius went to inquire about him. Having grasped his hand through the window, Confucius said: "It is killing him. It is the will of Heaven, alas! That such a man should have such a malady! That such a man should have such a malady!" [VI:8]

70. Though his food might be coarse rice and vegetable broth, Confucius invariably offered a little in sacrifice, and always with solemnity. [X:8]

71. When Confucius observed sacrificial fasting, his clothing was spotlessly clean, his food was different from the ordinary, and in his dwelling his seat was changed to another place. [X:7]

72. Confucius said: "He who sins against Heaven has none to whom he can pray." [III:13]

73. When Confucius was very ill, Tzu Lu asked that prayers be offered. Confucius asked: "Is there such a thing?" Tzu Lu replied: "Yes, there is. In one of the Eulogies it is said: 'A prayer has been offered for you to the spirits of Heaven and earth.'" Confucius said: "Ah, my praying has been for a long time." [VII:34]

74. Tzu Kung said: "The Master's views on culture and refinement we can comprehend. But his discourses about man's nature and the ways of Heaven none of us can comprehend." [V:12]

75. Confucius said: "I wish I did not have to speak at all." Tzu Kung said: "But if you did not speak, Sir, what should we disciples pass on to others?" Confucius said: "Look at Heaven there. Does it speak? The four seasons run their course and all things are produced. Does Heaven speak?" [XVII:19]

76. Confucius sacrificed [to the dead] as if they were present. He sacrificed to the spirits as if they were present. He said: "I consider my not being present at the sacrifice as if I did not sacrifice." [III:12]

77. The Master did not talk about weird things, physical exploits, disorders, and spirits. [VII:20]

The Gentleman

78. Confucius said: "When nature exceeds art you have the rustic. When art exceeds nature you have the clerk. It is only when art and nature are harmoniously blended that you have the gentleman." [VI:16]

79. Confucius said: . . . "If a gentleman departs from humanity, how can he bear the name? Not even for the lapse of a single meal does a gentleman ignore humanity. In moments of haste he cleaves to it; in seasons of peril he cleaves to it." [IV:5]

80. Confucius said: "The gentleman occupies himself with the Way and not with his livelihood. One may attend to farming, and yet may sometimes go hungry. One may attend to learning and yet may be rewarded with emolument. What the gentleman is anxious about is the Way and not poverty." [XV:31]

81. Ssu-ma Niu asked about the gentlemen. Confucius said: "The gentleman has neither anxiety nor fear." Ssu-ma Niu rejoined: "Neither anxiety nor fear—is that what is meant by being a gentleman?" Confucius said: "When he looks into himself and finds no cause for self reproach, what has he to be anxious about; what has he to fear?" [XII:4]

82. Confucius said: "The way of the gentleman is threefold. I myself have not

been able to attain any of them. Being humane, he has no anxieties; being wise, he has no perplexities; being brave, he has no fear." Tzu Kung said: "But, Master, that is your own way." [XIV:30]

83. Confucius said: "You may be able to carry off from a whole army its commander-in-chief, but you cannot deprive the humblest individual of his will." [IX:25]

84. Tzu Kung asked about the gentleman. Confucius said: "The gentleman first practices what he preaches and then preaches what he practices." [II:13]

85. Confucius said: "The gentleman reaches upward; the inferior man reaches downward." [XIV:23]

86. Confucius said: "The gentleman is always calm and at ease; the inferior man is always worried and full of distress." [VII:36]

87. Confucius said: "The gentleman understands what is right; the inferior man understands what is profitable." [IV:16]

88. Confucius said: "The gentleman cherishes virtue; the inferior man cherishes possessions. The gentleman thinks of sanctions; the inferior man thinks of personal favors." [IV:11]

89. Confucius said: "The gentleman makes demands on himself; the inferior man makes demands on others." [XV:20]

90. Confucius said: "The gentleman seeks to enable people to succeed in what is good but does not help them in what is evil. The inferior man does the contrary." [XII:16]

91. Confucius said: "The gentleman is broad-minded and not partisan; the inferior man is partisan and not broad-minded." [II:14]

92. Confucius said: "There are three things that a gentleman fears: he fears the will of Heaven, he fears great men, he fears the words of the sages. The inferior man does not know the will of Heaven and does not fear it, he treats great men with contempt, and he scoffs at the words of the sages." [XVI:8]

93. Once when Confucius was in Ch'en, the supply of food was exhausted, and some of his followers became so weak that they could not stand up. Tzu Lu came to the Master in disgust, saying: "Then even a gentleman can be reduced to such straits?" Confucius said: "A gentleman may indeed be so reduced. But when an inferior man is in straits he is apt to do anything." [XV:1]

Government by Personal Virtue

94. Chi K'ang Tzu asked Confucius about government. Confucius said: "To govern (*cheng*) is to set things right (*cheng*).⁵ If you begin by setting yourself right, who will dare to deviate from the right?" [XII:17]

95. Confucius said: "If a ruler himself is upright, all will go well without orders. But if he himself is not upright, even though he gives orders they will not be obeyed." [XIII:6]

96. Tzu Lu asked about the character of a gentleman [man of the ruling class]. Confucius said: "He cultivates himself in reverential attention. Tzu Lu asked: "Is that all there is to it?" Confucius said: "He cultivates himself so as to be able to bring comfort to other people." Tzu Lu asked again: "Is that all?" Confucius said: "He cultivates himself so as to be able to bring comfort to the whole populace. He cultivates himself so as to be able to bring comfort to the whole populace—even [sage-kings] Yao and Shun were dissatisfied with themselves about this." [XIV:45]

97. Confucius said: "Lead the people by laws and regulate them by penalties, and the people will try to keep out of jail, but will have no sense of shame. Lead the people by virtue and restrain them by the rules of decorum, and the people will have a sense of shame, and moreover will become good." [II:3]

98. Chi K'ang Tzu asked Confucius about government, saying: "Suppose I were to kill the lawless for the good of the law-abiding, how would that do?" Confucius answered: "Sir, why should it be necessary to employ capital punishment in your government? Just so you genuinely desire the good, the people will be good. The virtue of the gentleman may be compared to the wind and that of the commoner to the weeds. The weeds under the force of the wind cannot but bend." [XII:19]

99. The Duke of She asked about good government. Confucius said: "[A government is good when] those near are happy and those far off are attracted." [XIII:16]

100. When Confucius was traveling to Wei, Jan Yu drove him. Confucius observed: "What a dense population!" Jan Yu said: "The people having grown so numerous, what next should be done for them?" "Enrich them," was the reply. "And when one has enriched them, what next should be done?" Confucius said: "Educate them." [XIII:9]

101. Tzu Kung asked about government. Confucius said: "The essentials are sufficient food, sufficient troops, and the confidence of the people." Tzu Kung said: "Suppose you were forced to give up one of these three, which would

you let go first?" Confucius said: "The troops." Tzu Kung asked again: "If you are forced to give up one of the two remaining, which would you let go?" Confucius said: "Food. For from of old, death has been the lot of all men, but a people without faith cannot survive." [XII:7]

102. Duke Ching of Ch'i asked Confucius about government. Confucius replied: "Let the prince be prince, the minister be minister, the father father and the son son." "Excellent!" said the duke. "Indeed if the prince is not prince, the minister not minister, the father not father, and the son not son, then with all the grain in my possession shall I ever get to eat any?"[6] [XII:11]

103. Confucius said: "To have done nothing (*wu-wei*) and yet have the state well-governed—[sage-king] Shun was the one! What did he do? He merely made himself reverent and correctly occupied his royal seat." [XV:4]

Notes

[1]   A *li* is equal to about one-third of an English mile.
[2]   Classical music of the time of the ancient sage-king Shun (2255–2208 B.C.?).
[3]   This simple observation by Confucius was agreed upon as the essential truth with regard to human nature and racial difference by a group of international experts in the UNESCO "Statement on Race" published in July, 1950.
[4]   These four Chinese characters are often found written over the gates or on the auditorium walls of Chinese school buildings.
[5]   This is more than just a pun. Confucius was trying to get at the root of the matter by getting at the root of the word.
[6]   For then the country will be ruined.

CHAIRMAN MAO ZEDONG

QUOTATIONS

I. The Communist Party

The force at the core leading our cause forward is the Chinese Communist Party.
The theoretical basis guiding our thinking is Marxism-Leninism.

> Opening address at the First Session of the First
> National People's Congress of the People's Re-
> public of China (September 15, 1954).

If there is to be revolution, there must be a revolutionary party. Without a
revolutionary party, without a party built on the Marxist-Leninist revolutionary theory and in the Marxist-Leninist revolutionary style, it is impossible to
lead the working class and the broad masses of the people in defeating imperialism and its running dogs.

> "Revolutionary Forces of the World Unite,
> Fight Against Imperialist Aggression!" (Novem-
> ber 1948), *Selected Works*, Vol. IV, p. 284.

Without the efforts of the Chinese Communist Party, without the Chinese
Communists as the mainstay of the Chinese people, China can never achieve
independence and liberation, or industrialization and the modernization of
her agriculture.

> "On Coalition Government" (April 24, 1945),
> *Selected Works*, Vol. III, p. 318.

The Chinese Communist Party is the core of leadership of the whole Chinese
people. Without this core, the cause of socialism cannot be victorious.

> Talk at the general reception for the delegates
> to the Third National Congress of the New
> Democratic Youth League of China (May 25,
> 1957).

A well-disciplined Party armed with the theory of Marxism-Leninism, using the method of self-criticism and linked with the masses of the people; an army under the leadership of such a Party; a united front of all revolutionary classes and all revolutionary groups under the leadership of such a Party—these are the three main weapons with which we have defeated the enemy.

> "On the People's Democratic Dictatorship"
> (June 30, 1949). *Selected Works*, Vol. IV, p. 422.

We must have faith in the masses and we must have faith in the Party. These are two cardinal principles. If we doubt these principles, we shall accomplish nothing.

> *On the Question of Agricultural Cooperation*
> (July 31, 1955), 3rd ed., p. 7.

Armed with Marxist-Leninist theory and ideology, the Communist Party of China has brought a new style of work to the Chinese people, a style of work which essentially entails integrating theory with practice, forging close links with the masses and practicing self-criticism.

> "On Coalition Government" (April 24, 1945),
> *Selected Works*, Vol. III, p. 314.

No political party can possibly lead a great revolutionary movement to victory unless it possesses revolutionary theory and a knowledge of history and has a profound grasp of the practical movement.

> "The Role of the Chinese Communist Party in
> the National War" (October 1938), *Selected
> Works*, Vol. II, p. 208.

As we used to say, the rectification movement is "a widespread movement of Marxist education". Rectification means the whole Party studying Marxism through criticism and self-criticism. We can certainly learn more about Marxism in the course of the rectification movement.

> *Speech at the Chinese Communist Party's National
> Conference on Propaganda Work* (March 12,
> 1957), 1st pocket ed., p. 14.

It is an arduous task to ensure a better life for the several hundred million people of China and to build our economically and culturally backward country into a prosperous and powerful one with a high level of culture. And it is precisely in order to be able to shoulder this task more competently and work better together with all non-Party people who are actuated by high ideals and determined to institute reforms that we must conduct rectification movements both now and in the future, and constantly rid ourselves of whatever is wrong.

Ibid., pp. 15–16.

Policy is the starting-point of all the practical actions of a revolutionary party and manifests itself in the process and the end-result of that party's actions. A revolutionary party is carrying out a policy whenever it takes any action. If it is not carrying out a correct policy, it is carrying out a wrong policy; if it is not carrying out a given policy consciously, it is doing so blindly. What we call experience is the process and the end-result of carrying out a policy. Only through the practice of the people, that is, through experience, can we verify whether a policy is correct or wrong and determine to what extent it is correct or wrong. But people's practice, especially the practice of a revolutionary party and the revolutionary masses, cannot but be bound up with one policy or another. Therefore, before any action is taken, we must explain the policy, which we have formulated in the light of the given circumstances, to Party members and to the masses. Otherwise, Party members and the masses will depart from the guidance of our policy act blindly and carry out a wrong policy.

"On the Policy Concerning Industry and Commerce" (February 27, 1948), *Selected Works*, Vol. IV, pp. 204–05.

Our Party has laid down the general line and general policy of the Chinese revolution as well as various specific lines for work and specific policies. However, while many comrades remember our Party's specific lines for work and specific policies, they often forget its general line and general policy. If we actually forget the Party's general line and general policy, then we shall be blind, half-baked, muddle-headed revolutionaries, and when we carry out a specific line for work and a specific policy, we shall lose our bearings and vacillate now to the left and now to the right, and the work will suffer.

"Speech at a Conference of Cadres in Shansi-Suiyuan Liberated Area" (April 1, 1948), *Selected Works*, Vol. IV, p. 238.

Policy and tactics are the life of the Party; leading comrades at all levels must give them full attention and must never on any account be negligent.

> "A Circular on the Situation" (March 20, 1948), *Selected Works*, Vol. IV, p. 220.

II. Classes and Class Struggle

Classes struggle, some classes triumph, others are eliminated. Such is history, such is the history of civilization for thousands of years. To interpret history from this viewpoint is historical materialism; standing in opposition to this viewpoint is historical idealism.

> "Cast Away Illusions, Prepare for Struggle (August 14, 1949), *Selected Works*, Vol. IV, p. 428.

In class society everyone lives as a member of a particular class, and every kind of thinking, without exception, is stamped with the brand of a class.

> "On Practice" (July 1937), *Selected Works*, Vol. I, p. 296.

Changes in society are due chiefly to the development of the internal contradictions in society, that is, the contradiction between the productive forces and the relations of production, the contradiction between classes and the contradiction between the old and the new; it is the development of these contradictions that pushes society forward and gives the impetus for the suppression of the old society by the new.

> "On Contradiction" (August 1937), *Selected Works*, Vol. I, p. 314.

The ruthless economic exploitation and political oppression of the peasants by the landlord class forced them into numerous uprisings against its rule. . . . It was the class struggles of the peasants, the peasant uprisings and peasant wars that constituted the real motive force of historical development in Chinese feudal society.

> "The Chinese Revolution and the Chinese Communist Party" (December 1939), *Selected Works*, Vol. II, p. 308.)

In the final analysis, national struggle is a matter of class struggle. Among the whites in the United States it is only the reactionary ruling circles who oppress the black people. They can in no way represent the workers, farmers, revolutionary intellectuals and other enlightened persons who comprise the overwhelming majority of the white people.

> "Statement Supporting the American Negroes in Their Just Struggle Against Racial Discrimination by U.S. Imperialism" (August 8, 1963), *People of the World, Unite and Defeat the U.S. Aggressors and All Their Lackeys,* 2nd ed., pp. 3–4.

It is up to us to organize the people. As for the reactionaries in China, it is up to us to organize the people to overthrow them. Everything reactionary is the same; if you don't hit it, it won't fall. This is also like sweeping the floor; as a rule, where the broom does not reach, the dust will not vanish of itself.

> "The Situation and Our Policy After the Victory in the War of Resistance Against Japan" (August 13, 1945), *Selected Works,* Vol. IV, p. 19.

The enemy will not perish of himself. Neither the Chinese reactionaries nor the aggressive forces of U.S. imperialism in China will step down from the stage of history of their own accord.

> "Carry the Revolution Through to the End" (December 30, 1948), *Selected Works,* Vol. IV, p. 301.

A revolution is not a dinner party, or writing an essay, or painting a picture, or doing embroidery; it cannot be so refined, so leisurely and gentle, so temperate, kind, courteous, restrained and magnanimous. A revolution is an insurrection, an act of violence by which one class overthrows another.

> "Report on an Investigation of the Peasant Movement in Hunan" (March 1927), *Selected Works,* Vol. I, p. 28.

Chiang Kai-shek always tries to wrest every ounce of power and every ounce of gain from the people. And we? Our policy is to give him tit for tat and to fight for every inch of land. We act after his fashion. He always tries to impose war on the people, one sword in his left hand and another in his right. We take up swords, too, following his example. . . . As Chiang Kai-shek is now sharpening his swords, we must sharpen ours too.

> ""The Situation and Our Policy After the Victory in the War of Resistance Against Japan" (August 13, 1945), *Selected Works,* Vol. IV, pp. 14–15.

Who are our enemies? Who are our friends? This is a question of the first importance for the revolution. The basic reason why all previous revolutionary struggles in China achieved so little was their failure to unite with real friends in order to attack real enemies. A revolutionary party is the guide of the masses, and no revolution ever succeeds when the revolutionary party leads them astray. To ensure that we will definitely achieve success in our revolution and will not lead the masses astray, we must pay attention to uniting with our real friends in order to attack our real enemies. To distinguish real friends from real enemies, we must make a general analysis of the economic status of the various classes in Chinese society and of their respective attitudes towards the revolution.

> "Analysis of the Classes in Chinese Society" (March 1926), *Selected Works,* Vol. I, p. 13.

Our enemies are all those in league with imperialism—the warlords, the bureaucrats, the comprador class, the big landlord class and the reactionary section of the intelligentsia attached to them. The leading force in our revolution is the industrial proletariat. Our closest friends are the entire semi-proletariat and petty bourgeoisie. As for the vacillating middle bourgeoisie, their right-wing may become our enemy and their left-wing may become our friend—but we must be constantly on our guard and not let them create confusion within our ranks.

> Ibid., p. 19.

Whoever sides with the revolutionary people is a revolutionary. Whoever sides with imperialism, feudalism and bureaucrat-capitalism, is a counter-revolutionary. Whoever sides with the revolutionary people in words only but acts otherwise is a revolutionary in speech. Whoever sides with the revolutionary people in deed as well as in word is a revolutionary in the full sense.

> Closing speech at the Second Session of the First National Committee of the Chinese People's Political Consultative Conference (June 23, 1950).

I hold that it is bad as far as we are concerned if a person, a political party, an army or a school is not attacked by the enemy, for in that case it would definitely mean that we have sunk to the level of the enemy. It is good if we are attacked by the enemy, since it proves that we have drawn a clear line of demarcation between the enemy and ourselves. It is still better if the enemy attacks us wildly and paints us as utterly black and without a single virtue; it demonstrates that we have not only drawn a clear line of demarcation between the enemy and ourselves but achieved a great deal in our work.

> *To Be Attacked by the Enemy Is Not a Bad Thing but a Good Thing* (May 26, 1939), 1st pocket ed., p. 2.

We should support whatever the enemy opposes and oppose whatever the enemy supports.

> "Interview with Three Correspondents from the Central News Agency, the *Sao Tang Pao* and the *Hsin Min Pao*" (September 16, 1939), *Selected Works*, Vol. II p. 272.

Our stand is that of the proletariat and of the masses. For members of the Communist Party, this means keeping to the stand of the Party, keeping to Party spirit and Party policy.

> "Talks at the Yenan Forum on Literature and Art" (May 1942), *Selected Works*, Vol. III, p. 70.

After the enemies with guns have been wiped out, there will still be enemies without guns; they are bound to struggle desperately against us, and we must never regard these enemies lightly. If we do not now raise and understand the problem in this way, we shall commit the gravest mistakes.

"Report to the Second Plenary Session of the Seventh Central Committee of the Communist Party of China" (March 5, 1949), *Selected Works*, Vol. IV, p. 364.

The imperialists and domestic reactionaries will certainly not take their defeat lying down and they will struggle to the last ditch. After there is peace and order throughout the country, they will still engage in sabotage and create disturbances in various ways and will try every day and every minute to stage a come-back. This is inevitable and beyond all doubt, and under no circumstances must we relax our vigilance.

Opening address at the First Plenary Session of the Chinese People's Political Consultative Conference (September 21, 1949).

STRATEGIC PROBLEMS OF CHINA'S REVOLUTIONARY WAR

Mao Zedong

Mao Zedong (1893–1976) was born into a well-to-do peasant family in Hunan province and as a university student participated in the anti-Manchu revolution of 1911. During the next several years, while serving as a library assistant at Peking University, he was converted to Marxism and became one of the first members of the Chinese Communist party. Originally given responsibility for organizing urban labor unions, Mao gradually concluded that in China the peasants, a class whose capacity for revolution was discounted by orthodox Marxist-Leninists, would be the force to lead China to socialism. In 1927 he summarized his ideas in his "Report on an Investigation of the Peasant Movement in Hunan."

After the break from the Kuomintang, Mao established his small army in the remote and hilly region on the Hunan-Kiangsi border, where in 1931 he proclaimed the Chinese Soviet Republic. In 1934 Chiang Kai-shek's troops surrounded Mao's forces, but over 100,000 Communist troops and officials broke out of the Kuomintang encirclement and embarked on the LongMarch. This legendary trek lasted more than a year and covered 6,000 miles before a small remnant found safety in the distant mountains of Kansu province. Here Mao established unchallenged control over the party, rebuilt his army, and readied himself and his followers for what would be fourteen more years of struggle against the Japanese and the Kuomintang.

In 1936 Mao explained how this struggle was to be won in a series of lectures presented to the Red Army College and subsequently published under the Strategic Problems of China's Revolutionary War. *The following excerpts summarize Mao's basic ideas.*

The Chinese Communist Party and China's Revolutionary War

The chief enemies in China's revolutionary war are imperialism and the feudal forces. Although the Chinese bourgeoisie may take part in the revolutionary war on certain historical occasions, yet owing to its selfish character and its lack of political and economic independence, it is neither willing nor able to lead China's revolutionary war to complete victory. The masses of the Chinese peasantry and of the urban petty bourgeoisie are willing to take part actively in the revolutionary war and to bring about its complete victory. They are the main forces in the revolutionary war, yet small-scale production, which is their characteristic and limits their political outlook, renders them unable to give correct leadership in the war. Thus, in an era when the proletariat has already appeared on the political stage, the responsibility of leadership in China's revolutionary war inevitably falls on the shoulders of the Chinese Communist Party. At such a time any revolutionary war will certainly end in defeat if the leadership of the proletariat and the Communist Party is lacking or is forsaken. For of all the social strata and political groups in semicolonial China only the proletariat and the Communist Party are the most open-minded and unselfish, possess the most farsighted political outlook and the highest organizational quality, and are also the readiest to learn with an open mind from the experiences of the advanced proletariat of the world and its parties as well as to apply what they have learned in their own undertaking. . . .

Characteristics of China's Revolutionary War

1. The Importance of the Subject

People who will not admit, who do not know, or who do not care to know that China's revolutionary war has its own characteristics have treated the war waged by the Red Army against the Kuomintang forces as similar in nature to wars in general or the civil war in the Soviet Union.[1] The experience of the civil war in the Soviet Union directed by Lenin and Stalin has indeed a worldwide significance. All Communist Parties, including the Chinese Communist Party, regard this experience and its theoretical summing-up by Lenin and Stalin as their guiding compass. Yet this does not mean that we are to make use of this experience mechanically under our own conditions. China's revolutionary war is distinguished by many characteristics from the civil war in the Soviet Union. Failure to reckon with these characteristics or denial of them is of course erroneous. This point has been fully proved in the ten years of our war. . . .

2. What Are the Characteristics of China's Revolutionary War?

What then are the characteristics of China's revolutionary war?

I think there are four.

The first is that China is a vast semicolonial country which is unevenly developed both politically and economically. . . .

The unevenness of political and economic development in China—the coexistence of a frail capitalist economy and a preponderant semi-feudal economy; the coexistence of a few modern industrial and commercial cities and the boundless expanses of stagnant rural districts; the coexistence of several millions of industrial workers on the one hand and, on the other, hundreds of millions of peasants and handicraftsmen under the old regime; the coexistence of big warlords controlling the Central government and small warlords controlling the provinces; the coexistence of two kinds of reactionary armies, i.e., the so-called Central army under Chiang Kai-shek and the troops of miscellaneous brands under the warlords in the provinces; and the coexistence of a few railway and steamship lines and motor roads on the one hand and, on the other, the vast number of wheel-barrow paths and trails for pedestrians only, many of which are even difficult for them to negotiate. . . .

The second characteristic is the great strength of the enemy.

What is the situation of the Kuomintang, the enemy of the Red Army? It is a party that has seized political power and has relatively stabilized it. It has gained the support of the principal counter-revolutionary countries in the world. It has remodeled its army, which has thus become different from any other army in Chinese history and on the whole similar to the armies of the modern states in the world; its army is supplied much more abundantly with arms and other equipment than the Red Army, and is greater in numerical strength than any army in Chinese history, even than the standing army of any country in the world. . . .

The Chinese Red Army is confronted with such a powerful enemy. This is the second characteristic of China's revolutionary war. This characteristic inevitably makes the war waged by the Red Army different in many ways from wars in general, from the civil war in the Soviet Union and from the Northern Expedition.[2]

The third characteristic is that the Red Army is weak and small. . . .

Our political power is dispersed and isolated in mountainous or remote regions, and is deprived of any outside help. In economic and cultural conditions the revolutionary base areas are more backward than the Kuomintang areas. The revolutionary bases embrace only rural districts and small towns. They were extremely small in the beginning and have not grown much larger since. Moreover, they are often shifted and the Red Army possesses no really consolidated bases. . . .

The fourth characteristic is the Communist Party's leadership and the agrarian revolution.

This characteristic is the inevitable result of the first one. It gives rise to the following two features. On the one hand, China's revolutionary war, though taking place in a period of reaction in China and throughout the capitalist world, can yet be victorious because it is led by the Communist Party and supported by the peasantry. Because we have secured the support of the peasantry, our base areas, though small, possess great political power and stand firmly opposed to the political power of the Kuomintang which encompasses a vast area; in a military sense this creates colossal difficulties for the attacking Kuomintang troops. The Red Army, though small, has great fighting capacity, because its men under the leadership of the Communist Party have sprung from the agrarian revolution and are fighting for their own interests, and because officers and men are politically united.

On the other hand, our situation contrasts sharply with that of the Kuomintang. Opposed to the agrarian revolution, the Kuomintang is deprived of the support of the peasantry. Despite the great size of its army it cannot arouse the bulk of the soldiers or many of the lower-rank officers, who used to be small producers, to risk their lives voluntarily for its sake. Officers and men are politically disunited and this reduces its fighting capacity. . . .

Strategic Defensive

Military experts of new and rapidly developing imperialist countries like Germany and Japan positively boast of the advantages of strategic offensive and condemn strategic defensive; Such an idea is fundamentally unsuitable for China's revolutionary war. Such military experts point out that the great shortcoming of defense lies in the fact that, instead of gingering up the people, it demoralizes them. But that applies only to countries where class contradictions are sharp and the war benefits only the reactionary ruling strata or the reactionary groups in power. Our case is different. Under the slogan of safeguarding the revolutionary base areas and safeguarding China, we can rally the greatest majority of the people to fight single-mindedly, because we are the victims of oppression and aggression. The Red Army of the Soviet Union defeated its enemies also by defensive warfare during the civil war. It not only carried on the war under the slogan of defending the Soviets when the imperialist powers organized the Whites[3] for an onslaught, but also carried out military mobilization under the slogan of defending the capital when the October Uprising was being prepared. Defensive battles in a just war can not only exercise a lulling influence on the politically alien elements but mobilize the backward sections of the masses to join in the war.

When Marx said that once an armed uprising is started there must not be a moment's pause in the attack, he meant that the masses, having taken the enemy by surprise in an uprising, must not allow the reactionary ruling classes any chance to retain or recover their political power, but must seize this moment to spring a surprise attack on the nation's reactionary ruling forces, and that they must never feel satisfied with the victories they have won, underrate the enemy, relent in their attacks on the enemy, or hesitate to go forward so as to miss the chance of annihilating the enemy and court failure for the revolution. This is correct. This does not mean, however, that we revolutionaries should not adopt defensive measures even when we are already locked in a battle with an enemy stronger than ourselves and are hard pressed by him. Anyone who thinks so would be a prize idiot.

Our past war was on the whole an offensive against the Kuomintang, though militarily it assumed the form of smashing the enemy's campaigns of "encirclement and annihilation."

In military terms, our warfare consists in the alternate adoption of the defensive and the offensive. It makes no difference to us whether our offensive is regarded as following the defensive or preceding it, because the turning-point comes when we smash the campaigns of "encirclement and annihilation." It remains a defensive until a campaign of "encirclement and annihilation" is smashed, and then it immediately begins as an offensive; they are but two phases of the same thing, as one campaign of "encirclement and annihilation" of the enemy is closely followed by another. Of the two phases, the defensive phase is more complicated and more important than the offensive phase. It involves numerous problems of how to smash the campaign of "encirclement and annihilation." The basic principle is for active defense and against passive defense.

In the civil war, when the Red Army surpasses the enemy in strength, there will no longer be any use for strategic defensive in general. Then our only directive will be strategic offensive. Such a change depends on an overall change in the relative strength of the enemy and ourselves. The only defensive measures that remain will be of a partial character.

Notes

[1]   The reference is to the postrevolutionary struggle between the Bolsheviks and their opponents from 1917 to 1921.

[2]   The military campaign the Kuomintang pursued between 1926 and 1928 to break the hold of the warlords on central north China.

[3]   In the Russian civil war, the opponents of the "Reds," or Bolsheviks.

CHAIRMAN MAO DISCUSSES EDUCATION

Mao Tse-Tung

(February 13, 1964)

Talks with Party Leaders at Spring Festival Concerning Educational Work

"Today I want to talk to you about education. Today industry has made great progress and I believe that education should also have some reforms. However, education as it now is still leaves much to be desired.

"Period of schooling may be shortened.

"[The Government] may organize a women's militia or women's corps so that girls sixteen or seventeen years of age may experience a military life for six months to one year. I think those seventeen-year-olds may also serve in the Army.

"There are at present too many curricula that drive people to death. Students at primary and middle schools and colleges are living in a tense environment everyday. Their eyes are getting more near-sighted day by day because the school facilities are bad; lighting conditions are poor.

"Curricula may be reduced by half. It won't do to have students having no cultural recreation, such as swimming and sports.

"Historically, the highest graduates of the Hanlin Academy were not very outstanding. Li Pai and Tu Fu were neither Chinshih nor Hanlin. Han Yu and Liu Chung-yuan were only second degree Chinshih. Wang Shih-fu, Kuan Han-ching, Lo Kuan-chung, Pu Sung-ling and Chao Hsueh-chin were neither Chinshih nor Hanlin. All those who were awarded the degrees of Chinshih or Hanlin did not succeed.

"Among the emperors of the Ming Dynasty, only Ming Tai Chu (accession 1368 A.D.) and Ming Cheng Chu (accession 1403 A.D.) were successful. One of them could not read and the other could read only a few words. Later in the reign of Chia Ching (1522–1566 A.D.), intellectuals came to power.

This led to no good. The nation was badly ruled. Those who read more books could not make good emperors and were harmful to the welfare of the people. Liu Hsiu was only a grand secretary and Liu Pang a big bag of wind, yet both were excellent emperors of the Han Dynasty.

"The current examination methods contain many surprises, unusual questions and difficult problems. They are designed to deal with the enemy, not the people. These types of examinations were used in the old days in the writing of the eight-legged essays. I do not approve of them and think that they should be completely remolded. I suggest taking some sample examination problems and having them published. Let the students study and do them with open books. For example, we might consider preparing twenty questions about *The Dream of the Red Chamber.* If a student can correctly answer questions and if some of the answers are good and creative, he may be given 100 points. If he answers all 20 questions and the answers are correct but are ordinary without creative thinking, he should be given 50 or 60 points. In examinations, students should be allowed to whisper to each other and to hire others to take the examinations for them. If your answer is right, I copy yours. Copying is good too. In the past, whispering and hiring of examinees were done on the sly. Now let them be open. When I cannot do what you have done, then let me copy. It should be allowed. We should experiment with this system.

"Teachers giving lectures should allow the students to fall asleep. If the lecture is no good, it makes no sense to force others to listen. Listening to distasteful things with eyes opened wide is worse than sleeping in the class. Sleeping may help one to recover from fatigue. Students should be given the choice of not listening to monotonous lectures.

"The present methods are detrimental to talented men and youths. I do not think that people should study so much. Examinations are designed for dealing with the enemy. They poison people to death and should be abolished." . . .

"Actors, actresses, poets, dramatists and writers should be driven out of the cities and all of them should be sent down in groups to the rural areas and factories. They should not always stay in offices. If they do so, they can write nothing. Only when you go down to the rural areas should you be provided with rice.

"Li Shih-chen of the Ming Dynasty personally went to search for herbs in the countryside for a long time; Chu Chung-chih did not attend any middle school or college. Confucius was brought up in a poor peasant family. He was once a shepherd and never attended a college. At one time he was a trumpeter playing at funerals. He also practiced accounting, learned to play string instruments, shoot arrows and drive carts. Since he came from the masses, he knew the pains of the masses. Later on, when he served as an official in the State of Lu, he became a great intellectual and was alienated from the activities of the masses. This was probably so because he employed Tze Lu as his bodyguard who kept the masses away. Our policies are correct, but the methods are wrong. The current duration of schooling and curricula and the teaching and examination methods must all be reformed. All of them are very detrimental.

"Gorky attended school for only two years; his knowledge was gained entirely through his own efforts. Benjamin Franklin of America sold newspapers when he was young. James Watt, the inventor of the steam engine, was a laborer." . . .

"We should not read too many books. We must read Marxist books but not too many of them. A few dozen of such books will suffice. Reading too many books will lead the readers to take opposing views and to become bookworms, dogmatists or revisionists.

"Confucian teachings do not contain any instruction on industry and agriculture. Therefore, students of Confucius exercise their limbs less and know no names for grains. We must do something about this problem." . . .

"The problem now is that there are too many courses and too many books that overload the students. It is not necessary that all subjects have to be tested. For instance, middle school students should learn a little logic and grammar without being subjected to any test. They will comprehend these in time when they are engaged in practical work. It is enough for them to know what is grammar and what is logic."

UNIT FOUR
CULTURE AND CHANGE

CULTURE AND CHANGE

Editor's note: Stanley Rosen provides a thorough introduction in his foreword to the book from which the readings for this section were taken.

SELECTIONS FROM MAO'S CHILDREN IN THE NEW CHINA

Yarong Jiang and David Ashley

Foreword
Stanley Rosen

Oral histories, autobiographies and fictional accounts of the Red Guard generation have been appearing in China and the West since the 1970s. Far from abating, however, the outpouring of literature and film on this period seems to have gained momentum in the 1990s. Chinese participants in the Cultural Revolution (1966–1976) and its attendant "Up to the Mountains and Down to the Villages" movement (shang-shan xiaxiang yundong) (which lasted until 1978) have fascinated western readers and audiences with harrowing tales of their experiences in those years.[1] Critical acclaim for Jung Chang's Wild Swans: Three Daughters of China—a compelling account of the life histories of her grandmother, her mother, and herself in the turmoil of twentieth century China that has achieved bestseller status in many parts of the world—has noted the volume's power to express "the tragic quality of life in China," "the survival of a Chinese family through a century of disaster" and the "shocking story."[2]

While Jung Chang was describing three generations of oppression, not just her own personal suffering during the Cultural Revolution, Anchee Min's *Red Azalea*—another bestselling personal memoir from the 1990s—is limited to her own experiences as a Red Guard and "sent-down youth." If anything, Min's account is even more harrowing, as well as titillating. As a Red Guard she denounces her beloved teacher as a reactionary, thus putting that woman's life in danger. Sent to the countryside she toils in near-starvation while fighting off leeches. Not allowed contact with the opposite sex she has a passionate lesbian affair with her squad leader, constantly aware that discovery could mean execution. More adventures—both political and sexual—follow, as Min becomes the star of Madam Mao's opera "Red Azalea." The *New York Times* chose *Red Azalea* as a Notable Book and observed that it told "the true story of what it was like growing up in Mao's China, where the soul was secondary to the state,

181

beauty was mistrusted, and love could be punishable by death." The national advertisements used by the publisher—Pantheon—emphasized these same points, noting, again quoting the *New York Times*, how this remarkable story revealed both "the brutality of oppression and the incredible resilience of the human spirit."[3] Readers, to judge from comments on the Amazon.com website, had similar feelings. One noted how the book helped him "understand communism much better," while another found it "incredible to think these atrocities occurred in our lifetime . . . [It] makes you feel grateful to be residing in the United States."

More recently, Joan Chen's film *Xiu Xiu: The Sent-Down Girl*, based on Yan Geling's novella, *Tianyu* (Heavenly Bath), has received critical acclaim as a stark portrait of life in China, circa 1975, for a young girl sent to a remote area. As Roger Ebert noted:

> In a time of movies about sex and silly teenagers, here is a film that arrives with a jolt of hard reality, about a 15-year-old Chinese girl who was not lucky enough to be born into the consumer paradise of "American Pie". To those who find savage satire in "South Park: Bigger, Longer and Uncut" . . . here is a story about people who would weep with joy to have the problems "South Park" attacks.[4]

Joan Chen has defended her film from critics who object that this period has already been well covered in other Chinese films seen in the West, such as Zhang Yimou's *To Live*, Chen Kaige's *Farewell My Concubine*, and Tian Zhuangzhuang's *The Blue Kite*. As she puts it, "It's not just another Cultural Revolution movie. This was as important to my generation and my people as the Holocaust is important to the world. Why did Oliver Stone make three Vietnam pictures? Why do people still make World War II movies?"[5]

Joan Chen is correct to note the importance of this decade of upheaval for those who experienced it. Within China, former *zhiqing* youth—to use the term most commonly applied to those of school age sent to the countryside during the Cultural Revolution years—have produced an impressive collection of memoirs, reportage and historical fiction.[6] Chinese journals and magazines have also introduced feature stories on the Cultural Revolution experiences of the *zhiqing* and their current situation.[7] Up until now, however, with very few exceptions, the vast majority of westerners who have learned about this period have received their knowledge from a small number of widely circulated popular memoirs, novels or films. All the works cited above are extremely well done and provide important insights into various aspects of that period. But such polished accounts, written by expatriates and clearly prepared for a non-Chinese public, represent only one part of a much larger story. The twenty-seven interviews collected in *Mao's Children in the New China* certainly cannot compete with the dramatic, even lurid, details that emerge in books like *Red Azalea* or *Wild Swans*. On the other hand, as narratives related in conversations with Yarong Jiang, a native Shanghainese, these accounts are both more varied and, in a real sense, more "authentic" than even the best work published for western audiences. More importantly, unlike the accounts of Jung Chang and Anchee Min, both of whom end their story before the reforms, *Mao's Children* reveals the relationship between the Cultural Revolution years and the reforms that followed, bringing the individual stories that comprise the book up to the present.[8]

In most accounts of the Red Guard generation, including many written by participants, the Red Guards appear as thugs and the sent-down youth are portrayed as victims. In some cases, as in Ma Bo's *Blood Red Sunset*—another Cultural Revolution memoir that was very well received in the West—the protagonist is both a thug and a victim.[9] Unlike the works of Jung Chang and Anchee Min, Ma Bo's memoir was originally published in China, but it was quickly removed from circulation by the authorities. Indeed, given the restrictions that limit a thorough investigation of this complex and tumultuous era, the lack of understanding of the broader political context *within* mainland China, particularly among the younger generation, as illustrated by all the above-mentioned works, appears to rival that of the West. For example, in a recent book entitled *China Remembers*, that amassed a collection of thirty-four first-hand accounts of the crackdowns and campaigns that have shaped China since the founding of the People's Republic of China (PRC), An Wenjiang, a former Red Guard, explained why he wanted to tell his story:

> When I was teaching at middle school, one of my students wrote in an essay that the Red Guards were all thugs. She thought I was joking when I told her I was not only a Red Guard, but also the commander of a rebel group. It made me realize the importance of portraying a truthful picture of the Red Guards in history. . . . Perhaps my story will help people understand us better.[10]

Generations in post-1949 China

Mao's Children in the New China tells the story of the Red Guard generation, also called the "Third Generation." While westerners frequently use generational terms as shorthand—the familiar Generation X, the baby boomers and so forth—it is perhaps even more common to use such categories in China. Thus, those who became leading directors after attending the Beijing Film Academy in the first entering class after the Cultural Revolution, such as Zhang Yimou and Chen Kaige, are widely known as "Fifth Generation Filmmakers." Perceived membership in a common generation— what Strauss and Howe writing about generations in the United States call "Awareness"—is also familiar in China.[11] For Strauss and Howe it makes a great deal of difference whether a person was born in 1942 or 1943. In China, there is a similar shared awareness among those who entered university immediately after the entrance examinations were restored in 1977 or 1978, when there were as many as 6 million applicants for a small number of places. Successful applicants are widely known as *qiqi ji* or *qiba ji* (class of 1977 or 1978). These students were considered—and considered themselves—to be the best and the brightest of their generation, since they emerged victorious in the first open competition after ten years without such examinations.

There is also a shared awareness among those who "graduated" from secondary school in 1966, 1967 and 1968 as being from the *lao san jie* (old three graduating classes). Most of the interviewees in *Mao's Children* fall into this category. One can find specialized restaurants in Beijing and other cities named for this generation (such as *lao san jie* restaurant) or for the bleak areas of the hinterland to which many were sent in the late 1960s and early 1970s (such as *hei tudi* restaurant, named for the wilderness area of Heilongjiang province). These are gathering places for former sent-down youth, providing very simple fare similar to what was served during their Cultural Revolution exile. At the same time, however, it is important to distinguish between those in the Cultural Revolution generation of educated youth who were eventually able to attend college or rise through political channels and those who ended up as farmers or factory workers with few opportunities to rise. Both are represented among these interviewees and, in a sense, provide a partial explanation as to why this generation can be called both the lost generation (*shiluo de yidai*) and the thinking generation (*sikao de yidai*).[12]

To understand the place the Red Guard, or Third, Generation occupies within Chinese society it is necessary to situate this group within its larger generational context. The discussion below is of necessity presented in general terms. It is useful, however, as a starting point because it is based on the analysis prevalent in China today and is drawn largely from a variety of works by Chinese authors. After this overview, we will return to the more complex picture of the Third Generation that emerges from this volume.

There have been five generations that have shaped the People's Republic of China.[13] The First Generation founded the Chinese Communist Party and, through various armed conflicts, established the PRC on October 1, 1949. The most well-known members of this generation were Mao Zedong, Zhou Enlai and Deng Xiaoping. Chinese writers sometimes refer to this generation as "the Rebel Heroes." This was a generation that found it necessary to break with old traditions in order to create something new. They often betrayed their families, their education and their social class. As one author put it, there was no authority they could not overthrow, no myth they would not question. They are also seen as a romantic generation since their struggle required unlimited imagination. They were convinced that human volition could be transformed into material power, and that virtually anything—for example the Long March of 1934–1935—was possible. Despite some horrendous failures after achieving power—most notably the Great Leap Forward (1958–1961) and the Cultural Revolution—this generation has commanded and continues to command immense respect because of its revolutionary achievements.

If the First Generation were the Rebel Heroes, the Second Generation is often regarded as the Loyal Soldiers.[14] Although they also were born during hard times, they did not have the choices available to the First Generation. New authority structures were already in place by the time they reached adulthood. They came of age during the first seventeen years of "New China," before the Cultural Revolution. They accepted the leadership of the First Generation and many responded with both loyalty and enthusiasm to the call of Party and country. Because it was an era when the Chinese version of Marxism held sway, they had virtually no access to western or traditional thought alternatives. The only time this generation showed independent thought was during the Hundred Flowers Movement in 1956–1957, when some intellectuals raised criticisms of Party and state officials. After the anti-rightist movement of 1957, all such dissident voices were stilled. Politics, however, was very important in the lives of the Second Generation. Entering the Communist Youth League and then the Party was considered "glorious." As one commentator suggested, they were "collective animals," always putting state interests above individual interests. They were proud of their thriftiness and lack of material comforts. Their cultural lives were also circumscribed. They read Soviet literature and sang revolutionary songs. Even their family lives were politicized since political quality and social class background were priorities in choosing a spouse.

The Third Generation is often regarded as the generation that has experienced everything, having lived in three totally different eras. Indeed, it may be the only generation that Chinese writers have difficulty in characterizing. One author finds them "a combination of contradictions."[15] Yarong Jiang and David Ashley put it well in their introductory remarks to this book when they suggest that their subjects "develop themes that are contradictory, complementary and critical." It is a generation marked by paradoxes. Born in the late 1940s or early 1950s, it is often noted that the Third Generation experienced their happiest moments during their childhood, because they sensed the excitement of the 1950s. Some dissenting voices point out, however, that they were also confronted by the food shortages of the Great Leap Forward at an early age.[16] Still, most commentators suggest that elements of heroism and idealism have been deeply implanted within them and have affected them throughout their lives. As with the Second Generation, the Third Generation accepted mainstream state ideology unquestioningly. With the coming of the Cultural Revolution they transferred their complete devotion to Chairman Mao, competing to be the most loyal followers of the Chairman. Under these conditions they could commit the most violent crimes with the purest hearts. Objectively, therefore, these Red Guards should be seen as victims as well as criminals. They were compelled to forego their education and forcibly exiled to the countryside. When they were finally allowed to return to the cities, more than a decade later, there were often no jobs for them. Paradoxically, some of them are leading the market reform while others are unemployed. They are seen as realistic, flexible, highly adaptable and often nostalgic for an earlier era not tainted by corruption and material values. It is frequently suggested that it is the Third Generation that is managing China today, although some of the interviewees in this book take direct issue with that conclusion.

The Fourth Generation is made up of those who were born in the 1960s. While they may have some memories of the Cultural Revolution years, and some witnessed the persecution of family members during their impressionable childhood, they themselves were not direct participants. This spared them much of the pain experienced by the Third Generation. In school, however, their education was heavily influenced by Cultural

Revolution standards, offering little beyond Mao quotations or stories of model heroes and performances of model operas. When China opened to the outside world they began to be exposed to a wide variety of western thought and culture. For some, this generation is at the same time the luckiest and the most confused.[17] Many have become pioneers in China's reform program.

One way of distinguishing the belief systems that characterized the Second, Third and Fourth Generations is to examine the works of leading intellectual theorists associated with these generations. Second Generation intellectual thinkers such as Su Shaozhi[18] and Liu Binyan[19]—both currently in exile in the United States following the events of 1989—are still heavily influenced in their writings by socialist concepts. Despite—indeed, in some ways because of—developments in China, they appear to have retained a strong belief in socialism. The key theorists of the Red Guard generation, such as Yang Xiguang[20], the Li Yizhe group[21] and Yu Luoke[22], were different from intellectuals such as Su and Liu. Red Guard theorists might be characterized as very thoughtful individuals with limited knowledge, all trapped, to a greater or lesser extent, somewhere between Marxism-Leninism and its Maoist fundamentalist variant. Interviewee no. 8 in this book—the widely known and respected liberal Professor of History at Shanghai University, Zhu Xueqin—refers to his generation as "moral idealists" and, in a particularly apt expression, "amateur intellectuals."[23] Younger Fourth Generation theorists, such as Hu Ping[24] and Fang Zhiyuan[25], did not have the restrictions on information that had marked the Second and Third generations. A variety of translation series appeared in the 1980s, such as *Dangdai xifang wenku* (Collection of Contemporary Western Works) and *Zouxiang weilai congshu* (Toward the Future Book Series), exposing Fourth Generation theorists to more pluralistic ideas imported from the West.[26]

The Fifth Generation is made up of those born in the 1970s and growing up in the 1990s.[27] They are the generation most affected by "globalization." Thus, they are equally at home discussing the latest American films or the exploits of the superstars from the National Basketball Association. Michael Jordan, until his recent retirement, was one of the most popular and well-known individuals in China. The most desirable graduate degree is the Master's of Business Administration, or MBA. Indeed, "MBA" was listed in a survey of the ten most popular expressions used on the Internet in China.[28] At the same time, and perhaps paradoxically, the more they have learned about the outside world the more patriotic, even nationalistic, they have become. Finally, they are marked by a strong tendency toward self-interest, if not individualism. Surveys have shown that this generation acknowledges the increasing importance of money in social, economic and personal life, even rivaling friendship and ideals. What is particularly striking about this generation is the ability to hold simultaneously the contradictory values of nationalism/patriotism on the one hand, and pragmatism on the other. However, these values exist in a continuing tension with each other, although this tension has thus far been handled successfully by the Communist Party. After the American bombing of the Chinese Embassy in Belgrade, Yugoslavia in May 1999, Fifth Generation college students saw no real contradiction between their participation in violent demonstrations against the United States and their continuing desire to work for an American joint venture company or study in the United States. Not surprisingly, the interviewees in this volume are often quite openly critical of the value orientations and beliefs of the young generation.

The reader will notice that this brief overview of Chinese generations does not discuss one of the major events in PRC history: the student demonstrations in the spring of 1989, followed by the military crackdown on June 3–4. Unpublished public opinion polls conducted in China on the eve of the millennium that asked respondents to list the most important events of the past 50 years reveal that "June 4th" (*liu si*)—as the military's "retaking" of Beijing is commonly known in China—remains one of the five or six most salient events to Chinese citizens, particularly those in Beijing. Not surprisingly, the subject is seldom addressed in the open press in China, except to reiterate the "correct" decision made by the leadership to restore order out of "turmoil." Moreover, given the sensitivity of the issue, it is difficult to gauge accurately current attitudes about this period. Fortunately, a number of the interviewees in *Mao's Children* do address this issue and their views will be discussed in the next section.

As suggested above, it is common in China to think in generational terms and to compare one's own generation to those that came before or after. This is not particularly new. A traditional saying had it that "Each generation is worse than the last" (*yidai bu ru yidai*). Generational conflict is therefore not unusual. For example, members of the Fourth Generation have referred to their Second Generation counterparts as "the gray or gloomy generation" (*huise de yidai*) because they were—and, allegedly, in many cases remain—overly cautious, fearful of breaking political and social taboos, and "completely worn out" (*pibei bukan*). In its turn, the Second Generation criticizes the Fourth Generation for having no sense of mission or sense of responsibility. Indeed, they fail to see anything wrong with being cautious or with careful thinking. They criticize the Fourth Generation for being too much like western youth of the 1960s.[29] There is some evidence that they may be correct in this assessment. For example, a 1988 study of university students in Beijing found that 60.4 percent designated themselves as "the generation that pays no attention to authority" (*moshi quanwei de yidai*), while 76.7 percent demanded independent thinking. Only 7.5 percent said they were willing to obey authority.[30]

Chinese publications also reveal conflicts between the Third and Fourth Generations. Many young Chinese are critical of the Third Generation because they feel that the former Red Guards obstinately persist in defending their actions ("We were idealistic and enthusiastic") and claiming the status of victims ("We had no choice"; "we suffered in the countryside"). They are accused of an inability to reassess their past objectively or admit their mistakes and criminal acts.[31] The Third Generation is also attacked for its arrogance and conceit. Critics assert that this generation thinks of itself as the best and the brightest. Former Red Guards allegedly dismiss the oldest generation as good fighters in war but unsuccessful in constructing the nation. The Second Generation is regarded as too conservative and traditional, with no real ideas. The younger generation is seen as ignorant and naïve. Only the Third Generation, to hear their critics tell it, claims that it learned how to turn struggles into survival and suffering into maturity and flexibility.[32]

This harsh assessment suggests that some larger issues may be at play. In her thoughtful and highly entertaining book on Chinese urban popular culture, Jianying Zha, herself a member of the Third Generation, notes that "memory has generational gaps."[33] She feels that her generation may be fated to carry a heavier burden than their parents or younger siblings. Their parents often went to their graves with their faith in the revolution intact; the Red Guards lost their faith before reaching middle age. Their younger siblings, by contrast, often have little recollection of the Cultural Revolution. Their children may have no memory of the events in Tiananmen Square in 1989. Zha then provides an answer for critics of the Third Generation, such as those cited above. Her words are worth quoting directly:

This is a country where nobody confesses sins. Massive destructions have occurred, atrocities have been committed, millions have died of starvation and persecution, children have turned in their parents, husbands have denounced wives, people have sold friendships for a casual nod from a Party secretary—yet it has *never* been popular to acknowledge openly the wrongs you have done to others. The venerable form of "self-criticism" is practiced only when individuals apologize to the Party: you may say you're sorry to the system, even if you aren't really sorry. Other forms of confession or self-analysis, however, are neither encouraged nor expected. In fact, it's hard to talk about psychological issues in Chinese—the language just isn't well-equipped with words and expressions to discuss your inner demons. The common attitude is to leave the demons alone.[34]

The Third Generation assesses itself: viewing the mid-1990s while looking back to the past

Mao's Children in the New China, as the title suggests, tells the story of the first generation that grew up completely in "New China," after the founding of the People's Republic in 1949. Most were between the ages of 40–50 at the time the interviews were conducted in the mid-1990s. They were in the prime of life, at an age that often elicits self-awareness and self-reflection. Whatever youthful dreams they may have harbored, their lives were now anchored in hard realities. Having witnessed the entire history of the PRC, this generation has certainly earned the right to speak, and their reflections reveal a great deal, both about the Cultural Revolution years and about current conditions. Sorting through the memories of these twenty-seven ordinary citizens, the reader may find a China that looks different from what conventional wisdom—and many other sources—may have led us to believe. Particularly fascinating is the interplay between their experiences in the Cultural Revolution and the outcomes of their lives in subsequent decades down to the present. Thus, the individual stories about the Cultural Revolution era and life in the countryside are often at least as compelling as those from the present. What does the student of China learn from these interviews? Considering that the study was conducted in Shanghai, China's most "modern" city, with a unique political tradition, can we generalize beyond these cases to also say something about other parts of China?

First, we find a populace that feels quite free to complain and express open disappointment; both with the way their own lives have turned out, and with the current state of China more generally. Even those with good jobs often seem to be dissatisfied. In part, interviewees have revealed their honest opinions because they were simply talking to another Shanghainese. They were not told that their reflections would appear in a book published in the West. If they had been, they almost certainly would not have been so forthcoming. Should one conclude from their stories that most Chinese from the Third Generation are unhappy, particularly if they happen to live in Shanghai? While there is no clear answer to this question, it appears evident that Chinese citizens, at least among themselves, feel rather able to speak freely.

A second theme that resonates in a number of the interviews is the option—even in the highly politicized atmosphere of the Cultural Revolution—to ignore the call to "make revolution," and instead pursue one's individual interests. Ironically, to a certain extent, this appears to have been most possible for those of bad class origin. Certainly, the picture presented is far more complex than the familiar one offered in popular memoirs, novels and films that center on the life of one individual or family, and far more subtle than the generalized accounts that have appeared in overview histories and textbooks on this period. For example, there is the fascinating case of interviewee no. 6, a case study that offers several unexpected surprises. As someone from a wealthy—and even counter-revolutionary—family background, one would expect him to have suffered greatly in the past. Indeed, some of his story does echo familiar themes from this period, such as the constant danger of betrayal by a friend. Yet, despite the better conditions today, he reports that the Cultural Revolution years were the most fulfilling of his life. Although he was unemployed, he was left alone to write poetry and pursue ideas freely. Other interviewees—for example no. 10, whose father had been imprisoned in the 1950s and who used the Cultural Revolution years to study languages—reveal that, for an undetermined number, the "ten wasted years" were not really being wasted.

A third theme, one that spans the entire period, from the Cultural Revolution down to the present, is the possibility of "negotiating" with the regime to pursue individual interests. One perhaps is not surprised to find this today, nor is one surprised to discover that these "negotiations" are permeated with corruption. What *is* surprising is to encounter the same practice at the height of the Cultural Revolution, when "reason" was a more important negotiating tactic than bribery. A few examples from these interviews are illustrative. Interviewee no. 6, mentioned above, despite a bad class origin, refused to cooperate with the authorities in registering to leave Shanghai when job assignments were being handed out in 1968. He describes how he was able, when necessary, to raise his blood pressure so he could avoid being sent out of the city. Interviewee no. 10 recounts how his copy of Rousseau's *Confessions* was confiscated when a Workers' Patrol Team saw the words "Oh, Eternal Beauty," and concluded that the book was referring to God. However, by bringing his copy of Engels to the police station and showing the officers that Engels praises Rousseau, he was able to get the book returned. Interviewee no. 19, from a petit bourgeois background—his father owned a tailor shop before 1949—took the initiative to visit the job Assignment Work Team before they had made any decision about his future. Showing them a paragraph from Mao's "Analysis of Social Classes in China" that lists his particular family background as "half proletarian," he successfully argued that if Mao's thinking was correct—and who could possibly question that?—he should not be put in the same category as children from the bourgeois class. In the end he was sent to a factory rather than the countryside.

This suggests a fourth point: the arbitrary nature of the political system, marked more by the rule of individuals in official positions than by the rule of law. One example of this comes from interviewee no. 13, who was unable to get herself reassigned from the countryside back to the city because the petty official in charge of the Educated Youth Office in Shanghai insisted on exacting revenge for her sister's refusal to accept her assignment. It was only when this official was replaced that she could return legally. Nor could families plan strategies to keep their children in the cities. Policies shifted from year to year without warning. Interviewee no. 9 reveals how a shift in policy in 1968, requiring every graduate to go to the countryside, made it impossible for her family to plan on which of their five children they would try to keep at home.

As many of the interviewees suggest, the biggest difference between the Cultural Revolution and the 1990s may be the replacement of power by money as the main commodity governing social and political life. There is widespread condemnation of the corruption and lack of morality that exists today. What is particularly striking is how the 1990s, in the course of providing many more options for Chinese citizens, has created precisely the kind of social stratification that the Cultural Revolution was designed to prevent. Interviewee no. 17 notes casually how he and his wife bought a signed document of financial sponsorship through a dealer for 15,000 yuan on the black market so she could get a student visa to Japan. Several interviewees, including a high school principal (no. 18) and a college professor (no. 11) reveal details on the corruption of the educational system by money. As the latter notes, in his son's district key middle school only one in three students are there because of their test scores. The rest are sons and daughters of district government officials, rich merchants, army officials and others with privileges.[35] At the other extreme, the principal describes his difficulties at a school where neither the students nor their parents are concerned about education: 20 percent of the students come from broken homes and most students realize early on that they are not destined for university, only vocational training. Interviewee no. 4 provides details on how insiders manipulate the Shanghai stock exchange.

As money has become more important and social stratification has become more pronounced these informants offer a decidedly mixed assessment of "socialism with Chinese characteristics," as Chinese-style socialism is now characterized. Certainly, to many, there appears to be more emergent capitalism than remnant socialism in China. The large increase in foreign investment—expected to rise still further as China moves closer to membership in the World Trade Organization—the effects of globalization, and the resurgence of Chinese nationalism have all been major topics in the western press. How has the Third Generation responded to these developments? On the evidence of this book, the responses reveal the same kind of ambivalence that characterizes their attitudes about the reforms more generally. Interviewee no. 5, for example, studied in England and now works for a western company. However, he feels uneasy, perhaps even unpatriotic, about protecting his employer's interests in China. Like many others, he finds it difficult to reconcile Chinese national interest with the penetration of foreign capital and foreign products into the country. Interviewee no. 22, a local entrepreneur, is far harsher. He blames government concessions to foreign capitalists for the destruction of China's state-owned enterprises. He has refused offers from Japanese and Taiwanese companies because he "won't work with compradors and opportunists." Interviewee no. 24, a well-to-do lawyer, is particularly critical of the United States. He suggests that Americans "are too stupid" to realize that Chinese criticize their government because they're affected by its policies, contrasting this with American criticisms of China, made "to preserve its own cultural and political hegemony."

Indeed, the harsh views of interviewee no. 24 regarding the United States suggest the attitudinal change that appears to have occurred in China since the events that riveted the world in 1989.[36] He is one of five interviewees who briefly discuss their assessment of the "Beijing Spring." However, aside from interviewee no. 14, who was a graduate student in Shanghai at the time, interviewee no. 24 is the only one who acknowledges supporting the students. His view today—"another revolution wouldn't have done China any good"—is broadly similar to the comments offered by other interviewees. They note that there was too much turmoil during the Cultural Revolution and that China needs to concentrate on economic development now (interviewee no. 22), or that the ordinary working people will be the first to suffer if the country once again falls apart (interviewee no. 23). Even the former graduate student finds the events of 1989 a distant memory. The market economy, he notes, has dissolved the unity that existed then and ended the commitment to social causes.

There is a strong flavor of poignancy that pervades this volume, particularly as we read of the growing number of middle-aged residents confronted by unemployment as the reforms go forward. Interviewee no. 25, a member of the Shanghai Writers' Association, expresses this sentiment best, noting that history has singled out her generation to play a cruel joke. She contrasts her own "lost generation" to the Second Generation, using her mother—a former high-ranking official—as an example. Her mother doesn't like the present and doesn't pretend to understand it. Yet she's serene, has no regrets, and is content in knowing that the great challenges and crises of her life are all behind her. As for later generations, they're not out of place either. These times are custom-built for the young. She concludes that the members of her generation are "phantoms caught between two worlds. The shards of idealism are lodged in our hearts. But the world's not for idealists anymore." It is fitting that hers is the last interview in the book.

As the editors tell us in their introductory remarks, these interviews have been conducted in Shanghai, and most of the participants are natives of Shanghai. Since Shanghai is clearly not a "typical" Chinese city, it is useful to discuss how the choice of location for these interviews has influenced the results. In other words, what should the reader know about Shanghai that will help to place these stories into a proper context?

The name "Shanghai" is associated in the West with a variety of images, not all of them positive. As the metropolis with the largest foreign penetration, it became the center for China's modernization effort before 1949. It has always been a city of paradoxes. In the 1930s it was known as "the paradise for adventurers," and had the wealthiest members of society living alongside a large underclass of fringe members of urban society, including beggars, prostitutes and other members of the lumpenproletariat. It was a port city fraught with dangers, hence the term "shanghaied," which has entered the English language to describe the situation where a man is made unconscious with drink or drugs and then carried off to be a seaman on an outgoing ship. It has been a major center for industrialists, as well as literary figures and intellectuals. Leading political figures such as Sun Yat-sen and Chiang Kai-shek started their careers in Shanghai. It has also been the locus of China's working-class and revolutionary movements, serving as the birthplace of the Chinese Communist Party in 1921, the great strike waves of 1924–1927, and the base of the radical faction—later known in popular parlance as the "Gang of Four"—during the Cultural Revolution.[37] More recently, with some of China's most prominent national leaders—among them Party General Secretary Jiang Zemin and Premier Zhu Rongji—rising to the top as a result of their successful performance at the helm of Shanghai, it has become common to refer, perhaps only half-jokingly, to a so-called "Shanghai *bang*," or "Shanghai Mafia" running the country. Shanghai's seeming ability to accommodate such a varied political history suggests the first attribute that characterizes the city: a high degree of tolerance.[38] Yang Dongping, in his bestselling book contrasting the cultural spirit of Beijing and Shanghai, identifies six distinctive characteristics of the Shanghainese. As other writers have often noted these characteristics, they are worth citing in some detail:

> (1) "shrewdness," being capable, concise, excellent, flexible and clever; (2) "practical benefit," emphasizing concrete material interests (first estimating gain or loss, then judging people's value according to everyone's actual gains); (3) "rationalism," requiring everything in life to be as fair and reasonable as possible, e.g., reasonable prices, reasonable attitude toward life; (4) "standardization and etiquette," which attaches a great importance to regulations, rules, and order (this is a reflection of "the contract consciousness" in daily life necessitated by commercial actions); (5) "secularization," which means that because of the establishment of the basic value of a commodity economy, the political and ideological activities that once controlled society have gradually been replaced by new standards of the actual effect, achievement, popularism, and rationalism of the modern society;

and (6) "westernization," which is defined as a synonym for civilization and enlightenment.[39]

Can we see this distinctiveness in the experiences and attitudes of the subjects of this book? First, we must strike a cautionary note. As Yang Dongping suggests, during the pre-reform period Chinese national identity was fostered and regional identities were suppressed. People were expected to follow the "revolutionary center," which was located in Beijing where Chairman Mao resided. Thus, prior to the late 1970s, there was considerable tension between Shanghai and the central government, as the latter bled the city of resources, capital and skilled workers. With the onset of reform one begins to see the proud reassertion of these regional identities marked, for example, by the appearance of books "explaining" the differences between individuals from different regions. Books about the denizens of Shanghai—such as Luo Shuang's *"Dissecting" the Shanghainese*[40]—appear to have become particularly popular examples of this genre of literature.[41] At several points in these interviews the reader is aware that the comments offered reflect the situation in Shanghai rather than the country as a whole. For example, interviewee no. 4 discusses the workings of the Shanghai stock market. Currently, China has only two functioning stock markets, one in Shanghai and one in Shenzhen. A second difference is the number of college graduates in the sample—thirteen—and the number of respondents who studied abroad, or refer to friends who studied abroad. Indeed, interviewee no. 24, the well-to-do lawyer mentioned above, reflects the amazing changes that have occurred in Shanghai just in the 1990s. He starts the interview by noting how in 1990 a former classmate, the dumbest of their group, returned to Shanghai for a visit from abroad and regaled those left behind with stories of his "astronomically high salary" of US$28,000. Everyone was suitably impressed. When he returned again in 1996, his Shanghai friends were all doing so well that no one paid him any notice. In fact, we are told, "people in Shanghai have started making fun of students coming back from abroad." Self-confidence and perhaps a bit of arrogance are returning to China's most modern city. But the advanced nature and future potential of Shanghai is expressed best by interviewee no. 7, the general manager of a government-sponsored project, when he relates how he came to return to Shanghai. A friend convinced him that if he wanted to accomplish anything he would have to return to Shanghai. As his friend put it, "Don't go back to Anhui; Shanghai is China's America."

Notes

I would like to thank Mark Selden for his helpful comments on an earlier version of this introduction.

[1] For some of the earlier examples of such works, see Liang Heng and Judith Shapiro, *Son of the Revolution* (New York: Random House, 1983) and Nien Cheng, *Life and Death in Shanghai* (New York: Grove Press, 1987). More recent works have provided even more harrowing accounts, as in Zheng Yi, *Scarlet Memorial: Tales of Cannibalism in Modern China* (Boulder: Westview Press, 1998).

[2] Jung Chang, *Wild Swans: Three Daughters of China* (New York: Simon and Schuster, 1991). The quotes are from the back cover of the paperback edition and derive from the *Washington Post Book World*, *The New Yorker* and Mary Morris, the author of *Wall to Wall*. They are very representative of the critical commentary that greeted this book.

[3] Anchee Min, *Red Azalea* (New York: Pantheon, 1994). The quotes were taken from the Amazon.com website for this book. In June 1995 *Red Azalea* was released in a mass-market paperback for US$7.50. It has also appeared as an audiobook, read by actress Nancy Kwan, attesting to its success among western audiences.

[4] Roger Ebert, "Hearts of Darkness Revisited: A Stark Portrait of Life in China," *Chicago Sun-Times*, July 30, 1999, p. 30. In the film Xiu Xiu is sent off to the countryside with hundreds of other teenagers from Chengdu, the capital of Sichuan province. After a year of boring labor in a small town near the Tibetan border, she's ready to return to her family. Instead, however, she is sent even further away, to the Tibetan grasslands. Again, she expects to return home after six months, but no one comes for her. Various men pass by the lonely outpost and promise to use their connections to help her leave in return for sexual favors. She becomes an object of complete humiliation and scorn, repeatedly used and abused by any man who chooses to drop by. To virtually everyone else in the area this innocent and naïve young girl has become a shameless slut, an object of ridicule even to the local female medical staff, worthy of no sympathy. The home video version announces on the front that the film was "banned in China for political and sexual content."

[5] See the interview with Joan Chen in Scarlet Cheng, "Applying the Hard Lessons: Actress Joan Chen Didn't Let the Chinese Government Derail Her Acclaimed Directing Debut, 'Xiu Xiu'," *Los Angeles Times*, June 23, 199, Calendar, p. 1.

[6] See, for examples, Shi Weimin, ed., *Zhiqing riji xuanbian* (Selections from Zhiqing Diaries) (Beijing: Zhongguo shehui kexue chubanshe, 1996); Shi Weimin, ed., *Zhiqing shuxin xuanbian* (Selected Zhiqing Correspondence) (Beijing: Zhongguo shehui kexue chubanshe, 1996); Jin Dalu, ed., *Kunan yu fengliu* (Hardship and Heroism) (Shanghai:

Shanghai renmin chubanshe, 1994); Jin Yonghua and Jin Dalu, eds, *Dongfang shiritan* (The Oriental Decameron) (Shanghai: Shanghai renmin chubanshe, 1996); and Jin Dalu, *Shiyun yu mingyun* (World Destiny and Individual Fate) (Shanghai: Shanghai renmin chubanshe, 1998). This latter book, a study of the *zhiqing* today, perhaps comes closest to the present volume. Also see *Zhiqing dang'an* 1962–79 (Zhiqing Case Files) (Chengdu: Sichuan wenyi chubanshe, 1992); Deng Xian, *Zhongguo zhiqing meng* (The Dream of the Chinese Zhiqing) (Beijing: Rennin wenxue chubanshe, 1993) and the five-volume fiction collection entitled *Zhiqing wenxue jingdian* (Classics of Zhiqing Literature) (Lanzhou: Dunhuang wenyi chubanshe, 1998). I would like to thank Professor Richard King, chair of the Department of Pacific and Asian Studies at the University of Victoria, for bringing these sources to my attention. For translations of *zhiqing* literature in English, see Richard King, ed., "There and Back Again: The Chinese 'Urban Youth' Generation," *Renditions* Special Issue 50 (1998). Twenty-six writers of the *zhiqing* writers are interviewed in Laifong Leung, *Morning Sun: Interviews with Chinese Writers of the Lost Generation* (Armonk, New York: M.E. Sharpe, 1994). There is also some useful material in Sang Ye and Zhang Xinxin, eds, *Chinese Profiles* (San Francisco: China Books and Periodicals, 1987), which contains interviews with 100 ordinary Chinese citizens, some of whom are from the Red Guard generation. One of the earliest works of this type was B. Michael Frolic, *Mao's People: Sixteen Portraits of Life in Revolutionary China* (Cambridge, MA: Harvard University Press, 1980). The interviews for this book were conducted with Chinese émigrés in Hong Kong in the mid-1970s.

[7] For one recent example, see "Jiu ti xin lun: zhongguo zhiqing de zuotian, jintian he mingtian" (A Fresh Approach to an Old Topic: The Past, Present and Future of China's *Zhiqing* Youth), *Zhongguo qingnian yanjiu* (Research on Chinese Youth), no. 6, 1999, pp. 45–49.

[8] Jung Chang won a scholarship to Britain and left China in 1978; Anchee Min ends her story after the death of Mao and the disgrace of Jiang Qing. Although she spent another six years in China before moving to the United States, she summarizes those six years very briefly, providing few details on how the post-Cultural Revolution period affected her.

[9] Ma Bo, *Blood Red Sunset: A Memoir of the Chinese Cultural Revolution* (New York: Viking Penguin, 1995). This work was originally published in China in 1988 by the Workers Publishing House. Liu Binyan, in his review for the *New York Times Book Review*, noted that the book "echoes the realities of contemporary China." By the time the book had appeared in the West, Ma Bo was a writer-in-residence at Brown University.

[10] Zhang Lijia and Calum McLeod, *China Remembers* (Oxford: Oxford University Press, 1999), as cited in *Far Eastern Economic Review*, November 4, 1999, p. 65.

11   William Strauss and Neil Howe, *Generations: The History of America's Future: 1584 to 2069* (New York: William Morrow, 1992).

12   All members of this group are sometimes called the "thinking generation" because they were the first to gain broad experience and a broad knowledge of Chinese society under conditions that provoked many to question the ideology they brought to the countryside.

13   There are many books and articles published within China analyzing generations and generational differences. This section draws most heavily on the following sources: Wu Junping, *Di wu dai ren* (The Fifth Generation) (Tianjin: Tianjin jiaoyu chubanshe, 1998); Zhang Yongjie and Cheng Yuanzhong, *Di si dai ren* (The Fourth Generation) (Hong Kong: Zhonghua shuju, 1989); Song Qiang, Qiao Bian et al., *Di si dai ren de jingshen* (The Spirit of the Fourth Generation) (Lanzhou: Gansu wenhua chubanshe, 1997); Xu Sihe, "Qudong xin zhongguo lishi nianlun de si dai ren" (Four Generations That Have Moved China), *Qingnian tansuo* (Youth Studies), no. 4, 1994, pp. 12–14; and Liu Shaolei, "Xin de daigou: 60 niandai daxuesheng ji qi zinu" (The New Generation Gap: 1960s University Students and their Children), *Qingnian yanjiu* (Youth Research), no. 4, April 1996, pp. 24–28.

14   The expressions "Rebel Heroes" and "Loyal Soldiers" are drawn from Wu Junping, note 11.

15   See Zhang Yongjie and Cheng Yuanzhong, note 11.

16   See Xu Sihe, note 11.

17   Ibid.

18   Su Shaozhi was formerly the Director of the Institute for Marxist-Leninist Studies at the Chinese Academy of Social Sciences.

19   Liu Binyan, a reporter for *Renmin ribao* (People's Daily), was China's most famous muckraker and greatly admired and respected for his exposés of corruption.

20   Yang Xiguang was a secondary school student in Hunan during the Cultural Revolution who became famous for writing an "ultra-leftist" critique of China's leadership and society. It was entitled "Whither China?" and criticized some of the country's top leaders as "red capitalists."

21   The Li Yizhe group took its name from the three main participants: Li Zhengtian, Chen Yiyang and Wang Xizhe. Their wall posters on the streets of Guangzhou (Canton) in the mid-1970s, promoting socialist democracy and the development of a legal system, created national and international attention. For translations of their writings, see Anita Chan, Stanley Rosen and Jonathan Unger, *On Socialist Democracy and the Chinese Legal System: The Li Yizhe Debates* (Armonk, New York: M. E. Sharpe, 1995).

22 Yu Luoke was a high school student during the Cultural Revolution. His most important work was entitled *Chushen lun* (On Origin Theory) in which he questioned the emphasis on a person's class origin as the key determinant of his likely behavior. He was executed during the Cultural Revolution, but he has not been forgotten. Recently, some members of the Third Generation have compiled a book of his writings, along with critical commentaries from his enemies at the time, reminiscences and current assessments of his thought. See Xu Shao, Ding Dong and Xu Youyu, eds, *Yu Luoke: Yizuo yu huiyi* (Yu Luoke: Works and Recollections) (Beijing: Zhongguo wenlian chuban gongsi, 1999).

23 For a recent collection of Professor Zhu's writings, see Zhu Xueqin, *Shuzhaili de geming* (Making Revolution from within My Studio) (Changchun: Changchun chubanshe, 1999).

24 Hu Ping was a graduate student in the philosophy department at Beijing University specializing in Kant. He took a prominent role in the local National People's Congress election in 1980 and won his seat. However, he was denied work and eventually pressured into going abroad for further studies in 1986. He is perhaps best known for his article promoting freedom of speech, although he has written widely on events in China down to the present.

25 Fang Zhiyuan was among a small group of student leaders at Beijing University who had been active in the April 5, 1976 Tiananmen protests and at Democracy Wall in the late 1970s. Like Hu Ping, he was also a candidate for election to the National People's Congress in 1980.

26 For the great intellectual opening of the 1980s and the origins of these translation series see Chen Fong-ching and Jin Guantao, *From Youthful Manuscripts to River Elegy: The Chinese Popular Cultural Movement and Political Transformation 1979–1989* (Hong Kong: The Chinese University Press, 1997) and Edward X. Gu, "Cultural Intellectuals and the Politics of Cultural Public Space in Communist China (1979–1989): A Case Study of Three Intellectual Groups," *The Journal of Asian Studies*, 58(2), May 1999, pp. 389–431.

27 Because this generation has not yet received the detailed analysis accorded the first four generations by Chinese authors, I draw on my own forthcoming article entitled "Chinese Youth in the Year 2000" for many of the ideas in this paragraph.

28 See *Beijing qingnian zhoukan (Beijing Youth Weekly)*, 29, 1998, citing reports from the Internet survey network of Horizon Research, the leading private Chinese public opinion agency.

29 See Zhang Yongjie and Cheng Yuanzhong, note 13.

30   Cited in Stanley Rosen, "The Effect of Post-4 June Re-Education Campaigns on Chinese Students," *The China Quarterly*, 134, June 1993, pp. 310–334.

31   This paragraph is based on Song Qiang, Qiao Bian et al., cited in note 11, pp. 211–214 and interviews with Chinese youth in their twenties. It should be noted that the authors of this book had previously become widely known for their nationalistic tract, *The China That Can Say No* (*Zhongguo keyi shuo bu*), so their views perhaps do not represent the majority of Chinese youth.

32   For other contemporary comparisons of youth from different generations, see Xu Meng, ed., *Guanjian shike: dangdai zhongguo qite jiejue de 27 ge wenti (Critical Moment: The 27 Problems That Urgently Require Solutions in Contemporary China)* (Beijing: Jinri zhongguo chubanshe, 1997, pp. 538–556), which compares 1980s and 1990s youth, and Shi Chaoge, Zhang Meng and Zhu Min, "Dangdai daxuesheng dui qibashi niandai daxuesheng de kanfa" (The Views of Today's University Students about the University Students of the 1970s and 1980s), *Beijing qingnian zhoukan* (Beijing Youth Weekly), no. 41, October 13, 1998.

33   Jianying Zha, *China Pop: How Soap Operas, Tabloids, and Bestsellers Are Transforming a Culture* (New York: The New Press, 1995, p. 17).

34   Ibid., p. 18.

35   For a confirming account, based on data from Beijing, as well as more details on educational stratification and the role of money and power in choosing schools, see Stanley Rosen, "Education and Economic Reform," in Christopher Hudson, ed., *The China Handbook* (Chicago: Fitzroy Dearborn Publishers, 1997), pp. 250–261.

36   For some evidence of this attitudinal change among youth, see Rosen, "Chinese Youth in the Year 2000," cited in footnote 27.

37   The revolutionary nature of Shanghai's working class has been documented most effectively in the works of Elizabeth J. Perry. For example, see *Shanghai on Strike: The Politics of Chinese Labor* (Stanford, CA: Stanford University Press, 1993) and Elizabeth J. Perry and Li Xun, *Proletarian Power: Shanghai in the Cultural Revolution* (Boulder: Westview Press, 1997).

38   This point about the tolerance of the Shanghainese is also made in Yang Dongping, *Chengshi jifeng: Beijing he Shanghai de wenhua jingshen* (City Monsoon: The Cultural Spirit of Beijing and Shanghai) (Beijing: Dongfang Press, 1994). Chapter 9 of this book, "Shanghainese and Beijingese," has been translated in Cheng Li, ed., "City Monsoon: The Cultural Spirit of Beijing and Shanghai," *Chinese Sociology and Anthropology*, vol. 29, no. 2, Winter 1996–1997. Chapter 8, not translated, is entitled "New Beijing and the Third Generation," and discusses the characteristics of the "lost generation" and its

impact on the new culture of Beijing. I have drawn on Cheng Li's excellent introduction to this issue, pp. 3–17 for several of the ideas in this section.

[39]   This passage is quoted from Cheng Li's introduction in "City Monsoon," pp. 10–11.

[40]   Luo Shuang, chief editor, *"Pouxi" shanghai ren* ("Dissecting" the Shanghainese) (Beijing: Zhongguo shehui chubanshe, 1995). By October 1997 the book was in its third printing and the print run had reached 31,000 copies.

[41]   One could, however, also argue that some of the stories about the Cultural Revolution are influenced by the locale. For example, the ability to "negotiate" with officials who will listen to reason may be a reflection of Shanghai's vaunted tolerance and a higher educational level. It is likely that such "negotiation," particularly by those of bad class background, would not have been possible in less developed parts of the country.

LU XIN, FEMALE: NOVELIST

I was a simple-minded child.

My grandfather traded lumber in Nantong, Jiangsu province. The business was prosperous enough to support six children. His son—my father—left for Shanghai when he was very young and became an accountant. My mother was a *taitai*—a housewife with some status. She never worked outside the house until my father died from an illness in 1953. Then our lives suddenly changed.

My mother was a traditional Chinese woman with a very strong will. She came from an old family in Hunan and had attended school. After my father died she sold some of her jewelry so she could support the family while she trained as a nurse. Later, she found a position in a factory clinic. We moved into a poor residential area close to the factory where my mother had found her job.

The memories of my childhood are associated with a big dark room with old, creaking floors, situated on a noisy, crowded lane. Mother raised four children—my three brothers and me—by herself. She made no attempt to remarry. I suppose the responsibility of bringing all of us up was just so overwhelming she forgot herself completely.

Because of the absence of adult males in our family we were untouched by the purges of the 1950s and 1960s. The political struggles that left such a mark on others passed us by.

When I was young I believed everything the Party said. During the 1950s and 1960s, the government did make mistakes. But its policies also tried to give the working classes some security. Because our family lived in harmony with the new society we were supportive of government programs. I was seen as a very "progressive" kid—the term we used in those days. I was a student leader, a model child.

When the Cultural Revolution began I immediately became a Red Guard. Many accounts of Red Guard activity that circulate today are distorted. Most Red Guard organizations—particularly the ones in Shanghai—were not violent or monstrous. My friends and I were not hooligans. We saw the Cultural Revolution as an ideological struggle between right and wrong. I really believed that the Principal of my school was a bad person. To criticize him was to defend the highest ideals.

I was taught the most honorable way of living was to be a member of the working class. Xing Yanzi and Hou Juan were role models for the rest of us to follow.[1] Some now claim that the Up to the Mountains and Down to the Villages movement was Mao's attempt to get dangerous elements out of the cities. But Mao's policy was consistent with his attitude towards knowledge and education. He always believed intellectuals should serve workers and peasants.

Today, the Cultural Revolution is often characterized as a political movement designed to stir up infighting among the masses. It's untrue. The Cultural Revolution gave the masses the power to punish those who misbehaved. Although corruption and the bureaucracy in the Party were minor then compared to today, problems nonetheless existed. In those days people had high expectations and demands of Party officials—nothing like today's cynical attitude. We all took it for granted that the Party was good and that bad people didn't belong in it.

In the 1960s, many young students responded enthusiastically to the call to serve the less privileged because it seemed as natural to them at the time as it does now for students to go to college. But this attitude didn't start with the Cultural Revolution. It sprang from many years of education.

In 1968, I went to Heilongjiang province.[2] I could have waited another year, but I was determined to go to the countryside and wanted to leave as soon as possible. My eldest brother was one of those idealistic students who left to serve peasants in Xinjiang province before the Cultural Revolution began. When he got tuberculosis he had to return to Shanghai for treatment. After he recovered he persuaded several unemployed young people from our neighborhood to return to Xinjiang with him. He was a great influence on me. I thought I was going to change the backwardness of our countryside and transform the whole world. I was, of course, very innocent.

When millions of educated young people moved to the countryside they did begin to stimulate some changes, no matter how small these were. The students were the losers because they sacrificed their education. The countryside offered no hope of personal advancement. But we willingly adjusted to the harsh conditions.

All our energy was consumed by the primitive, endless labor. In winter, the temperature could fall to minus 40° centigrade. I didn't have a pair of boots or a sheepskin coat. My cotton-filled coat was useless because, after a couple of years, the cotton hardened into big lumps. The cold was unbearable, but we still had to work outside or in an unheated room. I was not spoiled as a child, but, before I joined the peasants, I'd never experienced real hardship.

Our farm, close to the border with the Soviet Union, was a militarized production corps administered by army officers. Because the soldiers didn't really know how to operate an agricultural enterprise it was reorganized later as a non-military state farm. I worked at various occupations, such as laborer, tractor driver, unit secretary and reporter for the farm's Public Affairs Department. Unlike many others, I made no attempt to return to Shanghai. The city no longer had any attraction for me. In any case, my younger brother—the only one of my siblings who had remained in Shanghai—needed our family's room.

During the Cultural Revolution I believed that the "Gang of Four's" ideology and policies benefited families and social classes such as mine. When the members of the "Gang" were overthrown I was bewildered. Our generation had grown up under their influence. They had become part of my body and soul. Some of the radicals on my farm couldn't take it any more and committed suicide. For the first time in my life I was forced to question some of my deepest beliefs.

In early 1976, I published a short story in one of the country's leading literary magazines. Overnight, I became famous. Everyone wanted to know who Lu Xin was. In high school, I'd not been particularly interested in literature— I'd wanted to be a scientist. But, at the farm, people spent a lot of time reading, and classical Chinese literature was often cited to help make a point. After I published that short story I was immediately moved up to the provincial Bureau of Public Affairs. My life as a professional writer began.

Just before the "Gang of Four" was arrested, the magazine that had published my short story recruited me as its editor representing peasants. After the arrests I assumed that the appointment would be retracted since the political situation in the country had changed. But I was told that, because I was a temporary employee, the appointment would stand. So I moved to Beijing at the end of 1976.

At the farm in Heilongjiang I'd "talked love" (*tan lian ai*) with one of my fellow students—a boy I'd known since middle school in Shanghai. In 1977, we were married. In those days, when you were attracted to someone you first began to "talk love" with them and then you entered a relationship that led to marriage.

I didn't know anything about sex or how a child was born. I thought that if a man touched a woman's private parts in a bus this could make her pregnant. Sexual desires were something dirty. I remember that words like "rape" and "adultery" in the posters about convicted criminals always confused and embarrassed me. When I was married at the age of 28 my mother, the nurse, had to tell me how a child was made. During my time in Heilongjiang I was psychologically and emotionally—as well as politically—frozen. I'd been stored in a freezer. A decade passed as if it were one day in my life.

After we married, my husband entered Fudan University in Shanghai, and I continued to work on the literary magazine in Beijing. The magazine wanted to give me a permanent position, but my registration as a rural resident couldn't be changed to that of a city cadre. I decided to go back to the farm and prepare for the College Entrance Examination, which had just been reinstated. In 1978, the Central Drama School in Beijing accepted me. I didn't have high scores on my exams, but my publication and work experiences were taken into consideration.

My new life at the university was a revelation. It was as if I'd awakened from a dream. I watched western movies, and I was stirred by a portrayal of emotion and behavior that previously had been suppressed. I read many Chinese and western novels that were unavailable in the past. I went to the Xidan "Democracy Wall" to read the Big Character posters, and I discussed political reform with my classmates. I felt like a newborn child.

I also attended dance parties. For the first time in my life I was hot and excited about being so close to strange male bodies. Like an adolescent, I was deeply confused by emotional and physical excitement. I'd previously lived in a shell that had protected me from the sexual confusion felt by normal adolescents. That's why I said I was like a child at the age of 30. Human sexuality is disturbing. Maybe I was lucky to have been so protected at an earlier age.

Even though my husband and I had to part immediately after we married I wasn't particularly upset. I don't know why. Perhaps, because I was tough. I know I wasn't sentimental. Not like now when I'm sensitive to everything. When life gets easier you become spoiled. Maybe it was because sex wasn't a major part of the marriage. I didn't worry my husband might be unfaithful. I just took it for granted we'd always be together.

After he graduated from the university my husband was assigned to Beijing as a corespondent for *Wenhui Daily*. We still couldn't live together though. I stayed in the university dormitory, and he lived in his work unit's dormitory. We visited each other at weekends. We were two native Shanghainees living in Beijing, where everything depends on political connections—more so than anywhere else in China.

I had my baby when I was 32—a year away from graduating. Because I'd had two miscarriages already we decided to keep the child, not have an abortion. At the time, my husband was assigned to report the activities of a Chinese expedition team to the North Pole, so I was alone. My mother came to Beijing to help with the birth. We rented a room from a peasant in the suburb. I didn't know how to look after a child. When my son was two months old he fell off the bed and broke his arm and leg. Even today, the guilt still bites at me whenever I look at him.

My baby was small compared to the other children. I think this is because, when I was pregnant, I didn't eat properly. You know what the food is like in student dining rooms. My friends sometimes criticize me about being too protective towards my son, but they don't know my past. The child had a hard time.

I know that westerners think it's normal for people to change their love and feeling towards one another, but this wasn't acceptable to me. I thought that once a man and a woman marry the most important thing is for both of them to work hard and be responsible towards one another. I never asked what my husband wanted from me as a woman. When he started an affair with someone else I was totally lost. I was so humiliated I couldn't even tell my mother and friends.

Why did this happen to me? The question tortured me. I'm the type of person who gets along well with everyone. I didn't demand anything special from my husband. Instead, I put him first in every single matter. I never thought I should be treated differently because I was a female—that it was all right for me to be a little weak or a little spoiled. All I wanted was to do everything I could for him and for our child. I was deeply wounded. The only way to escape the pain was to divorce him.

During many sleepless nights I returned again and again to the realization that my husband now belonged to another woman. Once we had been in the same middle school and high school; then we went to the farm together; finally, we made this child. A strange woman came. She knew how to talk in a sweet voice, and she knew how to use feminine guile to get what she wanted. My husband said he left me because he wanted some romance in his life. He told me I didn't understand what a man wanted. My devotion meant nothing to him.

After we divorced, my ex-husband wrote me letters saying he felt guilty that, all those years, he'd taken it for granted that I should wait on him. But he'd wanted it both ways. On the one hand he was happy when I played the role of servant and substitute mother, but on the other I was expected to be his fantasy lover. He was satisfied with me as the mother substitute but unhappy with me as the fantasy lover. But how could I have satisfied him? No one ever took the time to spoil me. My husband let me to do all the work, and then he turned around and told me I wasn't a proper woman. He once told me that a woman who doesn't know how to take care of herself couldn't expect to be loved by others.

I asked him whether he felt ashamed that he had betrayed me. He told me that what I'd done for him could have been done by a common housekeeper. My kind of love has little value today. Communist education always taught us to put others before ourselves. That kind of morality wasn't so different from traditional Chinese morality. I always subordinated myself to my husband. I'm a typical traditional Chinese woman.

I hate what he did to me. However, in a way, I'm thankful about what happened because it made me re-examine my life. After I recovered, I became a stronger person.

I don't want to get married again. First of all, I don't trust anyone to ignore my past or treat my child as his own. Second, I overcame a great deal of pain to get out of one marriage. I won't enter another as easily. Once I was told that marriage is the biggest punishment God places on human beings.

Many of my friends' marriages aren't happy. But as long as both partners make money and raise the family together you don't ask whether a marriage is happy or not. Why bother? In any case, when you get old you don't want to be alone. You start to worry about many trivial things.

The official divorce rate in Shanghai doesn't reflect reality because many people can't afford to divorce. What about their apartment, which was so difficult to obtain? What about their careers? Divorce is still a black mark for officials.

As a single, divorced woman the only relationship I can have with a man is as his "lover," not as his wife. I once believed that marriage alone could justify a sexual relationship between two people. But I have changed because society has changed. Now I, too, have a boyfriend or "lover." It was hard for me to take this step. I still have some reservations about what I've done.

Many people have complimented me on my independence. But they don't know how I feel. Many nights I cannot get to sleep. I long to have someone lying beside me, cuddling me and loving me. I miss the presence of someone who can share my concerns and help me make decisions. In China, very few women live by themselves. If I'm a heroine, I'm not one by choice.

Today, I'm often invited to give speeches about the "new modern female" (*xiandai nüxing*)—meaning a woman with "progressive" ideas that fit our new society. What a joke! The deformed capitalism we have in China has made things worse for women, not better. People spout nonsense about the "new" women who have become so "open-minded," so "cosmopolitan," so "well-educated," but all I feel are sadness and pessimism. When men gain wealth women lose ground.

Women who are strong and independent are now more isolated than ever. Society doesn't accept them. It's more accommodating towards females who are playmates and decorative companions. Today, we have a new type of career woman—the "Public Relations Miss" [*gongguan xiaojie*]. What's "new" about her is that she's the newest kind of prostitute. Her job is to accompany men and make sure their social and business activities are enjoyable. Between these two extremes are the majority of Chinese women. They're commonplace. Change doesn't touch them.

Under socialism, women's independence was valued. Women were treated equally. It's nonsense to claim that, after reform, Chinese women attained a higher status. But change was inevitable. We had to catch up with the rest of the world. However, we run too fast in no particular direction. The gap between the rich and the poor has become so wide. The privileged class is made up of the Party bureaucrats plus the rich businessmen. They make incredible amounts of money.

Then you have intellectuals such as me sitting here talking to you, emoting about "sentiment" and "humanity." Most Chinese people don't have that luxury. They're hard pressed to make a living. It's a continuous struggle. Few women have the time to talk about "rights" or independence. The more material society becomes the less independence women actually have. Money is everything today.

What became of the spiritual aspirations of my generation?

Let me tell you the hottest news in Shanghai media circles. It's about the man who used to be the Vice-Director of the municipal government's Overseas Chinese Affairs Office. He had a position anyone would envy because he traveled abroad frequently, socializing and doing little else. This man is now in jail for murdering his lover, and may soon be executed. Because he's a high-level Party official his crime is not reported, and it's forbidden to interview him. I heard he wrote a novel-length confession about his life. My journalist friends love him. He writes beautifully, and can give wonderful speeches. He was one of the rising stars of our generation: someone who recently achieved very high office.

This man's story reflects the tragic characteristics of our generation. He had a love relationship with his mistress that lasted many years, and she wanted to be with him forever. But he had to end the relationship. The woman had become a liability. I heard he offered her money and a two-bedroom apartment, but she refused. All she wanted was him.

It's sad isn't it? Most modern girls would have grabbed what they could and run to the next man. But this woman wanted her affair to lead to marriage. She expected to be treated equally. She'd had several abortions because our society doesn't permit illegitimate birth. If she'd had a child things might have been different.

I can understand why she couldn't step aside and let him go. The only way he could get free of her was to kill her.

Our generation is tragic. I've just finished a novel about the end of a heroic period. The teacher in my story is one of our generation and still has idealistic and revolutionary dreams. But when he tries to live up to his principles he fails every time.

Of course, there are those among us who've made a good adjustment. There'll always be opportunists. But let me tell you something: the best officials today are worse than the most corrupt cadres of the past.

Our generation—the Red Guard generation—cannot catch up with this world. Our thoughts are out of date. What we learnt in our childhood soaked into our bones. You'd have to install a new brain in us to change our way of thinking. Even if we move to the United States we're still the same. Many of my expatriate friends have told me that, although they understand American culture, they're still, at heart, "Chinese peasants." They cannot change their belief system or their mode of behavior—no matter how long they live in America.

You married a foreigner. Have you changed a lot?

Notes

[1]   Two "educated youths" who went to the countryside to live as peasants a few years before the Cultural Revolution began.

[2]   Heilongjiang or "Black Dragon River." A province in the far northeast of China. During the 1960s the government encouraged people to settle in this relatively under-populated region. In part, this was because of its proximity to the Soviet Union.

Students who ended up on state farms in Heilongjiang tended to be from "good" family backgrounds, i.e. from working-class or cadre families.

YANG YINZI, MALE: FACTORY TECHNICIAN

I've always loved *Dream of the Red Mansions*.[1] I've read the novel so many times. It has a special meaning for me because it's about a wealthy, influential, upper-class family that was ruined. My family's history resembles the story in this book. The difference, though, is that, whereas the Jias brought themselves down, our family was destroyed by historical events we couldn't control.

When I was very young my grandmother used to tell me stories about our family's past. At the time, I didn't understand much. Now, of course, I wish I could listen to her one more time. She died when I was 12 years old.

My great-great-grandfather was a high ranking Qing mandarin. During the reign of the Jiaqing Emperor [1799–1821] he was awarded the degree of *Jinshi*.[2] Later, in the Daoguang period [1821–1850], he was appointed Governor General of Jiangsu, Anhui and Jiangxi provinces. After the defeat of the first Opium War, he and the Manchu Commissioner Qiying represented the Emperor at the Treaty of Nanjing. So my great-great-grandpa's name is in the history books as the man who signed the first humiliating treaty with the British.

In 1851, the Emperor sent my great-great-grandfather to prevent Taiping rebel forces from crossing Hunan. Because my ancestor failed to stop the insurgents he was dismissed from imperial service and exiled to Xinjiang. After he'd served his seven-year sentence of banishment he came home and died the following year.

My family owned several mansions on Lake Poyang. Grandmother used to tell me all about them. She said we needed a room just to store all the keys. During the 1930s our estates fell into disrepair. Burglars broke holes in the walls and carried away whatever they could.

My grandfather sent his children to St John's College in Shanghai so they could get a western education. But he was the traditional Chinese intellectual. He spent his time drinking wine and writing classical poetry.

Grandfather served in the Nanjing Guomindang government but later quit, disappointed with all the corruption. He moved to Shanghai late in his life. Most of his friends and associates were writers, historians and actors. His brother was ambassador to France.

I remember the chest in which grandfather stored his published and unpublished writings. I didn't recognize the value of these materials when grandmother first showed them to me. The old-fashioned verses were meaningless to a small boy.

All I now recall about grandfather is that he was an old man with a long gray beard and an old-fashioned robe. The only keepsake of his I still have is the painting with his inscription you can see on that wall.

Two years ago I received a letter from a local historian in Jiangxi. The government had listed grandfather's name in *Who's Who*. He was described as a "well-known scholar and gentleman" who was executed during land reform in 1952.

No matter how apolitical he tried to be grandfather recognized that liberation augured a coming storm. His visits to our house became short and secretive, and he left quickly as if he didn't want the neighbors to notice him. But he always remembered to bring me some sweets.

Grandfather was indicted in Jiangxi province, where he owned his estates. He went into hiding. Understandably, he tried to keep our family out of trouble, and he broke off all communication with my father. Even grandmother, who, meanwhile, had moved in with us, didn't know what had happened to him. The news of his death didn't reach us until months after he'd been executed. Later, we learnt it hadn't taken long to track him down.

Grandmother was always bitter about grandfather's friends because she believed they'd betrayed her husband. But I don't blame them. In those days no one could afford to be loyal. Grandmother, herself, lived long enough to see her own son get himself and his family into trouble for trying to help a friend.

My father was an economist. He went to work for a bank in Nanchang, but lost his job during the civil war. When Shanghai was liberated he was working as a private English tutor. He disguised his qualifications, claiming he was only a primary school graduate. I think grandfather told him to do this.

At the time, my family still had quite a bit of money—enough to keep us going anyway. My parents didn't look for work until 1954, when the Shanghai unemployed were ordered to find jobs. Then, they took work as book-keepers.

During my childhood I lived in constant fear. I vividly recall the nights we sat around our table waiting for my father to come home. Whenever he was late we all assumed the worst. Finally, in 1958, our fears were realized.

Mother had cooked eggs and rice for father. It was late. We'd finished our dinner and our homework, but father still hadn't returned. I'd begun to read a book and was soon absorbed in it. Suddenly, father appeared under a dim light. Because his face was so grim we jumped up in alarm. "Eat first," my mother told him as she led us out of the room. Later, we learned father had been sentenced to three years in Dafeng labor camp.

Father's "crime" had been to assist a "counter-revolutionary fugitive"— an old friend. This man didn't live in Shanghai, and he'd had no contact with father for some time. One day he appeared at our door and asked if he could stay for the night. Of course, father said yes. He and father talked until midnight. I believe that next day father gave his old friend some money and took him to the railway station. Half a year later this person was arrested, and father was taken in for questioning. The authorities claimed that, by helping his old friend, father had revealed his "true face."

At my school, a young, stupid and insensitive teacher came up to me and asked: "Is your father going to Dafeng?" I nodded dumbly. The teacher seemed pleased: "He's got his iron bowl now" he noted. I felt as though ice water had been poured over me. My whole body went numb.

After my father left, my mother decided to take my elder sister and brother out of high school. She sent them to my aunt's home in Nanchang. So, my family was split three ways: mother, grandmother, my second sister and I were in Shanghai; two of my siblings were in Nanchang; and my father was in Dafeng.

I felt terribly lonely and depressed. I'd been very close to my elder sister and brother. I was their "little tail." They both liked reading and had spent all their allowance on books. They kept these books in a locked bookcase and had even made a "library card" for me to sign if I wanted to borrow anything. After they left home the house became quite different: it seemed large, empty and strange.

Every morning, my mother got up at four o'clock. She had to travel more than two hours to get to her workplace in Wusong. She was transferred there after my father got into trouble—obviously as punishment. Mother never got home until after seven. I sometimes woke up late at night to find her sitting under the dim light, writing letters to father, sister and brother or sewing or mending something.

Father served his term in the labor camp. During these "three years of natural disasters"³ food was in short supply and mother worried constantly. Father's letters said he got enough to eat but mother wasn't convinced. So she decided to send father some dried rice powder. However, she was afraid the postal officials wouldn't permit it. They checked all packages before they could be mailed.

Mother asked me to help. At home, we measured out a quantity of rice powder that weighed exactly as much as a thick dictionary. When we got to the post office we showed the clerk our package with the dictionary in it. After the clerk inspected, weighed and stamped this parcel he gave it back to us so we could sew it up. That was our chance to switch the book for the rice powder.

Father's time at the labor camp wasn't too bad. I think the authorities treated highly educated people leniently, and they made father keeper of the tool storage room. Father's co-worker in the storage room was once Sun Zhongshan's [Sun Yat-sen's] secretary.⁴ He'd known grandfather's brother—the Ambassador to France. Father never complained much about prison. I think he found it less stressful there. He returned to Shanghai in 1962.

Because of my family's background, I was, during my school years, very much the outsider. But I accepted the situation. Unlike my schoolmates, I had the freedom to make of my world what I wanted.

I had a very close friend in middle school. Before liberation, his father had been a rich merchant. His family still lived in a big house with a servant. He had lots of books. On Sundays, I would often walk a long distance to borrow some of them.

One day, I went to this friend's house, but he was not at home. While I waited for him to return, I started looking through some of his books. I came across a note written by him to the Youth League Organization at my school. It was about me. My friend had listed the books I'd asked about and had claimed he'd refused to help me. The books he'd cited—Dante's *Divine Comedy*, I remember, was one—weren't banned. But a good student wouldn't seek them out. If you were drawn to this kind of literature it indicated you probably had anti-social tendencies.

The report was only a draft. I suspect it was never handed in. But I left my friend's home before he returned and I never went back.

The incident scared me. It also hurt me dreadfully because one of the few friends I'd ever been able to make was planning to betray me.

When the Cultural Revolution began in 1966 I was in the second year of high school. You can imagine my fear: my father was an ideal target. Before long, people came to search our home. They stayed two days and nights.

Mother had prepared us. She gave me a Swiss watch and some money. She said the watch was a gift she'd planned to give the first child who went to university. She told me that, since this wasn't going to happen, I might as well have it now. She also told me to keep out of the house as much as possible.

We didn't know when the search team would arrive, so, for two weeks, I left home very early and didn't return until late. During this period I walked the streets aimlessly, with the watch strapped to my wrist. By the end of the day I was tired and hungry. My legs were as heavy as stone. But I defended my tiny watch as if I were guarding a kingdom of treasure.

In 1968, all Shanghai students were told to report to their schools for job assignments. Those with a "bad" family background, such as mine, were often sent to farms on Chongming Island.[5] But a few others and I refused to cooperate. Weeks passed and the number of students remaining in Shanghai dwindled. Finally, only two of us were left—a friend and I. Before long, we received an official letter telling us we had one week to go to the Security Bureau to cancel our Shanghai resident registration. That scared us a bit. We walked to the dispatch station with our registration books in our pockets. Reluctant to give in, my friend suggested that we draw a card to determine whether we should enter the building. We decided that if we picked the King of Clubs this would mean we should go in. Of course, the odds were against drawing that particular card. After we picked something else we let out a sigh of relief.

Now, I had to come up with an excuse for not going to the countryside. After discussing the problem with my parents I told the authorities I had chronic high blood pressure.

Obviously, this was a lie. I was ordered to report to the hospital for a test. People told me if I held my breath long enough while I was being checked the pressure would go up. I tried it but it didn't work. Then, a friend let me smoke one of his father's cigars until I felt my head spin. But that didn't raise my blood pressure either. Next, my mother was advised to give me lots of fatty pork—especially pig's head. So I started stuffing a large bowl of fat down my throat as often as I could. By the third day, just looking at the meat made me want to throw up.

I'd tried everything. No one in my family could get any rest. The situation was unbearable. I wanted to give up.

Mother said to me: "What I fear most is that if you go to the farm you may stay there forever, whereas other kids with good family backgrounds might have a chance to come back some day. If you stay at home at least we'll be together."

Finally, we found the solution to our problem. It was a medicine that temporarily raised blood pressure when taken in large enough quantities. Immediately, I swallowed some and went to the local district hospital to be tested. Before long I'd established a history of abnormally high blood pressure. When the doctor arrived at my home for an unannounced check my parents kept him talking downstairs while I rushed upstairs to swallow more medicine. After several such checks the authorities decided I wasn't malingering after all. I was left in peace.

Gradually, I settled into my life as an unemployed youth. You might not believe me if I tell you that the happiest and most fulfilling years of my life were spent during the Cultural Revolution. But it's true.

I was the complete outsider—both mentally and in every other way. I didn't belong to any organizations, and I had the freedom to do as I wished. I read, wrote and painted. Most important of all, I had a few very close friends. Every day we would meet and talk for hours. I used to look at other people in the street with pity. I thought my life was superior to theirs—even though I was supposedly the lowest in the society.

During the Cultural Revolution I wrote more than 300 poems. I had a lot of emotion bottled up inside me and this was the only way I could express it. I was very influenced by the poets of the 1930s. That was the only period we Chinese were able to pursue ideas freely. I used to go for long walks and stay up all night composing my verse. It was an intense, absorbing and exciting time for me.

No, I don't have those poems anymore. I burnt them. The finished verses were copied into little notebooks. I never anticipated that one day I'd have to destroy them.

What happened was this: I had an acquaintance not one of my close friends—with whom I shared books. He was particularly interested in aesthetics. He used to talk about girls—their shape, and the way they walked. I remember this because this kind of talk was unusual back then.

This man and I later fell out. He stopped returning the books I'd lent him. He even stole some books from my home—including a volume of poems I'd borrowed from someone else. That was the end of our relationship.

This acquaintance lived in half of a big room. The other half was a neighborhood inoculation station. It was separated from his living quarters by a thin piece of board with a small window in it. So, he and the nurses in the front room had few secrets from each other.

At that time, I was temporarily working in a neighborhood workshop. I polished razors on primitive machines in a cold, damp room for 70 cents [US 12 cents] a day. One morning, I was ordered to go to the public Security Bureau. My heart raced like a crazy horse's. I couldn't think of anything I'd done that might have caught anyone's attention.

The police immediately asked me whether I knew the acquaintance I just mentioned. Then, they ordered me to confess the counter-revolutionary activities I'd committed with him. After a day's interrogation, they finally released me at nine in the evening. When I was in the station what worried me the most was the poems I'd written. I knew that if the authorities got hold of them I'd definitely be in trouble.

I promised the police that, if they released me for the night, I would return home, think about the conversations I'd had with this man and return the next morning to report anything I thought might be significant. As soon as I got home I burnt my notebooks. Fortunately, it was winter, and I could let the smoke out of the house without attracting any attention.

Next day I went back to the security Bureau, no longer afraid. I'd turned my poems into ashes. The police finally explained why they'd pulled me in. The nurses at the inoculation station had told them my friend was listening to enemy radio broadcasts. The nurses had told the authorities they'd seen me visit him.

In the end, the police found no evidence a crime had occurred, and they gave up. But that was the end of my career as a poet. I tried to remember some of my verses and start writing again, but, somehow, it was different. I was always afraid I'd be found out.

During the Cultural Revolution father made good use of his spare time. I think the Dafeng experience taught him how to survive. He never much reacted to anything. When he was ordered to sweep the lanes or clean up sewage he did what he was told, without comment.

Later, after things quieted down, he began work on a Chinese-English dictionary. I know this meant a lot to him. He would spend a certain amount of time on this every day. The dictionary was written on the back of desk calendars. He didn't have the money to buy paper. I'll show you what I mean.[6]

I don't think his work was original enough to be published. However, it's worth millions to me. When father left China he asked me to throw his dictionary away. I couldn't. I'll show it to my child. It's part of my father's life.

In 1978, I took the College Entrance Examination. I did it for my parents. They wanted at least one of their children to get a degree. I was accepted by a university, graduated, and found work as a technician in a photographic paper factory. I've been in this factory since 1982 and now I'm head of a technical department.

The job's for making a living. I don't like it, and never will. I've no passion for numbers, which are what I deal with daily.

It's strange I miss the past so much. I view the time I spent during the Cultural Revolution as my golden period. Life since has become increasingly boring. I always feel I'm doing something I don't want to do. My real life was elsewhere.

On a superficial level, things are much better. I've got more possessions. Books are widely available. But I no longer feel there's any substance or intensity to my existence. My routine is colorless and without texture. Every morning when I wake up I feel the rush of depression.

Our factory isn't doing well. Secretly, I hope it'll close down. If it does I can end this kind of existence. It's not that I'll be better off leaving my job or that I have something else planned. It's just that I feel trapped and I don't have the courage to end things myself. I'll be relieved if events are taken out of my hands.

My brother and his family left for the United States. He found work in a factory in New York. Later, he sent for my parents. At last they have a better life. Now, they're US citizens, so I might get a chance to emigrate also. But I'm not that interested. It's too late for me now.

Notes

1 *Dream of the Red Mansions* by Cao Xueqin (1715–64) has been described as the greatest masterpiece in traditional Chinese literature. English trans., 3 vols, by Tsao Hsuch-chin and Kao Ngo, San Francisco: China Books and Periodicals, 1978.

2 *Jinshi*, the highest degree awarded by the Chinese civil examination system, was given to just one candidate out of 10,000.

3 This refers to a period of economic retrenchment (1959–1962) during which bad weather and the disastrous consequences of "The Great Leap Forward" led to severe food shortages. Millions of people died of famine during these years.

4 Sun Zhongshan (1866–1925) was founder of the Republic of China (1911–1949).

5 Chongming Island, the third largest in China, is situated across the mouth of the Changjiang River, a short ferry trip away from Shanghai. It was easy for the authorities in Shanghai to keep a close eye on students sent there.

6 He produced a sheaf of notes about a foot thick. These were written on the backs of calendars from 1970–1974. There were about 3,000–4,000 English words or idioms explained in Chinese, together with examples.

ZHU XUEQIN,[1] MALE: COLLEGE PROFESSOR

The article you mention focuses on a subgroup of Red Guards I call "1968ers" (*liuba nian ren*).[2] These Chinese 1968ers were unique in modern Chinese history. Like the 1968ers in Europe and North America, however, their influence was short-lived.[3]

My essay was written in response to the recent interest in the Three Old Classes. Frankly, I was disappointed at the naïveté of all those who participated in the discussion. But, at the beginning of the 1990s, everyone in China was hopelessly confused.

I think the chaos caused by the new market economy is responsible for the renewed interest in the past. Today, we have become nostalgic. "When the journey ahead is uncertain return to the shore" (*qiancheng mangmang, huitou shi an*). It's not just ex-Red Guards though. Many others, too, are in a mood of mourning.

My article was a requiem for the Chinese 1968ers, who've long since disappeared from the scene. These rebels were opinion-shapers who recognized that the Maoist dream of mass democracy was never realized in the cities.

The 1968ers were the first insurgents to challenge the Cultural Revolution. By 1968, most of them had been Red Guards for a couple of years. Typically, they were high-school students from key schools—very different from the brutish, mindless, thugs who were later portrayed in movies, TV shows and books. The 1968ers joined the Cultural Revolution as moral idealists, not as mob leaders. Their struggle and their critical attitude were genuinely spontaneous and largely unsupervised.

What was significant about 1968 was that this was the year the Up to the Mountains and Down to the Villages movement took off. Before long, hundreds of thousands of students found themselves in the countryside. This nurtured a unique environment that encouraged autonomy and self-reliance. These urban kids were removed from the political center. I would describe the rural settings in which they found themselves as decentralized "free-thought villages." I, myself, discovered the work of Hegel, Kant, Rousseau and Belinsky[4] when I was in a remote village in northern China.

In spirit, the Chinese 1968ers followed the heritage of traditional Chinese intellectuals: "Be the first under heaven to worry about social and political matters; be the last under heaven to enjoy what the world has to offer." They cared more about spiritual than material issues. They were willing to question everything.

They were nurtured by Marxist political thought—particularly by Marx's earlier more humanistic writings—and by Mao's belief in the value of continuous revolutionary struggle. Slowly, the discrepancies between Marxist thought and Maoist dogma became increasingly apparent to them. They dug deep into German philosophy, Russian eighteenth- and nineteenth-century literature, and French Enlightenment thought. All these works had some bearing on the Chinese Revolution, but at a distance, and, often, through the prism of official Party dogma. Of course, these kids were also the creatures of their own time and place.

Basically, the Chinese 1968ers were amateur intellectuals. During the daytime they were workers and farmers. At night, they were enthusiastic students of history, philosophy and politics. Not surprisingly, they had more questions than answers or solutions. The l968ers were not academically sophisticated. They were—let's not forget it—teenagers. I would say they were stuck at a stage of revolutionary populism.

Unfortunately, these amateur philosophers were quickly pushed aside by the corrupting materialism of the post-revolutionary period. You will not find many critical thinkers in China today. They've all disappeared, swallowed up in our current back-to-mediocrity campaign. History, of course, wields a sharp knife. It's not sentimental about having to dump you into the trash can. A culture of mediocrity does not, of course, foster any serious or painful historical inquiry.

I know that some commentators like to describe New China's Third Generation as the backbone of contemporary Chinese society. Many people claim that this generation now plays a major role in politics, the economy and intellectual life. This assertion is nonsense, however. First of all, in the political arena the Red Guard generation has been excluded from office. The so-called policy of "recruiting 'over-the-next century' people" (*kua shiji*) is designed to favor those who were born in the 1960s and educated in the 1980s. The members of this generation will reach the pinnacles of their careers at the beginning of the twenty-first century.

In other words, the up-and-coming leaders are members of a younger generation. They're also likely to be those petty bureaucrats who rose in the system by doggedly adhering to all the rules. This cohort is young and has no collective memory of the Cultural Revolution. Its members are very different from those born 1946–1953.

I'm not suggesting this is a conspiracy, but one thing for sure is that Jiang Zemin and the other top political leaders are nothing but careerists and bureaucrats. Naturally, they fear the Red Guard generation. There were two generations in China this century that had any first-hand revolutionary experience: one is the May Fourth generation and the other is the Red Guard generation.

May Fourth [1919][5] produced a generation that altered the course of Chinese history and managed to dominate Chinese social, political and cultural events for nearly half a century. The second revolutionary experience [the Cultural Revolution] didn't produce anything that lasted because it was imprisoned in the wrong body: the Chinese Communist Party. However, this second revolutionary experience left a legacy of "suspect-everything-and-down-with-everything." This rebellious inheritance makes a difference. High officials today believe that the members of the Red Guard generation can't be trusted with too much power.

In academic circles, too, the Red Guard generation has been passed over. I'm not suggesting that there are no outstanding scholars and scientists from that generation. But, in general, they missed the opportunity to reach the levels of scholarship attained by the older generation. Now they cannot compete with a younger generation. If you look at universities and colleges in China today, people in their thirties play a more important and visible role than those born around the time of liberation.

In the economic arena there are many people from the Red Guard generation who occupy middle-level managerial positions in state-owned enterprises. But the state-owned sector is in decline, so these people are stuck in positions of increasing irrelevance.

I don't believe the Red Guard generation has a significant role to play in contemporary China. They've outlived their era.

You raise the question of the Tiananmen Square demonstrators, which is an important one. At the beginning, I hoped the torch would be re-lit, and I was very much involved. I do believe there was a hand reaching out from the past, trying to reach the students. But, the connection wasn't made.

The 1989 movement was a complicated event. You cannot call it a "Movement for Democracy" just because "democracy" was painted on some banners. It was a marriage made of many parts. Some people from my generation tried to contact the student leaders and give some depth to their demands. Personally, I was disappointed.

Last year I was in the United States, and I saw a documentary about some of the student leaders who had fled China. Chai Ling made the worst impression on me. Her face had been cosmetically altered. As she flirted with the TV camera, she stroked a puppy dog on her lap and told her audience: "Don't just think of me as an activist; I'm a woman too." With the casualties of 1989 fresh in my mind, I felt deeply insulted and quite a bit nauseated.

Let's talk about history some more.

There were two movements around the time of May 4, 1919: the New Culture Movement of the pre-May Fourth period and the National Salvation Movement of the post-May Fourth period. The former movement aimed to establish a new civic culture. The latter was a political movement that tried to transform the state.

Those who led the New Culture Movement tried to change Chinese intellectuals from state bureaucrats to social critics. This created a new ideal for those who traditionally had been both associates and wards of the state. As reflected in Hu Shi's writings,[6] the spirit of the New Culture Movement was "a new attitude: one of faultfinding." Hu asked people to struggle for individual freedom. He thought only free individuals—those liberated from the patronage of the state—could create a decent society.

However, history never allowed the New Culture Movement to develop. During a period of national crisis it was far more important to rescue the Motherland from ruthless imperialist rape than to defend individual freedoms. Therefore, the post-May Fourth nationalist movement took precedence over the pre-May Fourth cultural movement. From that point on intellectual activities in China were dominated by power politics. In Mao's words, if you were not with "Yan'an," you were for "Xi'an."[7] Either Red or White! There was nothing in between.

What I am suggesting is that, under Mao, Chinese intellectuals played a traditional role. Their social participation once again was defined by how they could serve power and the interests of the state. Unfortunately, Chinese intellectuals have always lacked autonomy and have never really been able to act as social critics. The role of social critic has always been the most important and difficult one for them to assume.

Let me now answer your questions about the controversy caused by my writings on the French Revolution. As you know, many Chinese academics were surprised that I would try to make a comparison between events in France in 1789–1794 and the 1966–1976 Cultural Revolution.

My study shocked people because Chinese intellectuals are expected to accept the French Revolution as an exemplary moral narrative. Of course, if you find similarities between what people were taught was "good" [i.e. the French Revolution] and what they now see as "evil" [i.e. the Cultural Revolution] you are likely to be accused of denigrating the first or praising the second. At least, that's the kind of comment I get from my colleagues.

I don't believe the French Revolution was morally uncompromised. Nor do I see the Cultural Revolution as unambiguously evil. Serious historical research recognizes ambivalence. It doesn't favor one-dimensional forms of condemnation, nor can it be a simplistic accolade.

Two very different forces make human history. One represents the optimistic side of human nature. It's conformist and represents positive attitudes and constructive behavior. The other force is negative and represents the pessimistic side of human nature. It's critical, and suspicious about order. It recognizes the need for a complete structural revolution.

Most people are influenced by the first force. Only a few have sufficient ambition to try to reshape human society. Mao was one of them.

Towards the end of his life Mao claimed he had accomplished two great things. The first was to overthrow Jiang Jieshi [Chiang Kai-shek]; the second was to launch the Cultural Revolution. Mao was a revolutionary nihilist. His colleagues never realized how much he subconsciously suspected and distrusted established Chinese institutions. It's no coincidence that his favorite works of literature were *Water Margin* and *Dream of the Red Mansions*. The first is the story of a band of outlaws who fought against the political establishment in Song. The second ends with the exhausted hero of the story turning his back on the established cultural order.

In my work, I compare Mao's political thought with that of Jean-Jacques Rousseau. There are many similarities. Rousseau contrasted the "noble savages" with the corrupt individuals of the civilized world. Mao equated "the noblest with the stupidest; the most humble with the most intelligent." Not surprisingly, he ordered educated youths to go to the countryside to be re-educated by the peasants. Rousseau believed that science and art led to the decline of human moral life. Mao concurred. As he phrased it: "When the satellite is in the sky the red flag falls to the ground." Like Rousseau, Mao placed moral values above all else. He believed that the pursuit of material wealth was dangerous. Materialism would only stifle spiritual satisfaction.

Mao was a revolutionary purist. He couldn't compromise. What he wanted was moral perfection.

As well as looking at political ideology I also studied the similarities between the political activities of the Red Guards on the one hand and the Jacobins on the other. Anyone who knows about the French Revolution could easily make a connection between the bloody events in Paris of September 1792, and the terror in Beijing and Shanghai during July and August of 1966. Many of the Red Guards studied the French Revolution. The Jacobins certainly inspired their utopian idealism. The example of

Jacobin cruelty and revolutionary violence was important to all those who believed the Old World could only be smashed by force.

It's a question for psychologists why idealism and violence often go together. The more idealistic the students the more accepting they were of violence. Of course, if you're pessimistic about the existing order a refusal to compromise is the ultimate test of moral rectitude.

The Red Guards believed that the western world was demoralized and that the Soviet Union was equally decadent and corrupt. They rejected both political systems, as reflected in the popular slogan of the day: "We Oppose American Imperialism and Soviet Revisionism" (*fandi fanxiu*). In their innocent naïveté, they thought they'd discovered a third alternative—a new type of society that could save the entire world.

I'm not trying to defend the Red Guards. I condemn much of what happened during the Cultural Revolution. But, as a historian, you can't think like a moralist or a career politician, hemmed in by the need to give a "good" or "bad" slant on events. You want to understand *why* things happened as they did.

The third connection I make between the Cultural Revolution and the French Revolution has to do with the aftermath of revolution. The Jacobin effort to use violence in the service of liberty was ultimately thwarted by the Thermidorian reaction.[8] After Maximilien de Robespierre and other leftists were executed French society suppressed revolutionary energy and revolutionary memory, and the new leaders started to construct a safe, solid, national bourgeois order. In a similar fashion, after Mao died we got the "reform" to undo the revolution.

No matter how far revolution goes, Thermidor lies in wait. Mao once boasted that he wanted to release the nuclear energy of spiritual renewal. Such creative destruction creates heavy casualties and exhausts the survivors. When people can take no more the reactionary period comes into its own.

Do I have reservations about our Chinese Thermidor? Of course I do. If our "Jacobin" period revealed our capacity for aggression and cruelty, Thermidor shows how shallow and banal we can be. Today, many people want to repress all memory of the Cultural Revolution, as if this period were a natural catastrophe best forgotten. Remember how, almost overnight, the French gave up calling each other *citoyen* [citizen]—an expression that symbolized their newfound equality. Soon, they were back to "Sir," "Madame" and

"Count." The same thing has happened here. We no longer address each other as "comrade." Instead, *xiansheng* (master), *taitai* (madam) and *laoban* (boss) remind us of the persistence of social hierarchy. We do our best to erase the freedom of equality. Such liberty is what a mediocre society fears the most.

For my generation, no matter where we live, no matter what we do, we'll never escape the shadow of the Cultural Revolution. We'll live with it forever. If we reflect on its historical significance we can learn from it. If we refuse to come to terms with it we shall never be free of it.

Goethe once wrote: "I once had lofty ideals. To this day, I cannot forget them. This is my problem."

Yes. And this is my problem also.

Notes

[1]   Not a pseudonym.

[2]   Zhu Xueqin, "Of Those Missing in Chinese Intellectual History," *Dushu* (Digest), October, 1995, pp. 55–63.

[3]   Unlike other interviewees, Professor Zhu was given questions beforehand. Zhu Xueqin is Professor of History at Shanghai University. His book, *Collapse of a Moral, Ideal Kingdom: From Rousseau to Robespierre*, was published in Shanghai in 1994.

[4]   Vissarion Grigoryevich Belinsky (1811–1848), Russian literary critic, is described in the 1984 *Chinese Encyclopedia* as a major contributor to the Russian "national" type of social- ism. Belinsky's letter to the author Nikolai Gogol was regarded in China as a classic state- ment of "revolutionary populism."

[5]   The May Fourth movement began with student demonstrations in Tiananmen Square on May 4, 1919. The protesters were outraged that the Treaty of Versailles had trans- ferred Germany's rights in Shandong province to Japan.

[6]   Hu Shi (1891–1962), a writer and philosopher, studied at Columbia University with John Dewey. Hu was a leading figure in the May Fourth New Culture Movement. From 1938–1942 he served as the Nationalist government's Ambassador to the United States.

[7]   Yan'an, a village in Shanxi province, was the capital of the Soviet base governed by the CCP in the 1930s and 1940s. Xi'an was the capital of Shanxi province, held by the Guomindang.

[8]   So called because it began on 9 Thermidor, year II, of the new French calendar (July 27, 1794). The Thermidorian reaction in France led to the Directory, to the disarming of the Committee of Public Safety, and to Robespierre's arrest and eventual execution.

HONG YONGSHENG, MALE: HISTORIAN

I've been to America once—in 1992 when I spent three months at the University of Hawaii. I worked with a professor from the Institute of Far East Studies on *The Book of Changes*. That's my specialty. Last year, I published a book here called *Foreign Studies on The Book of Changes*.

Three months in Hawaii don't qualify me as an expert on the United States. I can only tell you how I felt when I was there. I was constantly reminded how lucky the American people are. Certain places do seem to show God's capacity for kindness. Hawaii has the most pleasant climate I've ever experienced. And, to my great surprise, there are no mosquitoes! I grew up in Shanghai, and the only other place I know is northern China, where nature is very harsh. For me, three months in Hawaii were like a Disneyworld vacation.

My wife wrote to me regularly. There were two main topics of discussion. One had to do with our little girl, and the other was whether I should return to China. I could have stayed in America—either legally or illegally, as do many visiting Chinese scholars. The university was willing to extend my visit. But I had to acknowledge that if I stayed in America illegally I would no longer be on vacation. I asked myself: did I want to sacrifice my career for a menial job in a Chinese restaurant? Besides, I didn't really belong in America. My roots are in this country. So I came back.

I come from a very poor family. Until 1953, when he became jobless, my father owned a tiny liquor store. The "store" was actually just a booth with a counter and several shelves set up in our family room.

I was the first son. Two brothers arrived later. Mother washed clothes for several families in the neighborhood. It was hard work, especially in winter. I always thought her hands were unusually large. In fact, they were permanently swollen because they were in cold water most of the time.

In 1957, the government tried to send some urban dwellers to the countryside. They targeted surplus residents (*xiansan renyuan*) such as my parents who didn't have formal employment. About a dozen families were transferred from our neighborhood to a village in Qingpu, a county outside Shanghai.

We traveled overnight in a small steamboat. I was five years old, and the river seemed very big and dark. Actually, it was only a small canal. Qingpu is water country. In those days you went about by boat. I wasn't a bit excited because I could sense how anxious and unhappy my parents were. Mother had wept and cursed as she'd packed our belongings.

My experiences in the countryside were immediate and vivid. During my first week I learnt about sex and death.

My parents and I shared one big storage room with two other families. Because I was in a strange place I was quite restless during the night. The couple next to my bed woke me up on several occasions. It didn't take me long to figure out what they were doing.

I quickly made friends with boys from the village. They liked to dig up abandoned graves. I followed them around and saw the skulls they'd found. These gave me nightmares. Later, I connected these rotten skulls with the fate of a boy who'd drowned in the river. This kind of incident happened often in the countryside because small kids were left to wander around by themselves. Children would go out to play or to wash in the river and never come back.

On one occasion I nearly drowned too. I'd followed the village boys to an abandoned temple. We had to cross a canal. I couldn't swim, but this didn't stop me from plunging ahead. In a second, I was under water, choking. A kid a year older than I gave me a push back to the shore. He saved my life. I didn't dare tell my parents what had happened.

My family lived in Qingpu County for about eight years. During this period I was in and out of six different schools. It was only in the last couple of years that my parents managed to settle down in Zhujiazhuang, a town near Lake Dingshan. There, I was able to go to school regularly. All the other village schools I attended had one thing in common: a single classroom containing children from the first to the sixth grade. The teachers would circulate from group to group, assigning various lessons. This gave me the opportunity to listen to what the others were doing. When I was in second grade I was already studying with the kids from the fifth grade.

I was particularly fond of one teacher. Every morning, he would take out a book and read stories for an hour. Sometimes it was a short story from *Harvest* literature magazine; at other times it was a long novel. Later, when I became a schoolteacher I did the same thing for my students. Every day, I picked a story from the Hans Christian Andersen collection. The children were so fond of these tales that I could easily control them just by warning them they might be banished from the next story-telling session.

The village schools I attended were primitive and backward. But, in certain respects, they resembled the private tutoring schools of old China. Rural teachers could teach whatever they wanted, and the kids certainly weren't under any academic pressure. I learnt something in those schools I've treasured all my life: a free and independent spirit of learning.

During my family's time in the countryside we often didn't have enough to eat. Father would dry edible plants and herbs, grind them, and mix them with flour. I thought this was quite creative of him. Sometimes, my parents would bring home baskets of carrots. We would wash them, slice them up, and put them out to dry. Then we would have carrots every day for weeks on end. When there was rice for dinner father and I were always served first. Mother made it clear that I was more important than my two younger brothers. It was taken for granted I would be the pride of the family.

In 1965, my father decided that he would appeal to the authorities to let him come back to Shanghai. But the request was denied. Finally, father and mother decided to return anyway, and we rented a small room in which to live. Mother took in laundry again. Father did all sorts of odd jobs. Among other things, he worked as a day laborer and as a stevedore. My brothers and I couldn't go to school because we weren't registered as city residents. Near our home was a key elementary school. I used to watch the kids through the fence and feel very despondent.

By that time, I'd already developed an interest in history and in classical literature. My uncle used to take me to Fuzhou Road, and we would spend the afternoon in the Bookstore of Chinese Classics and in the Cultural Relics Store. I would find a quiet corner and sit and read for the whole afternoon.

So when the Cultural Revolution began, I wasn't in school. At first, I really didn't understand what was happening. However, my parents were delighted by the sudden turn of events and joined others in the street to shout "Down with the Capitalist Roaders!" In the evenings they went to political meetings where they accused Party cadres of oppressing the masses.

At one such event mother broke down completely. She told everyone that officials in Shanghai had accused our family of taking rations away from city folk. She said that when we'd been ordered out of the city I'd burst into tears and told the authorities I could get by on tap water.

Actually, my parents weren't in the slightest bit political, but they hated the bureaucrats who'd sent them to Qingpu. The Cultural Revolution gave them a chance to voice their grievances. I don't see anything wrong with this. Before the Cultural Revolution Party officials often treated people such as my parents with indifference and contempt.

Looking back, I would say that the Cultural Revolution didn't significantly alter my family's situation. We did get our city registration status back in 1967. But, apart from that, our lives were unchanged. Before the Cultural Revolution we were poor and powerless. Afterwards, it was the same. If Mao wanted to bring democracy to the masses he failed.

I should have been in the class of 1968. However, as I hadn't formally graduated from an elementary school, the authorities decided I should be classified as a sixth grader. You might wonder why they bothered to make such a ruling, considering no schools were open at the time.

But the decision did have a major impact on my life. Instead of going to the countryside like the rest of the 1968 class, I was assigned in 1971 to a factory in Henan province. The factory was built by the Shanghai Steam Engine Plant to help develop heavy industry inland. It was staffed exclusively by Shanghainese.

I enrolled for a year's training in the Shanghai Steam Engine Plant, and, in 1972, I took the train heading north to Henan. I was singing and smiling all the way. I'd always wanted to go to northern China—the birthplace of our nation. Henan was rich in history. Could any other place have offered me so much?

For the first time ever I was given a desk of my own in a 14 square meter dormitory room I shared with a co-worker. How happy I was!

In Henan I made four good friends—all a bit older than I. One studied Chinese water painting, one learned English and the other two, like myself, were fond of classics and history. Later, three of us were appointed teachers in the factory's elementary school. We spent weekends and school holidays walking in the countryside and climbing mountains.

During my eight years in Henan province I visited nearly all the important historical sites. My friends and I also composed classical poems. I thought about seventy-five of mine were good enough to keep. I still have them. After I left Henan I stopped composing poetry, but now I've started again. Classical poetry best expresses my current mood.

I loved the time I spent in Henan. This vast land generously opened up to me its fullness of history, its space of imagination and its humanity. I love the people of northern China. They've inherited more of what is truly Chinese than the people of southern provinces, which were long influenced by alien cultures.

By 1978, I felt it was time for me to leave Henan. I chose Shandong province as my next destination: another important wellspring of Chinese culture. I took the College Entrance Examination and applied to the History Department in Shandong University. Unfortunately, I failed the political study and foreign language exams. I wasn't too upset because I was so sure of myself. However, it made me lose interest in studying as an undergraduate. I decided that if I ever wanted to go to university I would apply directly to graduate programs. I never took the College Entrance Examination again.

I started publishing some articles on Chinese history. Because of these, I was invited to lecture at history and sociology seminars organized by the Shanghai Academy of Social Sciences. I left the factory in Henan and moved back to Shanghai in 1980.

During this period I applied to several universities, but I was consistently rejected because I had no baccalaureate degree. Finally, in 1986, I was admitted as a graduate student in the Chinese Philosophy Institute at the Shanghai Academy of Social Sciences. In my entrance exams, I got the highest scores on all subjects, except political study. During my interview I was asked a couple of questions about Marxism. I talked non-stop for half an hour, trying to make a good impression. The examiners let me pass. Later, I was told that the chief examiner knew next to nothing about Marxism. Just as well!

I graduated in the summer of 1989. I was still a student when the student demonstrations broke out in the spring of that year.

The previous year I'd been a visiting student at Beijing University so I was quite involved in the events leading up to the occupation of Tiananmen Square. I had quite a few reservations about some of the student leaders.

In 1988, Beijing University was very lively. Students got together nearly every evening. The main topic of discussion was gossip about high-ranking officials. These top leaders were ridiculed for their ignorance and stupidity. The students believed the future was theirs. They were frustrated and felt they were not being taken seriously. They talked grandiosely and rather stupidly, making comments such as: "Today I study, tomorrow I save China." The following year this kind of attitude surfaced in the students' utter contempt for the government and in their aloof and elitist attitude towards the masses.

At the beginning of the 1989 student movement I was just an observer. However, on April 26, 1989, a *People's Daily* editorial declared that the students were "counter-revolutionaries," and, three weeks later, the government imposed martial law in the capital. This made me see things in a different light. I joined the demonstrations in Shanghai, and I signed my name and my wife's and child's names on petitions that opposed the official pronouncements about the students.

What really scared the government in 1989 was the emergence of independent workers' and students' political organizations that began to cooperate. This was unprecedented. It reminded the government of what was happening in Eastern Europe. It had to take a hard line.

We don't really know all that happened in Beijing on June 4, 1989. We got the news through the *Voice of America* and, of course, through the official media. On June 6 and 7, thousands of students and civilians in Shanghai held a memorial service in People's Square for those who'd died in Beijing. All traffic stopped for two days. Busses were left on intersections to block all roads leading to People's Square.

People were very anxious about the students' safety. Rumors spread that soldiers were moving towards Shanghai. People set up barricades and stopped trucks loaded with members of the Workers' Militia.[1]

Zhu Rongji [then Mayor of Shanghai, who became Chinese Premier in 1998] behaved very intelligently. He did what was necessary to defuse the situation. Basically, he gave everyone a chance to let off steam. But he insisted on mustering the Workers' Militia. These soldiers were armed with nothing but a helmet on their head. Nonetheless, the helmet was a symbol of authority and power. At first, people identified Militia members with the government and pelted them with objects. The Militia were caught in a bad situation. They'd been ordered not to let workers assemble in the streets.

By June 10 the street demonstrations in Shanghai came to an end.

Now you probably feel no trace of the excitement we experienced in 1989. There's nothing left. Nobody's interested in anything except making money. Wang Dan's sentencing didn't even cause a ripple among the students in Shanghai.[2] The market economy has dissolved people's unity and ended their commitment to social causes.

However, the market economy unexpectedly and positively impacted social science. Articles that are creative and independent are much more likely to be published now. No one's interested in official propaganda. This creates a good climate for us. We can say very critical things as long as it's phrased in academic terms. Read some of our articles for yourself. They're quite bold.

What matters to me are my own personal beliefs and standards. I think there's something deeper and wider than our limited life experiences. I've named this room "The Room of the Three Happinesses": Spiritual Happiness (my intellectual life); Physical Happiness (my family's life, our immediate environment); and Future Happiness (my child's life). I'm quite content, let me say.

Notes

[1]   Somewhat equivalent to the National Guard in the United States.

[2]   Wang Dan, a student leader during the protests in 1989, was given an eleven-year sentence on October 30, 1996. He was convicted of conspiring to subvert the government.

On April 19, 1998, Wang Dan was put on an airplane to the United States for "medical treatment."

LIN JUAN, FEMALE: EDITOR OF A WOMAN'S MAGAZINE

Both my parents came from very wealthy families. At home, *Waipo* (maternal grandmother) was in charge of everything. She put me under her wing from the day I was born. She really spoiled me. We had a live-in servant for the chores. I didn't have to do anything except my homework.

When the Cultural Revolution began I was in my first year of middle school. I wasn't directly involved in the movement but I did try to emulate the role models. That's why I ended up in Heilongjiang.

My class was "Completely Red." Everyone had to go to the countryside. I saw this as an opportunity to create some distance between my family and myself. I figured my parents would try to stop me leaving Shanghai because they knew I wasn't like the others. I planned to overcome my family's resistance, confound everyone's expectations and emerge as a model student. But things didn't turn out like that.

Because I was the best writer in my class I was asked to edit our school's Red Guard newsletter. One week, I had to attend a workshop that took me away from home for a couple of days. When I returned one of my teachers greeted me with a big smile on his face. "Congratulations!" he said. "Your father's such a good man. You can be proud of him." I had no idea what he was talking about.

It turned out that, while I was safely out of the way, my father had attended a mobilization session at my school. At this meeting he'd signed me up to answer the Party's call. He told everyone that his daughter might seem "progressive" in school but that she was a spoiled brat at home. He claimed I was lazy and had never laundered as much as a handkerchief in my life. He ended by telling everyone it wouldn't hurt a privileged kid like me to taste some "bitterness" in the country.

You can imagine how I felt. I was livid. My father had made me look so stupid. Actually he's a pathetic figure. Because of his "bad" family background all he could think about at the time was how to be politically correct. He wanted to demonstrate he was more revolutionary than the real revolutionaries. He put his own interests before those of his wife and children. I know he didn't care about me. What made me feel worse was that my mother didn't raise her voice against him.

Now, I had to decide where I should go. My father put on his democratic face and pretended to have a family council. He told me he wanted me to make the decision so I wouldn't be able to blame him if anything went wrong.

I chose Heilongjiang because I knew it was where the true revolutionaries went. I'd been strongly influenced by speeches given by some older Red Guard leaders. One of these had told us he planned to set up a *kangda* university in this faraway province.[1] His words were inspiring. In my mind's eye I could picture the vast land, the sweeping forests, the simple peasantry and the long border facing a hostile Soviet Union.

Grandma congratulated me on making a good choice. She pointed out that, if I joined a state farm, I wouldn't have to cook my own meals. She couldn't accept I might ever be capable of doing something for myself!

Five days later I boarded a train with other student-settlers, and I was on my way to help develop the Great Northern Wilderness.

First, it was a big train, which headed north for four days. Then we sat on a shabby, local train for another day. Next, we had a long journey on a broken-down old bus. Finally, we disembarked. The prospect wasn't encouraging. Everything was bleak and windswept. A tractor turned up for our baggage, and we were ordered to walk 7 miles to farm headquarters. By the time we arrived it was dark and cold. Most of the girls were in tears. I was beginning to suspect I could have made a mistake, but, unlike most of the others, I refused to cry.

On the tenth day, things got a lot worse.

We'd arrived in April, but the weather was still very cold. During the night it fell to minus 20° centigrade. Our dormitories were freezing. Someone suggested we keep the stove lit all night and redirect the vents so we could get more heat. While we were asleep some sparks escaped and set fire to a straw mattress. Before we knew what was happening our room was in flames. I had to rush outside in my underwear. Everyone else was screaming hysterically.

This was my opportunity. "Comrades," I shouted. "Stop crying! Let's sing a song." I led the group in verses from Mao's Quotations. Slowly, raggedly, everyone else joined in. When workers from other units rushed to the scene they were greeted with cheerful singing, not hopeless wailing. They saw me as I wanted to be seen. My spirits were uplifted. I'd transcended personal weakness.

Seven of the students were badly burned and were taken to the county hospital. Some cadres from Shanghai happened to be visiting the town and sent back news of the fire. By the time this news got home the story was that there'd been a major disaster and that only seven students had survived.

My father went to the Municipal Educated Youth Office with other parents. He'd appointed himself their leader. The parents were very upset and demanded to know what had happened to their children. My father told the authorities that he would pay everyone's train fare to Heilongjiang out of his own pocket. He made such a nuisance of himself that he was reprimanded for trying to stir up trouble and got another notation put in his record.

After a couple of months at the farm I no longer felt inferior. I told myself that I'd not only do everything well but also that I'd outperform everyone else. Before long, I'd become a "Five Goodnesses Soldier" (*wuhao zhanshi*) ["ideologically correct," "morally clean," "hardworking," "healthy in attitude" and "physically fit"]. But, because I was so driven, I wasn't particularly popular. My annual evaluations had comments in them such as "arrogant, and does not have a good relationship with the masses." I sincerely accepted these criticisms but didn't really know how to correct them. I couldn't help wanting to be the best.

What I missed most were my books. I was always a keen reader. In the third grade I'd read the "big books" (*dashu*) of Chinese classical literature written in the old style. Then, I discovered that one of the girls on the farm had a whole set of classical novels. Her sister had packed them for her. However, this girl wasn't able to read the difficult text. I told her that, if she lent me the books, I'd tell her the stories, chapter by chapter. She agreed. I ended up reading the stories so often I can still recall every detail.

Some of the officials in the farm were cadres from Shanghai. They'd been demoted and sent to this faraway land to become "king of the kids." Their families had accompanied them. Most of these cadres were college educated and had joined the Party before liberation. At first, I was attracted to them and felt I couldn't match their revolutionary zeal. I suppose I was looking for father figures that could give me some guidance.

Looking back, I realize these cadres were losers. They weren't committed to us, they didn't trust us, and they were always looking for an opportunity to get out—or, at least, get their children out. As soon as they could, these cadres assigned their own children elsewhere.

The first such chance to leave came when some of us were selected to be Worker-Peasant-Soldier students. Up to that point I'd been content, even though the life was tough. However, when I saw other people leaving I became resentful.

I asked for a three-month leave to go back to Shanghai. What surprised me was that as soon as I got home I was my old self again. I slept until midday, ate a lot, argued with my father and fought with my brother. I forgot about the farm. When it was time to go back I'd gained nearly 30 pounds and had a very fair complexion.

I should pause and tell you about my family. My father's father graduated from the Japanese Imperial University in Tokyo. He taught at Sichuan University in Chengdu. His two eldest brothers inherited the family's estates and were executed during land reform in 1952.

Land reform in Sichuan was unnecessarily harsh. Do you know why? It was because Deng Xiaoping came from a big landlord family in the province. In order to show he'd distanced himself from his "bad" family background Deng encouraged the movement to go way beyond what was constructive.

According to my father his uncles were enlightened landlords. After liberation they didn't dare oppose land reform. They handed their estates over immediately but it didn't do them any good. They were both killed anyway.

In 1958, my grandfather was sentenced to ten years in prison for his "criminal activities." He'd criticized land reform and organized a demonstration in front of the provincial government's building in Chengdu.

I didn't know about any of this when I was a child. After 1958, my father had cut off all relations with his family. It's difficult now to understand how people could behave like that. Father later told me he'd done it to help his family. But it didn't help me at all!

In 1973, when I was back in Heilongjiang, I applied to join the Youth League. I didn't mention my grandfather in the application because I knew nothing about him. I did list my father's "political problem." I'd had plenty of opportunities over the years to be reminded about that.

My father got a degree in economics before liberation. He joined an organization called the "Economic Development Strategy Advisory Committee" that was sponsored by the Guomindang. It was more political than academic. Father thought he was going to save China. Instead, he created a long-standing "problem" that was continuously being dredged up by people who didn't like him. Actually, most people didn't like him.

I never expected that father's background would affect my admission to the Youth League, and I was devastated when I was denied admission. I was reprimanded and told I'd concealed "serious family problems."

I sent a letter to my father demanding an explanation. As he'd been backed into a corner he had to admit that his own father was a convict. The farm in Heilongjiang sent two people to Chengdu to investigate my background. They discovered that the old man had died in jail in 1967. I don't know how father took the news. He never said anything to me.

In the late 1980s, I traveled to Chengdu to look up the house where my grandfather used to live. It's a big house. Strangers have taken it over. Grandma died shortly after her husband passed away.

In 1974, I began work as a teacher in a brigade elementary school in Heilongjiang. I wanted the job because I loved the idea of being a teacher. The previous teacher was a friend of mine. At the beginning of the Cultural Revolution both her parents had been sent to May Seventh cadre schools for two years. She was the oldest in her family, so she'd taken over the responsibilities of looking after her younger siblings. She was 14 years old when her parents left.

My friend had been a teacher for two years. Everyone had fallen in love with her. She'd cut the kids' hair and even made clothes for them. Of course, she'd had plenty of opportunity to work on these skills. Whenever it was raining or snowing she used to carry the small children to the school on her back. She'd spent her own money on pencils and books. When I assumed her position I realized I had an obligation to carry on the good deeds she'd started.

However, I knew I was a better teacher than she was because I'd read a lot and I wrote very well. I said to myself: maybe I can't make clothes for the children but I can certainly show them how to write letters for their parents. That's the most practical thing country kids can learn. I didn't want my students growing up like their mothers and fathers, who were mostly illiterate.

I was a good teacher. I'm not going to be modest about it. I loved being a teacher. During my time in that school I sent all the best kids to the county high school. I was well known as a model teacher in the county town, and I was often asked to give teaching demonstrations. The county government asked me to teach at the high school. I had to decline. The universities had just reopened and I wanted to enroll.

As soon as they heard that the College Entrance Examination had been reinstated, many people at the farm quit what they were doing. Many of them just packed up and went back to Shanghai to prepare for the exam. The farm was half deserted. I stayed in my school. I didn't have the guts to leave my job right away. Because of my sacrifice I unexpectedly failed the College Entrance Examination.

The following year, I spent more time preparing for the exam, and I passed. Northeast Normal University accepted me. I studied Chinese literature and language.

After graduation, I was assigned to work for the Women's Federation in Shanghai, and, in 1986, I was appointed Chief Editor of one of the Federation's magazines. That's how I got involved in women's issues.

Over the last five years my life has changed dramatically. I've shown I can adjust to a rapidly changing environment. I'm the kind of person who can't stand to be left behind. I look for opportunities and I grab them. Compared to many others I'm shrewd and business-minded. I'm catching up with the world. But the real masters are the members of the young generation. They have clear, material goals and they'll use whatever means are necessary to achieve them.

As the editor of a leading women's magazine I've established myself as an expert on women's issues. I'm often asked to give lots of speeches on the image of women, on their relations with men, on career choices, family, education, culture, shopping and so on. I've been on TV many times. Right now, I'm presenting a TV show that introduces people to new products. To tell you the truth, though, I'm not really interested in women's issues. Neither is the public.

At the age of 44 I'm still not married, so I can't claim to be an expert on motherhood. I didn't consciously choose to be single. Sometimes I think it has something to do with my father. I always saw him as a very weak figure. As far as our family's concerned, frankly he's useless. My disappointment with him probably affected my relations with other men.

I'm not saying I'll never get married. However, I don't think my life would be as good if I had a husband. As an acknowledged expert on women's issues I earn about 3,000 yuan a month, from speaking, consulting and TV fees. With no family to worry about, I can live comfortably and save up some money. I've worked hard. But I'm never going to make a killing.

As editor of a magazine I get a lot of under-the-table kickbacks. For instance, I can ask for a 10 percent commission fee from every advertiser who wants to do business with me. Many companies are eager to pay me to get the exposure they need. I admit I was a bit slow at first because I was still thinking "wrong versus right."

I make good money even though I don't make big money. But in my line of work you get a lot of extras, and you certainly get to attend a lot of dinner parties. That's income too, right? I'm still a salaried member of the Women's Federation, but I only have to come here once a week. Most of the time I'm running around the city going to meetings, giving speeches and attending dinner parties. I'm planning to start my own consulting business. There's lots of money to be made doing that kind of thing.

To answer all your questions, I'm neither satisfied nor dissatisfied with China. People should try to make the best out of a situation. There's no point bitching. If you want to know what I think might be missing from my life I'd say it's probably the lack of one friend on whom I can depend. Everyone today wants something from you. So, naturally, the same principle governs my relations with others.

I went back to Heilongjiang last year. Every student but one had left the farm. I went to visit her. She'd married a local farmer and was completely integrated into the community. Before I went to her house I warned myself to be tactful. I was expecting her to be unhappy. Much to my surprise, she seemed quite content. I'm much more successful than she is, but she'd prepared presents for me. I was quite touched.

She has a wonderful husband and a daughter who's getting ready to go to university. She laughs a lot. When I left her home I felt a little bit jealous.

And, suddenly, I didn't feel quite so sure of myself.

Note

1 The original *kangda* (anti-Japanese universities) trained military officers and political cadres in the Chinese soviet bases during the Sino-Japanese War (1937–1945).

ZHANG AIXIANG, FEMALE: SMALL BUSINESS OWNER

My husband's putting me on the spot. I guess he's right to say he can't tell you about his life without talking about me. We've been together a long time.

My father was a peasant from Shandong province. He joined the Liberation Army in the early 1940s. In 1958, he answered the Party's call to transform the "Great Northern Wilderness" (*beidahuang*) and, together with thousands of others, he moved his family to Heilongjiang. Father could've got a job in the county town but he got into an argument with his superiors over his job assignment. In a rage, he decided that he would settle in a remote village at the far northern edge of the province and become a simple peasant.

The village had about twenty families who lived in a mountainous area at the edge of a forest. The trees were so dense you couldn't even see your neighbor's house. At the time, I was 6, and I had an 8-year-old sister and a 3-year-old brother.

I wasn't able to go to school until I was nine. Because my mother had to work as a laborer I had to take my small brother and a new baby sister with me. My brother wasn't too bad, but my baby sister was a lot of trouble. She cried one minute and wet herself the next. It disrupted the class. When I complained to my mother she decided it would be best if I quit school. I wept, but I had to obey.

After I'd stopped going to school about a month, the teacher came to our home. He wanted me to return. "Come back," he said. "You can bring as many brothers and sisters as you want. We're all very poor in this village so it is all the more important that you learn."

The school was a one-room cabin. The teacher let me have a table to myself, so my little brother and sister could sit on either side of me. Altogether, I had six years of schooling.

When the first students from Shanghai arrived in our village in 1968 I was already a full-time laborer. By this time my mother had given birth to two more sisters. Now, we were a large family with six children.

Like everyone else, I was very excited about the new settlers. We used to cluster around the doors of the students' homes, peeking and chatting. Later, the students chose some villagers to be their friends. I became a frequent visitor to their collective households.

My husband came to the village with his sister. I was his sister's friend first. In 1970, I was appointed the first woman team leader in the village, and my future husband became the accountant for our work team.

The villagers chose me to be their leader because I had a reputation as an "iron girl" (*tieguniang*). I worked as hard as the men. After I became team leader I worked even harder. In autumn, we cut grass to prepare the winter food for our animals. If a male laborer cut 100 bundles of grass I'd cut 110— no matter how long it took. My parents said most people tried to get away from work but they had to try to get *me* away from work.

I remember one incident in particular. I was harvesting beans in the field, and it was getting late. My father came to check on me. He tried to pick up a bundle of beanstalks I'd cut, but he couldn't lift it. He took off his shoe and started beating me. "You work as if you don't want to live anymore," he cried. "You stupid little fool! Don't you know how to take care of yourself. If you're injured what are we going to do?" He felt he had to hit me to get my attention.

But I was born like that. I didn't change. People liked me, and thought of me as a hardworking and trustworthy person. I joined the Party when I was 19 years old. The following year I became Party Secretary of our brigade.

My husband and I liked each other the first time we met. We were both 16 at the time. I was a peasant and he was the city boy. But it wasn't until six years later that Chui and I opened our hearts to each other. That year his sister left the village to attend a college in the provincial city. I asked Chui if he was going to leave too. "No," he replied, "I want to stay here with you."

In 1977, before Chui and I could plan our wedding, the students in the village began to return to their families in Shanghai. A couple of them abandoned their peasant girlfriends and boyfriends. My husband was his family's only son. His parents put a lot of pressure on him to go back home. Chui's mother was planning to take early retirement so her son could replace her.

My parents were in panic. They warned me that I should not allow Chui to return to Shanghai. "If you let him go," they warned, "it will be the end of you. You'll be abandoned and humiliated and our family will never be able to hold up its head again. No other man will want a rejected woman."

I knew that Chui wanted to go back to Shanghai, and I also realized that, if I asked him to stay at the village, he probably would. I cried and cried. I never doubted that it was my duty to put him first. Finally, Chui did leave, but he also promised he'd come back to marry me.

My parents thought it was all over. They threw my belongings out of their home and ordered me to leave. They weren't going to shelter a disgraced daughter.

I picked up my stuff and moved into the brigade office. I recognized my parents probably were right and that, sooner or later, I'd get a goodbye letter from Chui. But I also realized it was pointless for me to try to force myself on him.

A month passed. One day I walked into the office and found that all my belongings had gone. My mother had sent my sisters to move me back home. I went to see my parents. They just said: "Now, please, do forget him."

Chui would send me letters often twice a month. In every one, he would repeat his promise that he was going to return to marry me. In 1980, almost two years after he had left the village, Chui asked me to come to Shanghai before the New Year. He wanted us to get married the day after the New

Year's Celebrations. Again, my parents were infuriated. "It's not possible," my father raged. "How can my daughter go to her husband's family without a proper greeting? It's embarrassing." I felt the same way. How could I go to Chui's home all by myself?

But Chui begged me not to worry. He didn't have the time or the money to travel to our village. If I could just forget about the ritual and the costume, he told me, we soon would be husband and wife. So I said goodbye to my parents and arrived in Shanghai on my twenty-eighth birthday. Two weeks later, Chui and I were married.

It was obvious no one in Chui's family approved of the match. I was greeted coldly by his family. We rented a place in a poor neighborhood and ate with Chui's parents. Two months later I was pregnant.

Shanghai's winter is very damp as well as cold—something I'd never experienced before. During winters in Shanghai it's the same temperature inside and outside the house. We were spared this in Heilongjiang because, there, all the houses are heated in winter. I couldn't speak the Shanghai dialect and was ignored by my in-laws. It was hard to sit with them at the dinner table as a total stranger. I wanted to cook meals for Chui and myself, even though it would have cost more. I also wanted to work—no matter what kind of job it was.

I didn't have Shanghai resident registration, so I couldn't be formally employed. The only jobs I could find were temporary. I had to beg for them. I did all kinds of work. But no matter what I did I was always given the worst job and paid the least. I was the scapegoat whenever things went wrong. "Crows are black wherever they go."

One boss gave me extra work during the lunch break. Other people were resting, while I was cleaning, sweeping and stacking things. I said to the boss: "You take advantage of me because I'm a temporary worker."

"That's right," he patiently explained. "That's how it works."

At home, I was often in tears. After my daughter was born the situation only got worse. My job paid less than 20 yuan a month. Our income couldn't support us. My mother-in-law's face got grimmer and grimmer.

One day, I said that I would like to go back to my village. This drew an immediate reaction. "Why don't you get a divorce?" my mother-in-law said. "You've created a lot of difficulties. Go back to Heilongjiang and find someone suitable for you. Chui can find a wife with Shanghai resident registration. You'd both be happier." I felt as if I was stabbed in the heart.

I ran back home and told Chui what his mother had said. He was very angry: "If she says this again," he said, "you can tell her that, wherever you go, I'll go with you." Later, he told his mother the same thing: "Don't turn me into a disobedient son. I'll never leave her." The topic of divorce was dropped.

I missed my family and the village very much. Sometimes in the street I heard people speaking the northeastern dialect (*dongbei hua*), and I would follow them to listen to the familiar and sweet sounds of my own tongue. In 1984, I did go back to the village with my husband and daughter. My child and I stayed for eight months. Then, something unexpected happened.

I became pregnant again. But I didn't realize it until four months later. I'd always had irregular periods. When my parents found out they were delighted. They wanted me to have the baby. I wrote to my husband—who'd gone back to Shanghai by this time—to give him the news. He and his parents were shocked. A letter arrived urging me to have an abortion.

I wanted to keep the baby, and my family supported me. "Give birth here," they told me. "No one in Shanghai will know. We'll raise the child if you can't." In Shanghai, a second pregnancy would have caused problems. But not in the village.

For several days, I debated with myself whether to have the baby. Sometimes I felt I wanted it and other days I worried about how I would cope. Time passed. The pregnancy entered its eighth month, and, by then, of course, it was almost impossible to abort the child.

Finally, my father-in-law sent me his verdict. He said that I was very foolish to keep the baby since my husband and I couldn't provide for our first child. My parents saw his letter and changed their minds. If I was still going to be his daughter-in-law, they said, I'd better obey him. Otherwise life would be very difficult for me.

I wrote to Chui and asked him to tell me face-to-face what to do. When Chui arrived in the village he was silent for a while. Then he exploded: "Why did you ask me to come?" he cried. "Now, I have to order you to have an abortion. Otherwise, how could I face my parents? If I'm not here I don't see and I don't know. You could have had the baby." He broke into tears.

The county family planning office said that it would be dangerous for me to have an abortion. They told me they would inform Shanghai that the local office had given me permission to have my child. They said that, since Chui and I were both Party members, we wouldn't be punished.

However, the pressure from Chui's family was unrelenting. He was reminded, once again, what a mistake he'd made to marry a peasant girl. I couldn't stand his sad and miserable face anymore, so I gave in. If I had to die I would. I felt I just didn't care any more.

The county hospital performed the abortion. I don't want to recall that day. I was in a coma for two days. Later, the nurse told me that my husband had passed out when he saw that the baby had thick, shining black hair. Chui didn't eat, sleep or talk until I came to. No one will ever understand how we felt. [She breaks down for a while].

Two months later I went back to Shanghai. I was still weak. But I had to look for work again. I heard that schools were trying to find people who could type their text materials. I thought I could get a typewriter and work at home. It was a good idea, but I didn't have the 700 yuan I needed for the typewriter.

My sister-in-law heard about my dilemma. She talked to her mother. One evening she came to our home with a typewriter. My mother-in-law had bought it for us. I was a bit moved.

The first month I only made 16 yuan and 80 cents (US$5.25). I typed very slowly, spending most of my time looking for characters. The second month I made more than 80 yuan. Gradually, I got some steady customers. However, half a year later, I figured out what I was doing wrong.

I was paid a maximum 1.20 yuan per page of typing—more often, 80 cents a page. I had to work almost non-stop to type 100 pages a month. But the people who did the printing were paid 3 cents per page. They were able to earn half my monthly income in one day. I decided I should do the printing as well as the typing. This meant I had to buy a cylinder press.

My husband said: "You're standing on top of one mountain and now you want to climb another. Why don't you just continue with what you are doing." But I insisted. I rented an old press to give it a try. As soon as I got this machine Chui became very supportive. He fixed and oiled it for me.

My first big job was to make 220 copies of a fifty-page lecture I first had to type. I worked half a month to finish the typing, and then printed and bound the copies in a week. When I delivered these copies I was paid 800 yuan. Can you imagine how I felt? I'd never seen so much money in my entire life.

I said to my husband: "800 yuan has made me crazy. I wonder if we could ever make 10,000?" I spent half my earnings on a new printing machine, and, over the next two months, I paid my mother-in-law back for the typewriter.

Six months later business started slowing down. People had begun to switch to power-driven printing presses. Several of my customers told me that they would give their business to someone else unless I could get one of these machines.

Either I had to find 12,000 yuan to buy a new printing press or I would have to acknowledge that my business had failed. I didn't have the money. All I had was 2,000 yuan. It was 1987. I thought at the time that no one could possibly have that much money.

It was summer. In the evening, everybody went outside to get some cool air. Some neighbors noticed my unhappy face. "What's wrong?" they asked. "You're so quiet." I told them my problem. "How much are you short?" they replied. "Maybe we can help."

I didn't really expect any assistance, but, to my surprise, two of these neighbors—one a truck driver, the other a retired worker—offered to lend me 3,000 and 4,000 yuan respectively. With almost 10,000 yuan in hand, I went to my in-laws for help. They came up with the rest of the money.

I turned half of our room into a workshop and moved the new machine in. I set out immediately to get orders. For the next three years my husband and I worked day and night. The printing press was never shut off. I worked from seven-thirty in the morning until one-thirty a.m. the following day. My husband had his regular job from eight to five. After dinner he went to bed and slept until one. Then he worked from half past one until seven-thirty.

Three years later we got three more presses and my two sisters came to work for me. I also hired two additional workers. The business moved to a four-room house. In my best year I made nearly 100,000 yuan. I bought a three-bedroom apartment.

My in-laws treat me quite differently. Now they smile a lot. Although I'll never be close to them I try to be fair. When air conditioners came on the market I put one in our new apartment. I cannot stand the summer heat in Shanghai. As I enjoyed the cool air I thought of my husband's parents. I told Chui we should buy one for them too. He couldn't believe his ears. "Are you serious?" he kept asking. He knows how much humiliation and pain I suffered because of them. Finally, he was convinced I was sincere. He was very excited. The next day he got up very early and stood in line for hours to buy a Japanese air conditioner.

People tell me I'm too kind to be a good businesswoman. I've helped seven other people open their own printing shops. "I've never seen anything so stupid," I was told. I did, of course, lose some business to those I helped. However, if there's enough rice everyone should get a bite. Maybe it's not how you should think if you want to run a business.

I've had a lot to worry about recently. We've been notified that we'll have to move our workshop. The new superhighway is going to run right through it. I've lived in uncertainty for two years. We were never sure what was going to happen. I prayed that the road would go a bit left so our print shop would be spared.

Now, I have to shut down—temporarily at least. Even if I find a new place my business will be cut in half. I get very little compensation from the government. It's difficult for people like me to get any assistance or consideration from the authorities. When you're in the way they move you out, regardless of the losses you suffer.

Is there any way you could help?

Chai Beihua, Male: Manager of a Printing Shop

My friends feel sorry for me. They think this job has forced me to sacrifice my passion for literature. My wife complains I spend all my time here: "It's a position the size of a sesame seed," she says, "but you act as if it were a watermelon." Like many of my friends, she thinks I'm a bit foolish. But there's a secret I've haven't shared with any of them: I'm happier now than ever before.

In 1984, I finished my manuscript on the history of Chinese contemporary literature. I'd worked on this project since 1972. During the Cultural
Revolution I read many writers from the 1920s and 1930s. They're not well
known because they're ignored in all the official histories. I discovered these
writers were diverse in outlook. Some were anarchists, others were more left
than the Communists; some were urbane, others traditional.

In the 1920s and 1930s, Chinese intellectuals experienced the kind of
freedom our ancestors enjoyed during the time of "One Hundred Schools"
in the period of Spring and Autumn [707–476 BC]. During the 1920s and
1930s China was in constant turmoil, and was often governed by warlords.
There was no centralized authority and no overall control of ideology. If
intellectuals ran into trouble in one place they could pack up and leave for
another. In Shanghai, writers would avoid Guomindang repression by moving from one foreign concession to another.

After I discovered these writers I became very excited. It was a surprise to
learn that intellectuals had an independent voice so recently in our history. I
began to collect all the materials I could find. See those twelve boxes up
there? They contain thousands of data cards.

I wanted to write a biographical history of these writers that didn't have
a political agenda. I tried to make it as accurate and as objective as possible.
After I finished my manuscript I sent it to the People's Publishing House.
Months later, they told me that they were interested but that the manuscript
needed more work.

I started revising the manuscript, but, then, something happened that
made me put my project on one side. I went to see an old professor in China
East Normal University to ask about some data. We chatted for hours.
During my visit, one of his old students showed up. This man was a member of a Research Institute [he names it]. He was asked to organize a business
venture that could generate some money for his Institute.[1] He'd founded an
organization in pursuit of this goal and had named it the "Educational,
Scientific and Humanistic Organization" (ESHO).

After he learned that I'd worked in the printing trade for more than fifteen years, this man asked me if I would help him start a printing shop.
Members of the Institute had translated several foreign works, and they were
eager to print and sell them. But, in order to do this, they had to use a state
publishing house's presses and share the profits. If the Institute could build

its own printing shop it could control the business from beginning to end. The plan intrigued me. Less than a month later I quit my job.

The capital for the printing shop was going to be raised by workshops ESHO would offer on philosophy, history, economics and literature. However, these seminars didn't make much money. Next, ESHO founded the Shanghai Entrepreneurs Friendship Club. This was designed to promote horizontal social exchanges among the managers of state enterprises.[2] The Club was popular, and generated a lot of money from membership fees. In 1985, ESHO purchased a building site in the Shanghai suburbs.

Investors were found who were willing to help fund the construction of an apartment complex on the newly purchased site. The printing shop would occupy the first floor of the building. Once construction was finished the investors would be repaid in apartment units.

For a while, everything seemed to be going well. The complex was nearly complete. However, some of the people running ESHO got out of control. They used Organization funds to invest in a township factory in Ningpo which, I believe, was run by their relatives. Before long, ESHO was bankrupt. Someone at the Institute wrote to the municipal government requesting an investigation. Because the complainant alleged that 1 million yuan of public money had been embezzled it didn't take long for an investigative team to show up.

This team reported that the Institute was illegally involved in the real estate business and had engaged in various kinds of mismanagement resulting in the waste of state property. It fined the Institute 700,000 yuan.

The members of the Institute couldn't pay this sum, so they made a deal with a joint-stock limited liability company. In 1988, the company was given this plot of land and the half-finished building complex. In return, it paid the fine. I said at the time that it was a big mistake. I was right. Four years later, that plot of land was worth 5 million yuan—not including this building.

ESHO already had purchased two printing presses. The company that now owned the building told me that, if I employed ten of their workers, I could use these machines and start the printing business as previously planned. I was paid a small salary, and I had to turn over all profits to the company. Company managers didn't think I would make much money but they were wrong. I managed to generate quite a good income for my employers. But, before I agreed to be manager, I insisted on three things. First, I wasn't going to join the Communist Party; second, I wouldn't do personal favors for anyone; third, I didn't want any political meetings on the shop floor.

In 1992, the company made a formal agreement with me. I could lease the printing presses and the first floor of this complex for 80,000 yuan per annum. Profits over and above this would be mine.

I have a good working relationship with company managers, who mostly leave me alone. As long as I hand over 80,000 yuan a year I can run this factory as my own little fiefdom. However I am supposed to attend management meetings.

Recently, at one of these meetings I got into an argument with the Chief Manager. He'd called the meeting to discuss a plan he'd put together to remodel the upper floors of this building as a hotel. He told us the project would require a 20 million-yuan loan.

It didn't need a person of superior intellect to see that the plan was doomed to fail. Right now, there are more than enough big hotels in Shanghai. Also, it would take the company fifteen years to pay back 20 million—assuming, of course, that the hotel made enough money to keep up with the payments.

I pointed out that no one in the room had any experience in the hotel business. "Where are the guests going to come from?" I asked. "This building is in an outlying suburb. Who's going to stay here, and why?" No one else asked any questions. They were all too busy arguing about what to call their new hotel.

My speech made the boss very uncomfortable. He warned everyone that he was in charge of this building, not anyone else. Hearing this, I got to my feet and walked out. I'm not a Party member, nor am I an employee of the company, so there's little they can do to me. A few days later, however, the boss called to tell me he'd appreciated what I'd said. He told me he now recognized I was the only one who'd made any sense.

Since I took over this business I've built it up. I've bought six new presses, and I now have significant reserves of paper and printing ink. I'm careful to avoid getting into "triangle debts" (*sanjiaozhai*). I only deal with businesses that can pay cash. Triangle debts are a very serious problem. They occur when one business isn't paid and, so, has to give IOUs to its suppliers. Immediately, the business is both a creditor and a debtor. It can't pay its debts because it's owed so much money. Before long, everything freezes up. Many state enterprises are ruined this way.

Why does this happen so often? I think the problem is the lack of overall supervision. Many projects are launched for no good reason and with little capital investment. Inflation is a big problem too. For instance, a company has 10 million to invest in a new factory. The actual cost is 15 million. The company borrows 5 million from a bank. A year later, the project is half finished but the cost has risen to 20 million. Now, the company can't pay the construction company. In order to keep the project afloat, the construction company stops paying its suppliers. When the factory finally is finished there's no money left to begin production. So, the company goes back to the bank. This time around, the bank raises its interest rates and shortens the loan period. This means bigger payments. Everyone is desperately trying to survive at the margins. If the new factory makes a good product, maybe everything's fine. But if the scheme was shaky from the start the company collapses very quickly.

The state-owned printing factories in Shanghai have gone bankrupt one after another. Now, there are only two left. Many factors contributed to this state of affairs. Competition from township enterprises is one such factor. Printing is not that complicated. A peasant can buy a printing machine and operate it at home.

Some cadres in Shanghai help township enterprises set up business. They act like sponsors, selling equipment to these rural businesses and making sure everything works smoothly. Cadres close to their retirement age [60] regularly do this kind of thing. Surely you've heard the expression "the 59 phenomenon." Often, the small businesses that cadres help start are really for family or friends. Nothing appears to be illegal. But the state-owned industries are hurt. They can't survive when cadres deliberately set out to undercut them.

State-owned enterprises are at a disadvantage in a competitive environment. The odds are stacked against them. The problem worsened after the state further decentralized economic management [in 1993]. The government hasn't just relinquished authority, it's also laid off many of its responsibilities.

About 75 million people work for state enterprises in the cities, and the numbers are falling. Nearly 30 million people work in private enterprises. Many of these private businesses are joint ventures or wholly foreign-owned enterprises. The state enterprises have to pay pensions and medical costs for millions of retirees. Since the recent reforms state enterprises are supposed to contribute to a fund that supposedly will pay 70 percent of medical expenses for public employees in the future. Patients and their immediate work units will pay the other 30 percent. I don't oppose such taxes in principle. But the reality is that state enterprises are burdened by increasingly punitive social security taxes.

The township enterprises and small factories in the countryside don't make any contribution to their employees' health or pension costs. In the private sector, employers can write whatever contracts they want with their labor force. Furthermore, small private companies often avoid paying any business tax at all, and joint or foreign-owned businesses in the Special Economic Zones pay much lower taxes than the state enterprises.

The only way to reform state-owned enterprises is to privatize them. Many state businesses are in a hopeless situation, and the majority are in debt. It's pointless expecting such industries to compete when they have much heavier costs to pay and when they're clustered in sectors of the economy that offer little opportunity for growth. The government should auction off bankrupt enterprises in order to try to revive them. The process has already begun. I think it's a step in the right direction.

Our government has made too many concessions to foreign capitalists. Some of the subsidies they give to foreign or joint enterprise businesses have damaged domestic industry and made robber barons of the foreigners. We're not a country starting from nothing. Before reform, we had an industrial base, and this shouldn't have been dismantled in the service of foreign capital. What happened was a disgrace. Many good Chinese products with a long history were pushed aside by foreign products.

I've had several dealings with foreigners. Once I was offered a salary of 5,000 yuan a month and a car. I refused all the offers because I won't work with compradors and opportunists. The people who approached me were Japanese and Taiwanese. The Japanese recruit Chinese students who are studying in Japan.

Both the Japanese and the Taiwanese had the same idea. They wanted to start a joint venture, and they planned to devalue the assets in this factory, so, by investing a given sum of money, they would have a bigger share of the business and a larger share of profits. When I refused to help one student told me I was making a big mistake: "You're not a Party member," he pointed out, "so why should you care?" I was outraged. I'm always criticizing the Party. But this isn't Party property. It was started with public funds, and so the assets belong to everyone. I told this Chinese middleman he should be ashamed of himself.

Despite everything, I'm very optimistic about the future. I think our country has completed the stage of primitive capital accumulation. It's a period of greed, cruelty and destruction that can't be avoided by any nation that wants to modernize. Now, I find that the frantic pursuit of money is slowing somewhat. People have begun to realize that not everyone can get rich quickly and that certain rules have to be followed. Let me give you an example.

Wenzhou [a coastal county in Zhejiang province] used to be known as the capital of pirated goods and counterfeit products. Many people were involved in various kinds of trickery, making money any way they could. The merchants in Wenzhou grew fat at the expense of their victims. But now we have entered a new phase. Capital is being put into legitimate, long-term business enterprises. The family businesses that used to specialize in shoddy, counterfeit goods have all disappeared. If you go to Wenzhou today you will find modern factories and good schools.

Fifteen years ago, the first entrepreneurs to take advantage of reform were the "bandits." Their only ambition was to grab money. Many of them actually *were* bandits—people with criminal records. They were without a sense of social responsibility. Their businesses tended to be exotic restaurants, massage parlors, private clubs and karaoke bars. They were people of poor quality, and a corrupting influence.

Today, a new group of entrepreneurs is coming to the fore. They have long-term business interests and a sense of decorum and responsibility. I'm not alone in thinking this way. Wait for another ten or twenty years. The business class in China will be quite different. Believe me!

My great-grandfather was a peasant turned businessman. During the Guangxu era [1898–1906] he owned two famous ham stores in Shanghai and Hong Kong. He also ran a pig farm and a ham factory in the countryside, so he controlled the whole operation from beginning to end. He was a thrifty person who lived simply. He knew how to build up a business.

After my father came of age he was sent to study business management at university. Both great-grandfather and grandfather recognized the value of a modern education. My ancestors were people with vision. Sometimes, I wonder what China would have been like if we'd not had a revolution. Before long, I think, we would have had many Chinese Rockefellers.

Father graduated with a business management degree, which was useless at the time. He taught political economy at a Party school for many years.

Now, father's retired. But he shows a lot of interest in this printing shop. In fact, he visits so often he's become quite a nuisance. He behaves as if we own the place. He told me once that he felt our ancestors' spirit was being carried on by me—a member of the fourth generation.

I have a big dream. One day, I want to run this printing shop, a publishing house and a bookstore. Then, I will control the product from beginning to end—just like my ancestor. My biggest fear is I'll never get the opportunity. I've only another fifteen or twenty years to make it happen. It'll probably take that long before privately owned publishing houses are permitted.

In 1989, I felt my dream was almost within reach. At the beginning of the year I was introduced to a Taiwanese professor. He wanted to invest in my factory and organize a publishing house here on the mainland. We had a long talk, and got on very well. He told me that, in Taiwan, ideological control was very strict. Presidents of Taiwanese universities all have to be members of the Guomindang. He was surprised to find there was more openness and freedom here than in Taiwan. He was going to use my presses to publish works that were outlawed in Taiwan. I was very excited because I thought I'd found a partner who shared my aspirations. This professor asked me to draw up a contract, while he traveled to Beijing to work on another business project. But after the crackdown in June he never came back. He sent me a message. It said: "I hope we'll get another chance one day."

In 1989, I didn't sympathize with the students. I saw enough turmoil during the Cultural Revolution. Mao was the greatest advocate of *geming* (revolution). I hate these two characters. China doesn't need any more revolution. What we want is *gailiang* (reform).

What happened in Tiananmen Square was turmoil. The students were activists (*huodongjia*), not leaders able to articulate solutions. Ordinary people were drawn to the demonstrations because of their opposition to corruption, inflation and the lack of democracy. After the students abandoned these concrete issues and began to play to foreign audiences their movement became fragmented and isolated.

The students were more interested in displaying their emotions than in addressing real issues. They were like the founders of Solidarity in Poland: activists with no ability to govern. When Solidarity took power it was a disaster. It would have been the same with the students. If we'd let them rule China they'd have become dictators too.

Economic development will bring political reform to China. It's just a matter of time. But I don't think we'll have a multi-party system. I believe reform will occur by strengthening the power and autonomy of the People's Congress. In the past, I've voted three times for representatives to Congress. On the first occasion, the government let us choose two out of three candidates. I didn't know any of them, so I crossed out all three names. The second and third times I handed in a blank ballot. Since then I haven't bothered to vote. One day, when the people can choose political representatives, I'll participate.

I've never been afraid to speak out. One day, two people from the State Security Bureau came to see me. They wanted to visit me on a regular base. They didn't want me to inform on others. They just asked me to speak frankly about certain policy issues. They questioned me about Taiwan. I said China would get Taiwan back when our economy overshadows theirs, and this will happen before too long.

I also told these officials that I'd heard that some female workers of my age had lost their jobs and could no longer support their families. They'd had to sell their bodies. I pointed out that if a mother and a middle-aged woman becomes a prostitute it can only be out of desperation. If the government can't, or won't, do anything for these poor women—well, that's the end of the Party. These visits lasted about six months. Later, I heard that my comments were sent to headquarters in Shanghai.

I spend most of my time in the factory. My apartment is next door. People can call on me whenever they want. I don't mind at all. On weekends, my wife and I take our daughter into the city center. We don't go shopping—it's too expensive. We just look around and then we go to a fast-food restaurant to have lunch. Our monthly income is about 2,000 yuan. We spend most of it on our child. She's in boarding school during the week.

That's my story. I enjoyed talking to you.

Notes

[1] Not an uncommon practice. Many Chinese universities, research institutes, etc., are expected to start their own business ventures so they can generate funds for themselves.

[2] Under centralized state planning, the managers of state enterprises usually communicate vertically with their Bureaus (upwards) and with suppliers (downwards).

WANG XIAOYING,[1] FEMALE: MEMBER OF THE SHANGHAI WRITERS' ASSOCIATION

A newspaper article recently described me as "a writer from the 'Three Old Classes' who writes about the 'Three Old Classes'." It's true. All my stories and novels are about people from my own generation. But after I read the article I said to myself: why *am* I so concerned with the past? It's an obsession shared by so many members of our generation. The world today is so lively and colorful, so full of promise and opportunity. Yet we turn our backs on it. We look inwards and backwards, not outwards.

As time's gone by we've become even more fixated on a past era. But why? Recently I figured it out. It's not that we don't understand the past. We can't come to terms with the present.

We're lost in the present. That's why we try to locate ourselves in things past. Let's face it. Our generation no longer has much of a role to play. We're actors and actresses in outmoded costumes, standing around, looking out of place and slightly ridiculous. We all see ourselves in this metaphor but we still can't believe what's happened.

After the Cultural Revolution came to its end we were described as a "lost generation." People thought that once Mao left the scene his "children" would become "lost sheep." But, by the mid-1970s, most of us were tired of the endless strife. We knew a crisis was brewing. When Mao died we didn't feel lost. We welcomed the prospect of change.

At first we were treated generously. People recognized the losses we'd suffered. In 1977–1978, I was among those who wrote "scar literature" (*shanghen wenxue*). But I wasn't just grieving about what had happened to me and to millions of others. I wanted to work through my experiences.

Our sense of loss came not in the 1970s but in the 1990s. Twenty years after the Cultural Revolution came to its end our society has completed its process of rebirth. Now it's a completely different environment. New China is about self-interest and the personal struggle to survive. As our society gets colder and crueler we'll just get older and less sure of ourselves. Now we're approaching our fifties. We've got parents to take care of as well as children. Many of us have lost our jobs. We're not in great shape. Our biggest problem is we've lost our bearings. To use one of our favorite expressions: *kanbudong* (it's all quite incomprehensible).

I do think history can single out a generation and play a cruel joke on it. It happened to us. We were raised as idealists, we saw the death of idealism and now we're spared to live in this materialistic world.

My parents' generation didn't experience anything like this. They became revolutionaries during a period of national crisis, and they were key players most of their lives.

My mother is a former high-ranking cadre. She has no regrets. She doesn't like contemporary China and doesn't pretend to understand it. But she's serene. She knows that the great challenges and crises of her life are all behind her.

The young generation's custom-built for the present, so they're not out of place either. We're phantoms caught between two worlds. The shards of idealism are lodged in our hearts. But the world's not for idealists anymore.

You probably think I'm becoming self-indulgent and sentimental. But let me tell you a story. This happened in the summer of 1969, nine months after I became a worker at Huangshan State Tea Farm.

We'd had several days of pouring rain. Early one morning, before it was light, we were awakened by shouts and whistles. Someone was screaming: "Get up! The water's rising!" We rushed outside. We could hear that the nearby mountain stream was running much faster than usual.

One team of twelve boys and girls was ordered to save rice bags and fertilizer from storage shed on the other side of the stream. The rest of us worked feverishly to create dikes to protect dormitories and offices.

In the middle of the morning, the loudspeaker crackled into life. An urgent voice ordered our team leader to come at once to farm headquarters. We knew something bad had happened.

Hours later, we learned that eleven people were missing. The rickety old bridge over the stream had collapsed as soon as the team set foot on it. By the time the students arrived its surface was already under water. Obviously, it was dangerous to attempt a crossing. But the team members didn't hesitate. Hand in hand together they plunged ahead.

When we heard what had happened we fell silent. Then, a few of us began to sob. The authorities sent out a rescue team. Only one boy had survived. He'd managed to cling to the branches of a tree. The others were washed downstream. It took nearly a week to find all the bodies. One of the dead was my closest friend: Lu Hua.

Lu should never have been at the farm. She was assigned to a factory in Shanghai. But she was the leader of our school's Red Guard Organization. She gave up her city registration and volunteered for the farm so she could stay with her friends. On the day we'd left Shanghai Lu had said: "Let's not cry. Our loved ones want to see us smile. We'll sing a song together." She cheered everyone up. She was such a brave person. She died when she was 22.

Today, people would say how stupid she was to risk her precious life for a few sacks of rice and some fertilizer. But, to her, the bags across the stream and the order to save them were more important than personal considerations.

I've just published a novel called *Once We Had Love*. The title refers to the idealism we all once shared. I spent six months interviewing people of my generation, and took another year to finish the book.

After it was finished I was invited to a book-signing ceremony. To my surprise, many, many people showed up. I had to go home and get my own 100 author's copies in order to satisfy all the demand. I was deeply moved. Nearly everyone there was from the Three Old Classes.

We're now told that the Cultural Revolution was a national disaster that victimized everyone except Mao, the "Gang of Four" and the Red Guards. But, during the Cultural Revolution, nearly all the nation's youth willingly joined Red Guard Organizations. We wanted to serve. The future we hoped to build never came, but this doesn't mean that all our sacrifices were meaningless and now are best forgotten.

Our generation represents the tragic spirit of an era. Overwhelmingly powerful and conflicting forces shaped us. Some were good, others evil.

A few weeks ago I was talking to my mother about the past. I asked her whether she believed she was a victim of the Cultural Revolution. She thought for a moment. "In one way or another," she replied, "everyone was a victim."

She was right. When a whole nation goes through a dark period no one is spared.

Thirty years ago I was a young activist. My father was a well-known poet who had joined the communists long before liberation. My mother was the Party Secretary of one of Shanghai's district governments. What mattered to us were loyalty to Mao and the Party. We had intense political discussions every weekend.

I had no doubt we were contributing to world revolution. The Party had told us that the two-thirds of the world's population that were oppressed would be liberated by us one day. Many years later, a friend in Huangshan—obviously more sophisticated than I—told me that working-class people in the west lived better than we did. She said *we*, not workers elsewhere, were part of the two-thirds of the world's population that were oppressed. At the time I was shocked.

During the Great Exchange, while I was still in high school, I went to Beijing to be received by Mao. When I returned to Shanghai the first thing I saw was a Big Character poster on the station wall. It proclaimed: "The Municipal Government is Rotten to its Core."

I knew at once that my mother was in trouble. If the Municipal Government was rotten to its core then, in all probability, so, too, were the ten district governments.

I rushed home and found no one there except our old nanny. She told me that my mother had been taken away in a truck to be exhibited as the Number One Capitalist Roader. They'd put a stone board around her neck. The string cut her quite badly. Members of the Workers' Rebellion Organization had taken Father prisoner in his work place.

I was devastated. I'd thought I was a revolutionary and that my parents were old revolutionaries. Suddenly I found out I was a whelp of counter-revolutionaries. But, even at that time, I didn't doubt Mao or the Cultural Revolution. I thought either my parents had done something wrong or the rebellious organizations had made a terrible mistake.

That's why I volunteered to go to Huangshan. My two sisters went to Heilongjiang. We just wanted to get out of Shanghai.

I would have to say that my life was sheltered before I left home. I really didn't know how ordinary people in China lived. I arrived at the farm with lofty and romantic notions. It didn't take long for the illusions to be dispelled. The work was demanding and the food was terrible. We had meat once a month.

Life in the countryside was monotonous. Often, both boys and girls turned to sex. We were about 20 years old and full of energy. What else were we supposed to do? We wanted companions as well as sexual partners. The companionship could be open. But the sex was forbidden. Only a few refused to cross that line. I was one of them.

However, I did form a partnership with a boy called Yijie. He was close to Lu before she'd drowned in that terrible flood. All three of us were from the same school in Shanghai.

Lu's body was recovered nearly a week after she died. I helped wash her, and I dressed her in her best clothes: a blue cotton jacket and green trousers. Yijie pinned a Mao badge on Lu's chest. In those days you honored someone by showing how loyal he or she was to Mao. Then we buried our friend on the mountainside.

The next day Yijie was charged with committing a counter-revolutionary crime. He was told he had revealed his hatred of Mao by burying his picture. The authorities ordered Lu's grave dug up and the badge returned.

Yijie was always the black sheep on the farm. In Shanghai he'd been involved in the Zhongshan Alliance. There were numerous investigations into his involvement with the anti-Zhang Chunqiao faction. Each had ended with an "inconclusive" evaluation. Basically, Yijie was on continuous probation. This time, too, he was let go with a warning.

Gradually, Yijie and I lost faith in Mao and the Party. I think, for us, the pivotal event was the Lin Biao incident. After that we became increasingly cynical about politics.

In 1972, some of the older students were given a chance to leave the farm. Two years later, most of my class had returned to Shanghai. I was on the list for transfer too, and I went to farm headquarters to tell them I wanted to give up my place to Yijie. The officials saw me as a stubborn young woman who'd fallen in love with an unworthy man. But, to our surprise, both Yijie and I were given jobs in Shanghai.

We left Huangshan Mountain in the summer of 1974, and were married two years later. In 1977, we enrolled in university. Yijie studied history at Fudan University, and I majored in literature.

In 1981, Yijie went to the University of Virginia as a graduate student in their History Department. I never went to visit him. I was too busy with my own work. I didn't want Yijie to stay in America, and I made it very clear to him that I would never leave China. I'm a Chinese writer, so what would I do in America? Yijie finished his Master's degree in 1983 and came home. We wanted to start a family.

Sometimes I feel I shouldn't have dragged Yijie back to China. I should at least have let him stay long enough to finish his PhD. Whenever I see him unhappy about his job I feel so sorry for him.

Last year, Yijie got financial backing from a Hong Kong real estate developer to establish a research institute on urban environmental planning. Since 1990 his main interest has been urban management. Chinese cities are developing rapidly, but no one knows how to tame these "monsters." Yijie wants to be a pioneer in the field.

Now we are experiencing a lot of difficulties with Yijie's university. I told Yijie that he should compromise with the bureaucracy. The most important thing is his project. He's nearly 50 years old now—there's not much time left if he wants to achieve something.

We're not Party members. Yijie applied, and was turned down, eight times—most recently in 1988. His persistence was the source of quite a few jokes among our friends. Now Yijie recognizes there's no reason for him to join the Party. He loves his country and that's enough. Once we were told socialism would save China. Today we're expected to believe that the market economy will solve all our problems. The trouble is that the propaganda is no longer persuasive. Probably the only thing that will hold us together is nationalism.

I was drawn to Buddhism six years ago. I was 41 at the time and badly wanted a child. I'd had one abortion when I was in the university because I didn't think I'd finish my studies if I had a baby. It was a difficult decision, and also the wrong one. Later, I miscarried three times. I was very upset and started to go to the temple to offer prayers.

Marx was right. Religion is for the vulnerable. Buddhism gave me the strength to keep going. I had my baby girl when I was 42. She's the gift of my faith.

Most of our income is spent on our daughter. She's in private school, which costs 300 yuan a month in tuition, plus other expenses. Yijie and I don't have many needs. Maybe it's because we grew up poor and never had much money to spend. Yijie won't even enter a restaurant.

The last two years I've worked on a long novel. A publishing house gave me 10,000 yuan to write it. Long novels aren't lucrative, but we're all right.

closed schools all boy & girls
work
army

Mother lives with us. Father died some years ago. We pool our money so we can have a good meal together every day. I think of myself as a lucky person.

Idealism → theory that ideas are only reality.

Note

[1] Not a pseudonym.

Qving (manchu) Dynasty (1644 - 1944)

Foot Sining Out lawed.

Infernal triangle

Opium wars - British Smuggling opium to China

Boxer Rebellion - (1849 - 1901) anti forien, anti christian, In response to imperialism

Sun Yat-Sen - Chinese revolutionary leader, refered to as the father of modern China

Chiang Kai shek - Commandent of KUOmintang's whampoa Military Academy.

Mao Tse tau (Zedong) - Comunist leader in Ching that lead the Communist to victory against KMT

~~The Long March~~

First Generation - revolutionaries

• The long march - massive military retreat undertaken by the red arm of the Chinese Communist party

• ~~The rape of Peking~~

Pu yi - last emperor of China

~~Second Gen~~

The great leap ~~forward~~ - economic & social plan 1958→ 1961

• Tienamin Square - large plaza near the center of pro democracy. Bejing China.

Red Guard → Police of communism for Moa, were students.

Death of Moa -

~~Rape of Peking~~ -

✓ Protest of 1976 1989

One child → poplation control, destricts number of kids.